The Bastille Effect

The Bastille Effect

Transforming Sites of Political Imprisonment

Michael Welch

UNIVERSITY OF CALIFORNIA PRESS

University of California Press
Oakland, California

Suggested citation: Welch, M. *The Bastille Effect: Transforming Sites of Political Imprisonment*. Oakland: University of California Press, 2022. DOI: https://doi.org/10.1525/luminos.124

Library of Congress Cataloging-in-Publication Data

Names: Welch, Michael, 1960– author.
Title: The Bastille Effect : transforming sites of political imprisonment / Michael Welch.
Description: Oakland, California : University of California Press, [2022] | Includes bibliographical references and index.
Identifiers: LCCN 2021062825 (print) | LCCN 2021062826 (ebook) | ISBN 9780520386037 (paperback) | ISBN 9780520386044 (ebook)
Subjects: LCSH: Prisons—History. | Memorialization—Case studies. | Memory—Sociological aspects. | Collective memory—History. | BISAC: SOCIAL SCIENCE / Criminology | POLITICAL SCIENCE / Human Rights
Classification: LCC HV8501 .W36 2022 (print) | LCC HV8501 (ebook) | DDC 364.6—dc23/eng/20220208
LC record available at https://lccn.loc.gov/2021062825
LC ebook record available at https://lccn.loc.gov/2021062826

31   30   29   28   27   26   25   24   23   22
10   9   8   7   6   5   4   3   2   1

To
Lennox Hinds, Angela Davis, and the Struggle

CONTENTS

LIST OF ILLUSTRATIONS

PREFACE

This book on the transformation of sites of political imprisonment has many beginnings. In 2014, I spent research time in Dublin and Belfast exploring the remnants of past conflicts as projected through various prison museums, historical collections, and memorial sites. Along the way, my observations deepened an appreciation for cultural sociology. The following year, that beginning got another start at a scholarly workshop sponsored by the Center for Cultural Sociology at Yale University. It was then and there that my reflections on a "Troubled" Ireland began to take shape, prompting me to begin a new way of thinking and writing. For that opportunity I am grateful to Phil Smith, Jeffery Alexander, and the room full of enthusiastic graduate students who peppered my presentation with sharp and witty insights.

This book is the product of not just one but two sabbaticals supported by Rutgers University. At the London School of Economics, Department of Social Policy, Mannheim Centre for Criminology, Tim Newburn and David Lewis provided me with a productive academic home. Also at the LSE, Conor Gearty and Sean Boyle contributed another layer of collegiality. In Belfast, Kieran McEvoy, Shadd Maruna (Queen's University), and Laura McAtackney (Aarhus University, Denmark) offered friendly research guidance.

Marking another beginning, the next sabbatical was based in the Facultad de Derecho, Instituto de Investigaciones, Juridicas y Sociales Ambrosio L. Gioja, Universidad de Buenos Aires. I extend enormous gratitude to Gabriel Ignacio Anitua, Diego Zysman, Leonardo Pitlevnik, and Bruno Nápoli as well as Maximo Sozzo (Facultad de Ciencias Jurídicas y Sociales, Universidad Nacional del Litoral, Santa Fe, Argentina). Also in Buenos Aires, Maria [Maru] Mendizabal granted me special access to Ex Centro Clandestino de Detencion, Tortura y Extermino: "Olimpo." In Chile, several colleagues and friends opened their doors for vibrant intellectual discussion, most notably Silvio Cuneo, Nicole Selame, and Marcela Aedo Rivera at Universidad de Valparaiso, Escuela de Derecho, Centro de Investigaciones de Filosofía del Derecho y Derecho Penal, Núcleo de Estudios Penitenciarios. At the Facultad de Ciencas, Juridicas y Politicas, Universidad Arturo Prat (Iquique, Chile), Roberto Dufraix, Daniel Quinteros, Romina Ramos Rodriquez, and José A. Brandariz coordinated exciting seminars and social events.

At Rutgers, my Canadian tutor Chelsea Rolin assisted the French translation of my work in Montreal. Not without some amusement, students in my classes patiently allowed me to test-drive some of my thoughts for the book. Correspondingly, segments of the project appeared in print in the following articles: Michael Welch (2020), "In the Sites of Operation Condor: Memory and Afterlives of Clandestine Detention Centers," *Social Justice: A Journal of Crime, Conflict, and World Order,* 47(1–2), 1–38; Michael Welch (2019), "Signs of Trouble: Semiotics, Streetscapes, and the Republican Struggle in the North of Ireland," *Crime, Media, Culture: An International Journal,* 16(1), 7–32; and Michael Welch (2016), "Political Imprisonment and the Sanctity of Death: Performing Heritage in 'Troubled' Ireland," *International Journal of Heritage Studies,* 22, 664–678. In its final incarnation, this volume has benefited from the careful oversight of the good folks at the University of California Press, namely Maura Roessner, Madison Wetzell, Julie Van Pelt, and Matthew Kudelka, who sharpened the work with fine copy editing. The University of California Faculty Committee, in turn, provided excellent recommendations for revision. Of course, three cheers to the anonymous reviewers who suggested new directions and inroads into theory and interpretation.

My long-term friend and colleague, Lennox Hinds, continues to be a source of inspiration dating back to 1993 when I entered the faculty of the Administration of Justice at Rutgers. In 2016, Lennox retired, but not without a final show of force. Along with Edward Ramsamy (who has taught me and my students about life under South African apartheid), Lennox joined Angela Davis on stage for a riveting lecture on "Justice in Action." Thomas Sokolowski, Director of the Jane Voorhees Zimmerli Art Museum (at Rutgers) began planning the exhibition *Angela Davis—Seize the Time.* The retrospective is a tribute to Angela as a political activist and central figure in the campaign to "Free Angela and All Political Prisoners." Sadly, the Rutgers community, in 2020, was informed that had Tom passed away. In a small way, may this book serve the memory of Tom, as well as my colleague Patrick Carr (a fine Dubliner), Timothy Sean McSorley (a fellow troublemaker), and my kid sister Margaret (a fearless ginger), all of whom died within weeks of one another that same fateful year.

On the upbeat, for keeping my life in harmony, thanks a bunch to AB, PP, SH, MC, and WD.

MW
Hoboken
July 14, 2021

PART ONE

The Sacred and the Profane

Cultural Afterlives

Renowned scholar Jacques Godechot is, indeed, correct in stating that by the end of the 18th century, the Bastille had emerged as more than just a prison. The infamous site had become a reminder of a feudal system that had grown increasingly obsolete, given its arbitrary power. The storming of the Bastille on July 14, 1789, is regarded as decisive event in the French Revolution even though it was less a strategic loss for the monarchy than an emblematic victory for the people. "July 14 thus marks the culmination of two great currents, the uprising of the people of Paris, which was one aspect of the great national uprising that had been underway for several months, and the defection of the troops, another aspect of the same national insurrection. The capture of the Bastille served as a marvelous symbol, for France and the world, of the triumph of this insurrection" (Godechot, 1970: 249).

The afterlives of the Bastille set the stage for this study of former prisons and detention centers that have been reconfigured into symbolic sites so as to emit narratives on social upheaval and repressive control. In the pages that follow, those transformations are explored in post-conflict cities in diverse countries where memorialization relies on the power of place to reflect on the injustice of political imprisonment. With cultural sociology at our disposal, this book unveils the enduring dynamics that animate these varied places of confinement. At a universal level, remnants of political imprisonment reveal the ubiquity of socio-religious forces, most notably the sacred vis-à-vis the profane. Those potent social themes are deeply embedded in forms of identity and heritage at the local level—whether it be Belfast amid the Troubles or Buenos Aires during the last dictatorship. This opening chapter invites us to consider those developments by taking into account the significance of cultural afterlives. Notions of place will guide our understanding of what we shall refer to as the Bastille Effect whereby former carceral institutions undergo a dual transformation. Those sites shed their violent past while opening themselves for public scrutiny and thoughtful re-examination of state crimes that occurred on those same premises. Transformed sites activate a collective imagination in ways that cast a powerful light on human rights and the contemporary struggle for democratic equality.

THE BASTILLE AND ITS AFTERLIVES

To chronicle the afterlives of the Bastille, sociologist Philip Smith (1999) delves into how the cultural meaning of place has changed over the course of history. The Bastille was a fortress prison where the monarchy had long disposed of political opponents and other nuisances. Durkheim would have considered the Bastille a profane symbol, or as Smith puts it, "a polluted place" (1999: 23). The Revolution with its patriotic heroes and blood sacrifice altered not only the nation but also the Bastille itself, allowing myth to transform it from a profane to a sacred place. Decades later, however, the site fell into neglect as its moats filled with stagnant water and patches of wild grass. That particular afterlife lost its capacity to evoke the sacred; the Bastille had become an ill-defined and desolate place (Lemoine, 1930).

Enter Napoleon, who was determined to reverse the Bastille's symbolic dysfunction. To commemorate his military adventures in the Orient, in 1806 he ordered that a giant fountain in the shape of an elephant be built on the site. Architects and other cultural advisers failed utterly to convince him that an elephant was not a fitting—let alone elegant—image for the tribute. "Project Elephant" moved forward, but instead of a fountain it would be a wooden and plaster model standing 24 meters tall. From 1817 to 1847, that behemoth occupied the place de la Bastille, where it decayed physically and aesthetically. "In 1847, the sad history of the elephant came to an appropriate end. It was finally thrown into the canal/sewer on the order of Prefect Rumbuteau. Crowds watched as rats escaped from the sinking monument" (Smith, 1999: 28).

Political campaigns aimed at scouring the site of its pollution and restoring its sacredness now gained considerable traction. In 1830, lawmakers approved a plan to erect the Colonne de Juillet. This memorial would be dedicated to the patriots who had sacrificed themselves on July 14 (1789) as well as to those who had perished during the "Three Glorious Days" in July 1830. The 50-meter column in center of the place de la Bastille rises from a tomb in which the remains of 504 fighters are buried. Their names engraved on the foundation make a clear cultural statement about its appropriateness as a sacred place. "The monument is both a shrine to fallen heroes and a demonstration that liberty rises from the sacrifices of the fallen. . . . It is a monument whose aesthetic resonates past against present, drawing intertextually upon the narrative of the Bastille, tuning into, configuring and amplifying the popular mythologies of the site" (Smith, 1999: 29). The sculpture is topped by the Genie de la Bastille (or Genie de la Liberté), who hoists a torch in one hand and a broken chain in the other. Hence, the site of a former prison now embodies the revolutionary spirit. Themes of ascent are evident: the memorial now serves as an expression of the sovereignty of the people and a rallying point for revolutionary activity. In 1848, the bodies of 52 protesters shot by the military were arranged around the column to the cries of "Vengence! Aux barricades." The solemn procession was capped by an act of profane purification: the throne of Louis-Phillipe was torched. Rituals of revolution again were ignited at the place de la Bastille in 1871 when the Communards erected their own barricades there (Sewell, 1996). To appreciate the importance of cultural afterlives, we turn to a sociology of place.

PLACE, SPACE, AND GHOSTS

Smith (1999) recognizes that the iconography—or representation—of space has caught the interest of scholars from an array of perspectives: cultural, postmodern, and ideological. Taking a decidedly Durkheimian stance, Smith insists that place is formed by myths and narratives that become institutionalized through monuments, the mass media, and various other routines. Such rituals, however, hold differing meanings for different observers. As we will discuss in greater depth, the Troubles in Northern Ireland illustrate that "divergent typifications can lead violent and symbolic struggles over the meaning of places" (Smith, 1999: 16; Welch, 2019). As a way forward, Smith offers a template for discerning how identities of place are transformed and preserved through action. Accordingly, place identity is constructed in four basic domains: the sacred, the profane, the liminal, and the mundane.

The sacred lends purity to special places, enabling close contact with the transcendental and producing emotional reactions such as awe and reverence. Its opposite, the profane, contains pollution and evil so that the psychic register migrates toward revulsion. Everyday places are best understood as mundane; in these, ordinary behavior goes on without much reflection. As a departure from the mundane, liminal places thrive in suspending everyday rules and traditional moralities. In such places, narratives of the quasi-ritualized carnivalesque add cultural energy to the out-of-the-ordinary. "They are often comedic in character, offering a ludic conception of place, or else 'absurd' in the sense that they are fragmented and defy any easy classification or ontological grounding except that they are 'other' to the everyday" (Smith, 1999: 20). This fourfold framework is not static since places have the dynamic capacity to morph into other types depending on a mobilizing action or event. Once that rupture occurs, a new place identity is reinforced by rituals and monuments that serve as cultural markers, in this way institutionalizing the narratives of place (see Bell, 1997; Sewell, 1996).

It is easy to use the terms space and place interchangeably. Nonetheless, there are some distinctions to make, as Michael Mayerfeld Bell suggests: "Space refers to the three-dimensional coordinates of things. A place is a particular space that has meaning" (1997: 833). Bell is quick to caution that such distinctions ought not to be reified because, like many categories, they tend to dissolve at the margins. Therefore, according to Bell, "when I speak of place I am emphasizing issues of meaning more than I would be if I were speaking about space" (1997: 833; see also Agnew and Duncan, 1989). For Bell, place is rife with meaning. More to his point, places are occupied not only by objects, images, and people but also by ghosts. Without resorting to superstition, ghosts can be defined as imaginary entities that inhabit places. They cannot be seen yet their presence is felt. For example, a somewhat mystical experience occurs when we revisit an old "haunt" of our youth: ghosts emerge as memories of people who are no longer around. That moment is likely to deliver an emotional charge, be it positive or negative. With respect to historical sites, ghosts contribute to the specificity of places. "Places are, in a word, personed—even when there is no one there" (Bell, 1997: 813; see also Mayerfield and Murray, 2001).

Ghosts are ubiquitous in places in ways that give them life, Bell insists, making space a place. The Bastille, even after its demolition, remained haunted by the ghosts of its many colorful prisoners, including de Sade, Voltaire, and the "Man in the Iron Mask" (BnF, 2010). Visitors to the place de la Bastille activate the social relations of memory by imagining the physical site as it might have appeared during its tenure as a prison. Many observers are keenly aware that the boulevards surrounding the Colonne de Juillet are paved with the Bastille's original stones, and this enables them to connect with history. As Bell further notes, "the ghosts of place are not only ghosts of the past; they can as well be of the present, and even the future" (1997: 816). With profound sadness and sacredness, many of these places become memorials to those who were sacrificed in a place that had been profoundly profane. As a place, ESMA in Buenos Aires was transformed from a rather mundane institution for training naval cadets into a profane place of state terror where victims were detained, tortured, and exterminated. The compound retains the ghosts of its polluted past while forging ahead as a sacred place of memory. The top floors of the site seem especially haunted. In some areas, placards and storyboards steer visitors through spaces where detainees were confined; other areas are devoid of any narration. Empty sectors of a larger place are more likely to be "personed"—or seemingly inhabited by ghosts and spirits (see figure 1). Bell reminds us that we experience places as having ghosts because those sites are engaged socially. Simply put, we experience places as we do people. "Through ghosts, we re-encounter the aura of social life in the aura of place" (1997: 821).

A sociology of place, space, and ghosts extends beyond sites to encompass entire communities. In his ethnography of Belfast during the Troubles, Feldman encountered the saturation of death, or what he calls "symbolic genocide," the "erasure of ethnicity and ethnic spaces," and "the cartography of death events—

FIGURE 1. "ESMA: Former Detention Space." On the top floors of the Casino at ESMA, the former detention space seems especially connected to its profane past. © retrowelch 2022.

the spaces of the dead" (1991: 65). Below, that sense of collective defilement is accumulated into an Irish death-warning tale, followed by a ghost story:

> The night before Francie Legget got dead, a girl from this area was coming from her friend's house. . . . She seen a banshee sitting on the wall. . . . [I]t was a wee small withered woman crying with tears and mourning. . . . [T]he following Friday morning Francie Leggett was shot dead on the spot.

FIGURE 2. "Memorial to Gerald McAuley." In a Catholic community in Belfast, a memorial to Gerald McAuley, a victim of the Troubles, is open to the public. © retrowelch 2022.

> There have been so many horrendous deaths in this district over the years that there has to be ghosts. (Catholic housewife, St. James district; Feldman, 1991: 66)

Feldman writes that the presence of ghosts in such communities is attributed to the sheer magnitude and randomness of death within a limited space and time. "In folk explanation, ghosts are the inevitable excess of the defilement which emerges from the flooding of social space with death" (1991: 67). The banshee and the ghost become free-floating signifiers within a liminal place where the conventional order of time and space no longer governs. Places of death often spawn places of resistance where forces of the sacred, the profane, and the mundane not only intersect but also interact. In Belfast, special gardens memorialize the victims of political violence. In 1969, Loyalist rioters targeted the Catholic community, burning down homes, most notably on Bombay Street. The "onslaught entered nationalist folk history as the 'pogrom'" (Taylor, 1997: 52). Among those who perished was Gerald McAuley, a 15-year-old who was shot dead by a Loyalist gunman. The tragedy was deepened as it become known that McAuley was helping residents flee their homes on Bombay Street (Coogan, 2002; Quinn, 2019). At the neighborhood memorial site, a large billboard reenacts those events. The space marks a cultural transformation from the profanity of sectarian violence to a sacred place. It is dedicated to the memory of Gerald McAuley (see McKittrick, Kelters, Feeney, and Thornton, 2001; figure 2).

CULTURAL TRANSFORMATIONS

The afterlives of place are informed by historical thought and concepts of memory. Pierre Nora reminds us that history tends to attach itself to events whereas memory clings to places. Given that power of place, it is within "les lieux de memoire where memory crystalizes and secretes itself" (1989: 7). History remains a representation of the past; memory is affective and nourishes recollections that may be out of focus, thereby "tying us to the present" (8). Nora deepens our insights by casting history as prosaic, particularly against the rich dynamics of memory, which bind certain people together since "memory takes root in the concrete, in spaces . . . [becoming] sites for anchoring its memory" (1989: 9). That cultural transformation is evident in sites of political imprisonment, which have the potential to be reinvented for contemporary remembrance.

Such transformation, by design, produces reflection. For our purposes here, reflection has two meanings: first, contemplation; and second, the mirroring of something else. Former prisons and detention centers have been rebuilt as memorial spaces that encourage visitors to reflect on past atrocities. To facilitate that experience, those sites often contain artifacts intended to represent other things. Instruments of torture, for example, are commonly displayed in memorial spaces. Once on display, those objects attain special meaning as something worthy to consider since they represent the suffering experienced by prisoners. For that transformation to occur, the torture device must pass from use-value to signifying-value (Welch, 2015; Williams, 2007). In its previous incarnation the device was used to inflict pain; having undergone cultural conversion, the same object has become a symbol of state repression. Indeed, entire sites pass through a similar form of cultural transformation in ways that demonstrate how signifying-value can facilitate use-value—for example, by offering lessons from the past. At the ESMA memorial space, visitors are frequently reminded that they are entering a reconstruction of the detention, torture, and extermination center administered by the last dictatorship. In this way, visitors are able to experience "safe contact" with a site that no longer harms people. The site then offers enough evidence of pain to prompt reflection. Whereas dark tourism often delivers cheap thrills, the Bastille Effect aims at a higher degree of enlightenment (Lennon and Foley, 2010; Welch, 2020). Through cultural maneuvering, profane places are transformed into sacred spaces as well as places for learning. It is the reconceptualization of sites that has inspired this book. Allow me to explain how we go from here to there.

FROM HERE TO THERE

This journey through various cities requires some signposting in order to clarify where we are going and why. As we transit from place to place, it is important for us to realize that these sites are selective, based on my own scholarly interests in post-conflict societies. In particular, Belfast and Buenos Aires: two very different cities that were plunged into turmoil under very different circumstances. From the 1960s until the late 1990s, a low-level war—the Troubles—in Northern Ireland divided a country and its cities, where political violence was a daily event. In the 1970s, Buenos Aires became the focal point of a dictatorship that would consume Argentina well into the 1980s. It is difficult to compare the two societies in terms of the sheer magnitude of the human rights atrocities they faced; we can, though, say they shared a common and openly expressed sense of loss and memory. Visitors to Belfast and Buenos Aires who are willing to take notice encounter significant manifestations of past injustice. This book examines the sites and symbols of those conflicts in Belfast and Buenos Aires, and in other cities as well. What follows is my story, which contains many stories. Those stories offer narratives about the Bastille Effect as former prisons and detention centers undergo cultural transformations in ways that enhance the pursuit of justice.

This book represents a deliberate effort to build on my previous book, *Escape to Prison: Penal Tourism and the Pull of Punishment* (2015). Among many things, that volume offered an in-depth analysis of Robben Island and the Old Fort in Cape Town, and Johannesburg, respectively. Those former prisons—and their cities—are synonymous with Nelson Mandela, who served 27 years in captivity, becoming one of the world's most famous political prisoners. *Escape to Prison* also includes my experience at a comparable institution in Seoul, South Korea, the Seodaemun Prison History Hall. The afterlife of that site remembers the fate of thousands of Korean political prisoners persecuted by Japanese imperialists before and during the Second World War. Having finished that book, it was time for me to move on to other things, or so I thought. As it turns out, the idea of political imprisonment would take hold as my next major undertaking, though I would not neglect the lessons of penal tourism and the pull of punishment.

To concentrate more fully on the historical and cultural implications of political imprisonment, I adopted Paris as a summer research home for five years. During that stretch of time, the meaning of the Bastille captured my attention, especially in light of its mythic presence in the popular imagination. Moreover, I realized that its representation as a sign of repression was rivaled by the triumphant forms of resistance it embodied. That yin-and-yang dualism might be better interpreted sociologically by way of the sacred versus the profane, especially in post-conflict societies. With the benefit of what I learned in Paris about the Bastille, I moved on to a series of cities to study other sites and symbols of political confinement. In Dublin, the Kilmainham Gaol is widely regarded as the "Bastille of Ireland." The former prison, with its striking Victorian architecture, has reopened its gates to loads of tourists interested in expanding their knowledge of Irish political history against the backdrop of British colonialism. Heading north on the Emerald Isle, the Crumlin Road Gaol in Belfast offers more Victorian narratives on empire. That site, and various historical collections scattered around the city, paved the way for an informed interpretation of the Troubles, thus demonstrating how political imprisonment has contributed to a heritage that is cherished as well as contested by Irish and British identities (Welch, 2019).

In 2017, I relocated (again) to Buenos Aires, where several former detention, torture, and extermination centers have been resurrected as memorial spaces. For months, I scoured the city for the afterlives of places of confinement, finding clear patterns of profanity overcome by the sacred. Those sites in turn joined a vast network of memorial spaces in neighboring nations also ravaged by repressive regimes. To immerse myself in those post-conflict societies, I moved to Santiago (Chile) to examine the various places where victims of Pinochet were confined, including the National Stadium, where sectors of the concourse have been preserved as they existed during the coup of September 11, 1973 (known as the Chilean 9/11). Since the Argentine and Chilean dictatorships had formed coalitions with other military despots, I spent considerable time visiting similar sites in Asunción (Paraguay) and Montevideo (Uruguay) as they projected a collective memory of pain and anguish (Welch, 2020).

Along the way, I realized that these cities and their transformed sites of political imprisonment contain evidence of cultural influence from abroad, most notably Europe. Since the late 19th century, Buenos Aires has welcomed Irish immigrants, affectionately referred to as "Los Irish Porteños." During the "dirty war," some of them—particularly those belonging to the activist clergy—were swept up along with thousands of others who disappeared. At former detention sites, memorials have been raised to honor them. Their ranks include Patrick Rice, an Irish Catholic priest who devoted his life to serving the poor as well as families victimized by the military (see Welch, 2020). Similar ethnic markings are visible in Montreal, where the local Irish took up arms with the Québécois to fight British rule in the 1830s. As so often happens to defeated insurgents, the Irish in Quebec faced political imprisonment followed by summary executions at a site renamed La-Prison-des-Patriotes. In its current incarnation, the place reflects on events that could have changed the course of history, but didn't.

Throughout my travels, I learned a great deal about how these cities serve as vibrant backdrops in support of the afterlives of former prisons, memorial spaces, and historical exhibitions. In *Artifacts and Allegiances: How Museums Put the Nation and World on Display* (2015), Peggy Levitt relies on cities to decipher local—and global—stories as told through various cultural institutions. As a like-minded sociologist, Levitt points to the enduring contributions of Robert Park, who in 1915 described the city as a "state of mind, a body of customs and traditions, and of the organized attitudes and sentiments that inhere in these customs and are transmitted with this tradition" (qtd in Sennett, 1969: 91). Toward that same end, trusted urban explorer Lewis Mumford invites all of us to appreciate cities given that their stories "can be read through a succession of deposits: the sedimentary strata of history" ([1938]1970: 223). Having said all that, cities, like the nations wrapped around them, undergo transformation due to an array of forces. Political upheaval is just one of those forces and remains the underlying condition for this project as we travel from city to city in search of the afterlives of confinement.

Let me summarize the path ahead. In the next chapter, we delve into the nature of confinement as contoured along political lines and how the categories of *criminal*, *subversive*, and even *terrorist* remain in flux. Some additional historical lessons allow us to sort out those complexities. The discussion then turns to select autobiographies in tandem with related works focusing on Northern Ireland and the southern cone of Latin America. From there, I introduce a series of case studies that illuminate how post-conflict societies grapple with memory and transform sites accordingly. It has been said that an essential feature of the city is drama—especially *social* drama (Mumford, [1938]1970). In chapter 3, the social drama of the city pivots on the Troubles as those events have shaped Dublin and Belfast. By its very nature, the word "Troubles" speaks to tense entanglements among a cast of characters, their dialogues, and their audiences. While that euphemism has been used to describe the more recent conflict in Northern Ireland, the expression was common in all of Ireland, particularly during the 1916 Easter Rising, followed by the War of Independence and the Irish Civil War. The cultural residue of the Troubles reaches so deep into Irish society that it invokes socio-religious meaning; correspondingly, references to sacrifice and martyrdom are firmly embedded in a collective memory of political imprisonment. In both Dublin and Belfast, assorted cultural emblems have been folded into transformed sites so as to sway recognizable expressions of heritage (see Welch, 2016a).

With the benefit of knowing how the afterlives of cultural sites have emerged in Ireland, chapter 4 concentrates on the southern cone of Latin America, where Operation Condor and a series of "dirty wars" have shaped a wider consciousness about human rights atrocities. The afterlives of detention, torture, and extermination centers are examined in the capital cities of Buenos Aires, Santiago, Asunción, and Montevideo. In those places, critiques of the dictatorships are delivered through a cultural system of messages about death as well as survival. Those testimonies constitute what Pierre Nora (1989, 2002) detects as an upsurge in memory that refutes the "official" versions of history perpetuated by military and financial elites. The ensuing discussion sorts out the various strains of remembering and forgetting.

Chapter 5 recounts the economic disaster that would define Irish history: the Great Famine. In Dublin, in an effort to conceal so much poverty, British officials transformed the imposing Kilmainham Gaol into a "warehouse" for the poor.

From that very site, many Irish were transported to the colony of Australia, where they worked as prisoners, producing financial gain for the British Empire (Welch, 2015). Similar struggles are examined in Montreal, where La-Prison-des-Patriotes narrates the rebellions against British ruler in the 1830s. Returning to the southern cone, controversies over fiscal crises as perpetuated by proponents of the Chicago School of Economics (i.e., Los Chicago Boys) are examined in the context of military dictatorships and their reliance on political imprisonment as well as a methodical disappearance of the "subversive" population. The chapter ends by drawing attention to the economic transformations in South Africa that favor wealthy institutions in a post-apartheid society.

The repression that became part and parcel of the last dictatorship in Argentina went beyond political and financial restructuring. As will be shown in chapter 6, the junta harbored elements of a conservative Catholicism that condoned the scapegoating of civilians as well as activist religious workers, tarring them as "subversive." In Chile, by contrast, the Catholic Church took a very different stance, even confronting the Pinochet regime through legal action. To decipher all of this, I will examine historical developments in Montreal during the rebellions of 1837 and 1838 as well as in Belfast during the more contemporary Troubles. The chapter exposes how those events determined *how* political imprisonment would be administered—as well as resisted. This interpretation anticipates a cultural sociology dealing with the sacred and the profane (Smith, 1999; 2008).

In chapter 7, the last in "Part Two: Diagrams of Control," I unpack the many ways in which architecture itself has shaped political imprisonment. In Victorian times, the British built their prisons along the lines of a panopticon, thus injecting geometry into prisoner control, as so clearly illustrated at the Kilmainham Gaol (Dublin), the Crumlin Road Gaol (Belfast), and the Women's Jail (Johannesburg). Parallel architectural innovations were built into other institutions holding political prisoners in Seoul and Montevideo; the repurposing of Chile's National Stadium (Santiago) in wake of the 1973 coup serves as another example. The chapter explains how the dictatorships in the southern cone performed power by establishing a society of spectacles fastened to an economy of looks and looking. By doing so, authorities directed citizens to internalize the gaze of their repressors.

Much of this book focuses on how sites of political imprisonment are culturally repurposed, yet it is also important to examine other forms of transformation. The third set of chapters sheds crucial light on the "Technologies of Power." Chapter 8 theorizes on tactics of censorship and propaganda aimed at transforming the mind; accordingly it highlights the significance of Goffmanesque inquiry. Such dramaturgy in the southern cone underscores the various performances embodied in authoritarian regimes, which go to great lengths to mystify their atrocities. Censorship and propaganda also became tools of the British authorities in Northern Ireland. During the Troubles, state-controlled media were carefully managed by then-Prime Minister Margaret Thatcher and her cabinet. As a countermove,

Irish Republicans launched a public relations campaign to expose the inhumanity of political imprisonment. This publicity was carefully tailored for a sympathetic audience at the local and international levels.

Another technology of power is torture, a brutal method of transforming the body. Chapter 9 considers Foucault's notion of the body as the ultimate material seized by all political, economic, and penal institutions (see Garland, 1990). Former detention centers in the southern cone not only memorialize the victims of repression but also offer detailed lessons on the legacies of mistreatment. Likewise in Northern Ireland, controversies over the "five techniques" (or "deep interrogation") inflicted on political prisoners continue to spark social activism. To provide some theoretical grounding, the discussion blends Foucauldian perspectives on power, technology, and the body. As a method of critique, the chapter introduces the idea of "Foucault's Museum" in which former penal institutions serve as sites for progressive commentary that condemn human rights abuses (see Lord, 2006).

In the final installment on the technologies of power, chapter 10 outlines ambitious plans to transform entire societies through extermination. Genocide and denial are mutually reinforcing. A case in point is the extermination of the indigenous people of the southern cone, which even today is dismissed by a litany of denials. Similarly, the death flights conducted by the Argentine military were justified as "humane" acts of elimination. Likewise, in Chile, the Caravan of Death and Operation Colombo carried out by Pinochet's dictatorship also have been defended by those holding a nationalist identity. As a socio-historical backdrop, this chapter's discussion addresses themes of fascism, given that many Nazi war criminals fled to Latin America and once there were granted safe haven from post-war tribunals. Apparently, Baudrillard's (1994) warning—that forgetting the extermination is part of the extermination—was disregarded in the southern cone. There, military officers both embraced and denied their own participation in genocide. The chapter also deliberates on the unfolding controversy over the children born in captivity. At ESMA, the notorious detention, torture, and extermination center, infants were confiscated from their mothers, who were then murdered by the junta. Without their knowledge, those children were raised by other families under an illegal adoption program coordinated by the last dictatorship.

"Performing Memory" is played out in Part Three, in which Durkheimian thought continues to guide a sociological interpretation. In chapter 11, concepts related to the sacred and the profane are again interpreted through the prism of consecration and desecration (see Smith, 2008). The sanctity of death is contemplated at the Kilmainham Gaol and throughout a network of heritage sites in Dublin, where socio-religious rituals uphold the demand for proper memorialization (Welch, 2016a). Yet such sanctity is culturally contested in Belfast as partisan memories continue to clash in the collective consciousness. Memory of the 1981 hunger strike at the Maze prison hardens the ethnic and political divide. Bobby Sands and the nine other political prisoners are mourned as martyrs by the Republican community but scorned by Loyalists. In the southern cone, the sacred is ritualized to consecrate the victims of mass murder by the dictatorships, a heinous act of profanity and desecration. In that context, interpretation relies on the afterlives of sites to translate the quasi-spiritual foundation of political confinement.

The concluding chapter returns to the power of place and the performance of memory. In Buenos Aires, shaming repressors has become a brash form of activism. In what they call *escraches*, the grown children of the disappeared publicly humiliate former military officers complicit in the last dictatorship. As a collective, they use profane acts of street theatre to dispense their version of justice (Kaiser, 2002, 2020). Returning to Belfast, the city contains places of memory as well as places of resistance. In several museums devoted to Irish Republicanism, well-chosen images and objects are displayed as part of a ritual of resistance. Political posters, in particular, are a significant source for symbolic campaigns, becoming institutionalized within a partisan heritage. Reproducing themes of ascent, political prisoners in Belfast are celebrated for their daring escapes. Those prisoners have become legendary, even larger than life. The book concludes with some afterthoughts on the cultural afterlives of the sites and symbols of political imprisonment.

CAPTURING THE BASTILLE EFFECT

So we have lots of places to go to, lots of things to look at, and lots of ideas to think about. But let's not lose track of the significance of transforming sites of political imprisonment. Toward that end, my project begins with a basic question. What historical and cultural effect did the storming of the Bastille have on other places where political prisoners were confined?

Upon exploring those sites, I found a great deal of intriguing symbolism that narrates particular struggles. What I conceptualize as the Bastille Effect has emerged in various cities but under very different circumstances. However, what many of those transformed sites seem to share is a critique on justice as it prevails over injustice. Indeed, a dual transformation is evident in the manner in which sites are purified of their profane past as they cease to function as places of confinement. In the process, the site's place identity is reconfigured into a sacred space that invites visitors to reflect on the atrocities that occurred there. Those former prisons and detention centers also become metaphors for progressive social change in post-conflict societies whether in Northern Ireland, the southern cone of the Latin America, or elsewhere. To capture the Bastille Effect, the forthcoming chapters invite us to remain mindful of how these symbolic sites enter into the collective consciousness, promoting a greater awareness of human rights as a theme of ascent.

2

States of Confinement

Paris in the wake of the Revolution serves as a starting point for this journey into the Bastille Effect. Even while French architects were making plans to preserve of the Bastille as a monument to a fallen despot, the site was swiftly being demolished, due in large part to Pierre-François Palloy, who went by the self-appointed title "Patriote Palloy." This well-connected entrepreneur had his fingerprints all over a newly formed cult of the Bastille, which would quickly emerge as a global symbol of liberated humanity. Debris from the site was carted away and circulated around Paris as popular souvenirs. Palloy proudly promoted and meticulously regulated the business behind remembrance, using masonry from the ruins to make medallions and authentic replicas in the shape of the Bastille (BnF, 2010; Schama, 1990). At the Museum of the National Archives (Hotel de Soubise) in Paris is a model of the Bastille made by Palloy dated 1790, formed from stone recovered from its ruins. That mesmerizing remnant speaks to a dual transformation: the masonry of the former prison has abandoned its use-value and acquired signifying-value: thus, its afterlife celebrates the triumph of the Revolution and the storming of the Bastille. Secured as it is in a plexiglass vitrine, the object is clearly something important for visitors to gaze at. At a higher level of cultural commentary, that finely crafted model represents a transition from the profane function of incarceration to the sacred current of liberty in the French Republic (see figure 3).

Going beyond such cultural transformations, this chapter considers the important role of the state in political imprisonment by drawing attention to the subjective nature of such confinement. Efforts to nail down precisely who is a political prisoner are difficult and often self-defeating. To provide some perspective on that predicament, I will be turning critical attention to the United States, South Africa, and France. Along the way, we will remain mindful of themes of ascent in terms of the high status of some prisoners relative to the low status of other convicts, who are subjected to degrading treatment as they descend into the profane. After that, I will offer select readings on political imprisonment that contend with the

FIGURE 3. "The Bastille, a model by Palloy." An original model (1790) of the Bastille made by Palloy with stone recovered from its ruins is on display at the Museum of the National Archives (Hôtel de Soubise) in Paris. Maquette de la Bastille réalisée à partir d'une pierre de la forteresse par Palloy*, 1790, Archives nationales, AE VI a 79. © retrowelch 2022.

perennial struggle for justice against the misuse of state power. To provide context for that discussion, I will briefly summarize autobiographies of famous political prisoners alongside related writings on the Troubles in Northern Ireland and the "dirty wars" in the southern cone of Latin America.

THE STATUS OF POLITICAL IMPRISONMENT

Consider, if you will, the task of defining political imprisonment and determining who qualifies as a political prisoner. Compound the chore by expanding your audience to members of diverse ideological, religious, socio-economic, racial, and ethnic backgrounds. The exercise is likely to be stalled by the polarizing nature of what constitutes political imprisonment and who qualifies as such a prisoner. The popular adage that one man's freedom fighter is another man's terrorist remains undiluted. Which side to take is very much a subjective decision, and that judgement depends on one's point of view. A sociology of culture allows us to recognize that one's point (or points) of view often rests on themes of soaring ascent as well as spiraling descent (Smith, 1999). Some observers might regard a particular political prisoner as noble, heroic, and patriotic; others, as a criminal, a thug, or a subversive.

Let's situate the controversy over political imprisonment specifically in the United States. Historically, foreign visitors were quick to detect a particular point of view with respect to the politics of confinement. French writer Alexis de Tocqueville in *Democracy in America* helped explain how Americans saw themselves in the 19th century. A Continental European, Tocqueville was surprised to realize there were no political prisoners in America. The long, well-guarded French tradition was to treat an elevated class of offenders better than common criminals; American authorities had opted for a different path. James Q. Whitman, in *Harsh Justice*, clarifies the cultural divide between America and Europe as encountered by Tocqueville. From the American perspective, "the idea of subjecting the tiny minority of honorable prisoners to the sort of cellular confinement seen in either the Auburn system or the Pennsylvania system was unacceptable and indeed almost unimaginable" (2003: 125).

Let's fast-forward to more contemporary times to test this theory of cultural relativity. In 1978, during an interview with a French journalist, Andrew Young, a prominent African-American and at the time the US Ambassador to the United Nations, said: "After all, in our prisons too, there are hundreds, perhaps even thousands, of people whom I would call political prisoners" (Young, 1978). Enter Lennox Hinds, author of *Illusions of Justice: Human Rights Violations in the United States*, who reminds us that Young's remarks "reverberated throughout the world like a verbal rocket. In this country, it precipitated emotions ranging from appreciation of his candor to moral outrage" (2019: v). Calls for Young's resignation led to an impeachment resolution introduced in the US House of Representatives. Congressman John Conyers injected himself into the controversy by insisting that anyone familiar with the historical experience of Blacks and minorities in the US should not be shocked by Young's comments, especially given the widespread government abuses that had taken place in response to political dissent in the 1960s and 1970s (Hinds, 2016, 2019; see also Goodell, 1973).

Let's look more closely at the US from the point of view of the international human rights community. Albie Sachs, who would rise to serve on the Constitutional Court of South Africa, reminisces about the day he discovered he was a terrorist. He recalls with some bemusement that while teaching law in England, he was invited to attend a conference at Yale University. When he applied for a US visa, he was told he was ineligible because he was a "terrorist." Apparently, the US Department of State had classified the African National Congress (ANC) as a terrorist organization, and its members—including Sachs—as terrorists. Terms such as terrorist and political prisoner are rarely set in stone, however, and Sachs was eventually permitted to attend the conference at Yale. "And so, I discovered I wasn't a terrorist, and yet the description resonated, and irritated"

(Sachs, 2007: 355). Continuing to reflect on the matter, he noted his involvement in an unsuccessful bid to persuade Amnesty International to adopt Nelson Mandela as a prisoner of conscience. "Today—oh, how they wish, how they wish, how they wish they had adopted him! But AI didn't" (Sachs, 2007: 355–56). Amnesty International decided that because Mandela had planned violence against the state of South Africa, he did not meet the criteria of a prisoner of conscience. Sachs seems to confirm the theory of cultural relativity by pointing out Mandela's predicament:

> If his conscience had simply left him immobilized, sitting his house and doing nothing against apartheid, and he was picked up [arrested], then you could adopt him [as a prisoner of conscience]. But if his conscience led him to give up his career, break up his family, go underground, and take all the risks that he took—changing his name, his appearance, dedicating his life to bringing about change; if his conscience could tell him to do all that *and* risk his life physically by confronting the state that was denying him and his people their rights, then he doesn't qualify. (2007: 356)

Returning to Sachs's own predicament, he actually did qualify as a prisoner of conscience due to his detention under Ninety Day Law of South Africa. That law allowed the state to hold citizens for 90 days if it was suspected they might have knowledge of plans to overthrow the state. Accordingly, the state maintained the authority to order persons arrested and placed in solitary confinement without charge and without access to legal counsel. In the aftermath of apartheid, Sachs helped draft a new constitution that reversed the direction of state power. "No detention without trial" is now in that constitution, since as Sachs remembers, the practice of holding persons without access to the courts "was the weapon, the instrument that was used to pervert the whole of our criminal justice system" (2007: 359).

As for Mandela, the state would continue to dictate his status in South Africa as well in the US, but not without some twists and turns of cultural relativity. In 1964, Mandela was convicted of sabotage for targeting the state electrical grid, though no one was harmed in the operation. Mandela was imprisoned until 1990, when he was released at the age of 71. Four years later, he was elected President of South Africa. While he was imprisoned on Robben Island, the US had placed economic sanctions on the white minority government of South Africa for its policy of racial apartheid. However, in the 1980s, the US appeared to reverse its course by banning the ANC. Oddly, Mandela and other ANC officials appeared on the terror watch list even as President George Bush welcomed President Mandela to the White House in 1990. It wasn't until 2008 that the ANC was finally removed from the list of terrorist organizations monitored by the US government. By then, Mandela was 90 years old, having stepped down from the presidency nine years prior. Condoleezza Rice, Secretary of State in the George W. Bush administration, complained to Congress that her department was required to issue waivers for

ANC members to travel to the US. "This is a country with which we now have excellent relations, South Africa," Rice added, "but it's frankly a rather embarrassing matter that I still have to waive in my own counterpart, the foreign minister of South Africa, not to mention the great leader Nelson Mandela" (Windrem, 2013; see also Waxman, 2018; Mandela, 1994).

Making sense of this cultural relativity as it pertains to political imprisonment can be tricky, so let us turn once again to Whitman (2003) and his analysis of the divide between America and Europe. From the standpoint of comparative history dating back to the 18th century, the traditions of social hierarchy on the Continent stem from an "aristocratic element" in legal culture. By contrast, in America the absence of such elevated respect and dignity moves punishment toward a harsher and more degrading form of justice. To degrade someone is to reduce that person's status to an inferior level, thus widening the gap between the high-status punishments in Europe and the low-status ones in the US. Whitman points out that in European law there is a drive toward a high-status egalitarianism that raises everyone's social standing, not only for political dissenters but also for criminal offenders (see Elias, 2005). "Nothing of the kind has happened in the United States . . . and this reflects the fact that the history of social status in the American world is very different" (Whitman, 2003: 11).

From its early days, America embraced the norms of low-status penalties. According to Whitman, the historical reasons for that leveling down are complex; yet we can say here that the legacy of slavery looms large in the realm of incarceration, with racial minorities facing demeaning treatment. In sociological terms, the administration of justice in Europe embraces themes of ascent, whereas themes of descent are characteristic of the US. Acts of mercy are not uncommon in the American courts, but they are much more institutionalized under European law. To explain the cultural divide, Whitman revisits the role of history in Europe in regard to how it has shaped status hierarchy. He insists that France—and Germany—are much stronger states than the US as well as relatively autonomous, in the sense that "they are relatively free to intervene in civil society without losing political legitimacy . . . [and] are relatively immune to the vagaries of public opinion" (Whitman, 2003: 13–14).

High status, as pegged within a European social hierarchy, throws historical light onto political imprisonment. In medieval society, aristocrats defeated in battle risked being taken captive and held for ransom. As war booty, those prisoners added to the symbolism of royal victory. Their high status also ensured that while in captivity, they would be treated well, often within the protection of a fortress. Fortress confinement, as embodied most famously in the Bastille, would survive for centuries, with high-status prisoners—political dissenters, philosophers, literary figures—retaining their honor and enjoying privileged accommodations (BnF, 2010; Spierenburg, 1995). Their special treatment was rarely challenged because they weren't *really* criminals. By the 1960s, "that high-status imprisonment [had] been generalized to all in France. The French pattern of leveling-up in status runs from *aristocrats and the like; to political dissenters and debtors; to everybody"* (Whitman, 2003: 108). Hence, common criminals benefited by being identified with the "politicals," who were viewed as opponents of the state.

In 1960s Paris, upheaval against the Algerian war only fueled that shift toward leveling up, for when the French authorities resorted to the mass imprisonment of protesters, those protesters once behind bars expected better conditions in accordance to the old French tradition (Spire, 1991). As these events unfolded, Michel Foucault and like-minded activists pushed for even more sweeping prison reforms (Welch, 2011b, 2010a). Left-wing militants who opposed the colonial war in Algeria demanded "special treatment" as political prisoners. The French state capitulated, and soon after, laws were passed that extended a dignitary regime to prisoners nationwide. "For the old privileges of 'political prisoners' were at last extended to 'ordinary' confines of the 'droit commun.' In effect, one of the most radical demands of the 1960s was successfully realized in France, all prisoners came to be treated as political, as rebels against the established order" (Whitman, 2003: 130; see also Vimont, 1993, 1990). Of course, depending on one's point of view, those developments speak to themes of ascent in which humanity brings an end to the degrading treatment of *all* prisoners, regardless of their status. Regrettably, though, as this book will reveal, political prisoners as well as civilians have been swept into detention, with the state exercising brutal forms of power that are not limited to mistreatment, torture, and death. Themes of descent with all its degrading forces are the subject of deep reflection in this book. To widen our understanding of those matters, let us delve into the memoirs and other writings that contemplate political imprisonment.

READING THOUGHTS ON POLITICAL IMPRISONMENT

The journey along which we reflect on the transformation of sites and symbols of political imprisonment benefits from my previous work that recognizes how former prisons in their afterlives have reemerged as storytelling institutions, emitting signifying-value (Welch, 2012, 2013, 2015). Indeed, the Bastille Effect is animated by stories, legends, and tales that rely on themes of ascent as well as descent to express the duality of political confinement. From that perspective, this book is a book about stories and the role institutions play in telling those stories. When we absorb those stories, our exploration—however vicarious— becomes all the more meaningful. In this section, we turn to some of the literature, which I have grouped into three areas specific to this project: autobiographies, the Troubles in Northern Ireland, and the last dictatorships in the southern cone of Latin America.

Memoirs figure prominently in the literature on political imprisonment. But these works create an unavoidable paradox for readers. Stories of political confinement are enthralling; we want to know what these prisoners think of their personal ordeals. Yet themes of ascent—of survival, for example—are routinely accompanied by those of descent, including suffering. Readers find their own point of view shaped by both. Mandela's *Long Walk to Freedom* (1994) is one of the most renowned autobiographies of a political prisoner, and rightly so. Its sweeping narrative begins with his early childhood under apartheid, then tracks his transformation into a freedom fighter. The arc of the story extends to reconciliation, or what Mandela refers to as "talking to the enemy." In between these stages of development are moving passages that allow readers to appreciate the polarity between justice and injustice. Life as a political prisoner serves as Mandela's main literary device for sharing his insights. When he was processed at the notorious Robben Island prison, he was assigned the number "466/64," indicating that he was the 466th prisoner admitted in the year 1964, and ordered to strip naked. The ritual reminds readers that stripping is just one of the "indignities of prison life" (1994: 334). Foucault (1979) theorizes that the minute dispensation of punishments down to the smallest detail amounts to a micro-economy of perpetual penality. At Robben Island, prison uniforms both illustrated and reflected apartheid's stringent regulations. Whites and Asians were issued long pants. By contrast, Black prisoners were given short pants. Mandela writes that being assigned shorts was intended to instruct Africans that "we were 'boys'" at least from the point of view of the guards. This might sound trivial, relative to the systemic inhumanity faced by political prisoners at Robben Island, yet it was consistent with the degrading treatment that saturated the entire apartheid system of control.

Angela Davis begins her autobiography with her childhood in a time of violent segregation. Through those early experiences she developed a consciousness critical of the establishment. The book blends a literary style with edgier rhetoric that inspires an activist audience. Davis's imprisonment followed by her trial is remembered in dramatic prose. Among her memories as a prisoner is the enormous outpouring of support, including a letter from James Baldwin that reads:

> Some of us, white and black, know how great a price has already been paid to bring into existence a new consciousness, a new people, an unprecedented nation. If we know, and do nothing, we are worse than the murderers hired in our name. If we know, then we must fight for your life as though it were our own—which it is—and render impassible with our bodies the corridor to the gas chamber. For, if they take you in the morning, they will be coming for us that night. (in Davis, 2016a: 306)

Davis went on to form a collective that published a book chronicling the stories of other political prisoners. After Baldwin, the anthology is titled *If They Come in the Morning* (Davis, 1971). After her famous victory in court, Davis was launched onto an international stage. With forces of ascent, Davis continues to speak passionately about justice and equality (2016b). In 2021, a major exhibition, *Angela Davis— Seize the Time*, began its tour. The retrospective invites viewers "to re-imagine the construction of the image of Davis as a political icon of the left, symbol of Black

FIGURE 4. "Angela Davis Poster in Paris." A vintage poster of Angela Davis decorates a café in Paris. The caption borrows from a quote in Davis's autobiography: "Walls turned sideways are bridges" (2016a: 347). © retrowelch 2022.

radical resistance, female empowerment, and a threat to the white patriarchal status quo" (Sokolowski, 2019). The materials on display document the campaign to "Free Angela and All Political Prisoners" as well as Davis's own writings and actions related to freedom, oppression, feminisms, and prison abolition (Davis, 2016c; see figure 4).

The global war on terror, initiated by the US government, has generated streams of human rights abuses relevant to a discussion of political imprisonment (Welch, 2006, 2009a). In *Guantanamo Diary*, Mohamedou Ould Slahi delivers a tale of misery so compelling that it seems like a work of fiction. It is not. The heavily redacted journal chronicles his personal plight through what spy novelist John Le Carré calls "a vision of hell, beyond Kafka: a perpetual torture prescribed by the mad doctors of Washington" (Slahi, 2015: back cover). After more than 14 years of torture and confinement without charge, and even after finding relief in the US federal courts, Slahi faced an uncertain future that is still difficult to comprehend. Slahi spent his time in solitary confinement learning English well enough to write a book-length diary. The bizarre circumstances of Slahi's confinement offer an opportunity to theorize a little on state power—and as we shall see, those lessons are applicable to similar problems in Northern Ireland and the southern cone of Latin America (see Fletcher and Stover, 2009).

In her critique of socio-legal transformations in a post-9/11 world, Judith Butler theorizes that the war on terror is being administered by newly created petty sovereigns who are mobilized by tactics of power they do not fully control. In the process, they are granted the power to render unilateral decisions, "accountable to no law and without any legitimate authority," becoming "a 'rogue' power par excellence" (2004: 56). That "rogue" power determines the process of classifying certain persons as high-value detainees and unlawful enemy combatants. It is important to emphasize that those decisions take place in the context of a "state of emergency" that has set the conditions for removing accountability from the field of operations. The "emergency" ushers in rules (governmentality) that replace laws (juridical), thus reinstating sovereign power that distributes managerial authority even as it enjoys full and unreviewable discretion. As a result, pseudo-institutions are produced for the administration of the war on terror, most notably "a law that is not a law, a court that is not a court, a process that is not a process" (2004: 62; see also Welch, 2008, 2010b, 2014, 2016b).

Turning attention to the ways in which political prisoners reflect on the state of confinement in Northern Ireland during the Troubles, we find Bobby Sands. In his *Writings from Prison*, Sands issues short stories and uplifting poetry to condemn the historical injustice of British colonialism in Ireland. Challenging the British state that has labeled him a criminal and a terrorist, Sands replies: "I am a political prisoner. I am a political prisoner because I am a casualty of a perennial war that is being fought between the oppressed Irish people and an alien, oppressive, unwanted regime that refuses to withdraw from our land" (Sands, 1998: 219). His readers already anticipate his death as a hunger striker, which makes the collection of entries all the more meaningful to tacticians of resistance. Sands's memoir paves the way for other first-hand accounts of political prisoners in Northern Ireland, including *Cage Eleven* (Adams, 1997) and *Nor Meekly Serve My Time: The H Block Struggle (1976–1981)* (Campbell, McKeown, and O'Hagan, 1994). Their narratives are often descriptive in style and content, offering a unified vision for a peaceful Ireland—a sentiment that continues to resonate.

Setting aside memoirs, the scholarship on the Troubles in Northern Ireland is extensive. As guideposts for this project, we turn to some selected books that prompt us to think along the lines of concepts and theory as well as processes of social and cultural transformation. Feldman's *Formations of Violence: The Narrative of the Body and Political Terror in Northern Ireland* is a daring exercise in urban fieldwork, offering readers a terrifying look at the Troubles in real time. His study consists of confidential interviews in 1985 and 1986, a time when Republican and Loyalist paramilitaries were operating under high alert. Feldman, an anthropologist, deciphers political violence and political imprisonment through representations of the body as text. In helping us develop a critical understanding of the Troubles, he describes his work as "an ethnography of surfaces—those sites, stages, and templates upon which history is constructed as a cultural object" (1991: 2).

In the massive *Paramilitary Imprisonment in Northern Ireland: Resistance, Management, and Release* (2001), Kieran McEvoy complements his research with a keen knowledge of the Troubles. With his focus on various activities behind prison walls, McEvoy recognizes that those dynamics fueled a larger political conflict across Northern Ireland. Correspondingly, the infamous Maze prison provides a site of resistance that is not unlike the legacy of the Bastille (see Wylie, 2004). With even more emphasis on culture, Laura McAtackney's *An Archaeology of the Troubles: The Dark Heritage of Long Kesh/Maze Prison* (2014) gravitates toward the significance of afterlife and how even (partly) demolished institutions resonate with meaning. Much as happened with the Bastille, remnants of the Maze have been dispersed to heritage sites elsewhere (see Welch 2016c). For broadening our point(s) of view of the Troubles, the investigative journalism of Peter Taylor is indispensable. Years of exhaustive coverage have produced a trilogy of books exploring each side of the low-level war. Beginning with *Provos: The IRA and Sinn Fein* (1997), followed by *Loyalists: War and Peace in Northern Ireland* (1999) and then *Brits: The War against the IRA* (2001), Taylor places the conflict into an international forum for serious reflection (see also Beresford, 1987).

Those writings on the Troubles in Northern Ireland provide some basis for understanding the southern cone of Latin America, where political violence ravaged the region around the same time (the 1970s through the 1990s). *The Condor Years* (Dinges, 2004) and *The Pinochet File* (Kornbluh, 2013) demonstrate the importance of cross-national journalism conducted by writers who have devoted their careers to investigating controversies in Latin America. Dinges, himself targeted, abducted, and detained at the notorious Villa Grimaldi (Santiago), explores the underground history of Operation Condor and role played in it by US intelligence agencies. In the course of his work, he traces vectors of accountability in cases of crimes against humanity. *The Pinochet File* exposes the dictatorship in Chile as well as the clandestine Operation Condor, an illustration of

"State-Sponsored International Terrorism." From declassified documents held in US archives, Kornbluh details Pinochet's criminal activity, including his implication in a scandal in which he funneled more than $26 million to a US bank. Naomi Roht-Arriaza's *The Pinochet Effect: Transnational Justice in Age of Human Rights* (2005) chronicles the enduring legacy of the 1998 arrest of Pinochet in London that sent shock waves through the international community.

Conceptualizing state violence and political imprisonment in the context of Latin America's southern cone, this project closely adheres to the lessons drawn from *Disappearing Acts: Spectacles of Gender and Nationalism in Argentina* (D. Taylor, 1997) and *Accounting for Violence: The Memory Market in Latin America* (Bilbija and Payne, 2011). Those two books offer a critique of gender, nationalism, and memory. Taylor keeps her focus on the last dictatorship in Argentina, underscoring the cultural importance of hypermasculinity vis-à-vis feminism. *Disappearing Acts*'s use of the spectacle as an organizing principle is reconfigured herein by a decidedly Goffman-esque perspective on performance. *Accounting for Violence* examines the marketing of memory in a Latin America torn by mass violence. The volume serves as an important safeguard for memory studies by unveiling a range of motives for remembering as well as forgetting. In the later chapters of this book, discussion will similarly turn to the performance of memory not only in post-Condor cities but also in Belfast, where sites and symbols of the Troubles have been transformed.

A final grouping of works—by Marguerite Feitlowitz, Rebekah Park, and Susana Draper—establish a foundation for witnessing and interpreting discourse, sited-ness, and the afterlives of former detention centers in the Southern Cone. *A Lexicon of Terror: Argentina and the Legacies of Torture* (1998) is a classic work on the torture carried out by state operatives as explained by Feitlowitz, who captures the surreal vocabulary concealing human rights atrocities. Park, in *The Reappeared: Argentine Former Political Prisoners* (2014), tracks the pathways from political imprisonment back into free society, where "life after prison still feels like imprisonment" (2014: 108). *Afterlives of Confinement: Spatial Transitions in Postdictatorship Latin America*, by Draper, strongly shapes our comprehension of the spatial transitions of former penal sites once used by military and later repurposed for memorialization. As we transit through post-Condor cities, we will also remain mindful of Jacobo Timerman's *Prisoner Without a Name, Cell Without a Number* ([1981]1998). That powerful memoir benefits from the flair of a seasoned journalist, who details his horrific ordeal under the last dictatorship in Argentina. The book remains a benchmark in the human rights literature, appealing to a global audience (see Almada, 1993; Feierstein, 2014). This book does not attempt to compete with these impressive autobiographies and scholarly works. Rather, it absorbs their insights into a sociological context for cultural inspection of transformed sites of political imprisonment (see Newburn and Sparks, 2004).

RESTATING THE BASTILLE EFFECT

Early in this chapter, we reflected on how Patriote Palloy created a cult of the Bastille so that it became a broader metaphor for liberated humanity. In doing so, he transformed the use-value of the infamous site into enduring signifying-value. As an example of the Bastille Effect by which the former prison shed its profane past and acquire sacred status, a stone from the prison's foundation was carved into a bust of Mirabeau, a celebrated ex-prisoner. The statue was honored at Mirabeau's historic funeral in 1791, thus gaining even greater distinction. In a similar ritual of transformation, a sword was bestowed on Lafayette made with four bolts from the Bastille. Lafayette, in turn, presented George Washington with one of 27 keys to the Bastille as a gesture of revolutionary goodwill. Demand for Palloy's mementos continued to mount outside of France; New York's Society of St. Tammany requested one. On site, former guards—converted Patriots—offered visitors graphic accounts of the torment and torture of legendary prisoners once held there. With the power of place, performances surrounding the former prison struck a delicate balance between the horror of imprisonment and the euphoria of its demise. On the first anniversary of the Bastille's fall, hundreds of thousands of provincial guardsmen made a pilgrimage to its grounds. Perhaps more memorable, July 14th would be commemorated as Bastille Day, which continues to be celebrated around the world (BnF, 2010; Fournel, 1892; Schama, 1990).

While offering added thoughts on cultural transformations and the afterlives of the Bastille, this chapter has addressed the subjective underpinnings of political confinement, especially given the state's complex role in determining—or denying—political status. After outlining lessons in the US, South Africa, and France, it turned its attention to controversies in other societies where the degrading treatment of political prisoners demonstrated the degree to which the state undermined justice. Along the way, human rights campaigns gathered leverage, prompting social and democratic reforms. In the chapters to follow, greater interest is focused on those developments in Northern Ireland and the southern cone of Latin America. As we shall see, the sites and symbols of political imprisonment, as embodied in sacred memorials, articulate those crucial shifts in history.

PART TWO

In Search of Signs

3

Sites of Trouble

Apparently operating on the logic that the Bastille was built to keep prisoners in while keeping intruders out, the authorities deemed it a safe place to store 250 barrels of gunpowder. As urban unrest in Paris grew uglier by the week in 1789, that assumption was sorely tested. On the 14th of July, a crowd swarmed the Bastille, eventually breaking through its supposedly impassable gate. Hours later, nearly 100 citizens lay dead and the gunpowder had been seized. The rest is history. The Bastille had long enjoyed an evil mystique, yet the record indicates that by the time of the revolution it was almost empty. A grand total of seven prisoners—four forgers, two madmen, and an irritant held at the request of his family—were honored for surviving the monarchy's repression. In a picture to mark the occasion, one ex-prisoner, an Irish lunatic known as Major Whyte, is shown leading a procession through the streets of Paris. His long beard, bony body, and dazed demeanor are consistent with the popular imagining that the Bastille was a site of tyranny. Thus its grim legacy has been perpetuated (BnF, 2010: 167; see also Funck-Brentano, 1979, 1898).

In her cultural characterization of Ireland, Jessica Scarlata writes that "imprisonment is a central trope of Irish nationalism, often deployed to portray the injustice of an Ireland occupied by foreign rule. Irish nationalism celebrates people jailed for resistance to British forces" (2014: front flap). The events of 1916, a year of immense trouble, figure prominently in the collective consciousness of the Irish as manifested in local heritage. Heritage is treated as something of value to be cherished and curated, yet the concept has been retheorized to suggest that "there is no such thing as heritage" (Smith, 2011: 69). Rather, heritage is a cultural performance that takes the stage at various sites such as memorial spaces and historical museums. The process of performance attaches meaning to things and places, particularly as they are converted from use-value to signifying-value. Those transformations have a considerable hold among certain people, yet they are often subject to alternative interpretations and counter-arguments and at times are rejected outright.

"Sites of trouble" play a significant role in the Bastille Effect, through which the power of place facilitates narratives on justice and injustice. In Ireland, profane sites have been transformed into sacred spaces. Such cultural transformations facilitate the emergence of heritage and identity among different groups. To understand these complicated matters, it is important to take into account the importance of boundaries, borders, and walls. The physical lines demarcating space and territory produce another yin-yang duality in that they both separate and unite. To illustrate these historical and contemporary transitions, we focus on Dublin, a city of early Trouble, followed by Belfast, a city of later Trouble. Along the way, we will find that transformed sites contribute to a Bastille Effect, becoming metaphors for nation-building in the aftermath of social and political conflict.

THE DUALITY OF BOUNDARIES, BORDERS, AND WALLS

As we consider the significance of boundaries, borders, and walls as they have shaped Ireland—North and South—the scholarly work of Juri Lotman enables us to comprehend an array of social dynamics. In his *Universe of the Mind* (2000), Lotman interprets culture as information manifesting as collective memory that is acquired, preserved, and transmitted by certain people. Signs, symbols, and language are the vehicles for transmitting that culture, giving unique form to heritage and identity—with all their political, religious, and ethnic complexities. Our social worlds, Lotman recognizes, do not stray from their duality. He emphasizes that we live in realms of culture that are predicated on contradictions. Our social worlds are unequal yet unified, asymmetrical yet uniform. And while those social worlds are holistic and social, they are composed of individuation in ways that give rise to self-description expressed through first-person pronouns.

Enter the boundary, where individuation is heightened—or as Lotman puts it, "the boundary can be defined as the outer limit of a first-person form" (2000: 131). The boundary intensifies culture and territorial space between "our" internal space that is "my own," "safe," and "harmoniously organized" and "their" external space, which is deemed "hostile, dangerous, and chaotic" (131). The edges of a boundary are the "hottest spot" for linguistic and symbolic activity; with an inherent sense of duality, such a boundary "both separates and unites" (136). Unsurprisingly, Lotman's contributions have penetrated urban studies, especially given that cities embody various forms of communication and identity within a confined social space (Remm, 2011; see also Lotman, 2004, 2005).

In previous chapters we saw how cities are animated by social drama (Mumford, 1938). Thus Lotman's account of boundaries helps us refine our approach to both

Dublin and Belfast, where notions of unification and separation are continuously performed through heritage. As intangible as those activities are, they nonetheless occur at specific places, creating forms of sitedness that are either sanctified or condemned, depending on one's political and ethnic orientation. In a word, heritage as it exists in Ireland is *troubled* (Welch, 2016a, 2019). As we shall see, there are often a clashes of performances, which surf the tensions of heritage and identity as expressed through sites and symbols. Those performances amplify both monologues and dialogues about who "we" are, and why, in contrast to who "they" are, and why (see Smith, 2011; Waterton, 2008; Welch, 2016a).

DUBLIN: CITY OF EARLY TROUBLE

In Dublin, Irish heritage is convincingly performed at the former Kilmainham Gaol. Known as the "Bastille of Ireland," that site currently serves as a history museum as well as a storytelling institution (O'Dwyer, 2010). There, imprisonment in Ireland is a topic around which nationalism and identity are carefully organized. Confinement, in Ireland, was a patently political act of colonialism, but beyond it lay another act, of economic exploitation. While the story of how the British seized Irish land and property has long been told, Kilmainham goes to great lengths to connect the dots between incarceration, penal transportation, and famine (see Cook, 2014; Foster, 1988). What is commonly known among the Irish as the "Hunger," the Great Famine was caused by a failed potato crop, which deprived the majority of the people of their staple food. The "Hunger" consumed over a million people between 1845 and 1850; another million and a half emigrated.

With reminders of death in the foreground of the museum, one can sense that in its current form the gaol has passed through a cultural process in which the profane has been replaced with the sacred. Memory of that humanitarian crisis is activated through various curatorial techniques embedded in Kilmainham's exhibition hall. At Kilmainham, the storyboards on display acquire greater authority by introducing the Irish language first, followed by English. "The Government proved inadequate in dealing with the crisis. Nothing illustrates this more clearly than the Vagrant Act of 1847. Intended to clear the streets of unsightly poor, its effect was to swamp the prisons with those found begging in the streets. In prison, they were either saved by the luxury of a meagre but life-saving prison diet, or succumbed to the disease-ridden overcrowded conditions." The collection includes a stark drawing of a mother clutching her dying child. With more technologically powered imagery, a series of video monitors post biographical details of those swept up in the machinery of punishment:

James McDonnell (18)
Plasterer
In possession of stolen peas and apples
Sentence: Fourteen Days

Betty Toole (56)
No Trade
In possession of stolen potatoes
Sentence: Two Days

The curators at Kilmainham deliver a narrative on punishment that aligns major events in Irish history with a wider message on injustice, as an emergent Bastille Effect. A few steps away from the exhibit on "the Hunger" is a panel devoted to "Transportation," which tells us that more than 4,000 Irish were shipped from Kilmainham to Australia to work as penal convicts for the British Empire in the early 19th century. "The nature of the crimes for which sentences of transportation were handed down varied greatly. This was due largely to the judiciary's arbitrary attitude to sentencing." Among those transported were the "Young Irelanders" who "enthused by the spirit of revolution in Europe . . . organised a rebellion in 1848." When the rebellion collapsed, its leaders William Smith O'Brien and Thomas Francis Meagher were held in Kilmainham and then transported to Tasmania. Maintaining his rebellious streak, Meagher escaped to the United States, where he led the Irish Brigade for the Union during the American Civil War (Kilmainham Gaol, n.d.; Touhill, 1981). Yet the vast majority of the Irish convicts consigned to the Antipodes were ordinary poor people caught up in a colonial system that exploited them for their economic value. Forced migration to Australia was especially punitive, considering what is commonly referred to as the *tyranny of distance* (Blainey, 1966).

With its sacred aura, the Kilmainham Gaol reveals its signifying-value in its afterlife so as to provide lessons on Irish history. "From the 1790s onwards, freedom from British rule, as a republic, became the form of political independence favoured by radical Irish nationalists. More moderate nationalists aspired to 'Home Rule', or constitutional independence for Ireland within the British Empire. A remarkable number of leading figures of Irish nationalism were imprisoned at Kilmainham Gaol, and some were executed here" (Visitor's Guide, n.d.; see also Cooke, 2014).

Kilmainham opened as a prison in 1796 and closed in 1910. From 1916 to 1924, it was recommissioned to incarcerate political prisoners, another reminder of its complicated heritage. During the War of Independence (1919–21), political prisoners were held by British forces. During the Civil War (1922–24), the Irish Free State Army took control of Kilmainham to imprison its rivals, who opposed the Anglo-Irish Treaty (1921). Adding to those controversies, the Free State Government executed 77 Irish Republicans at the gaol. Those bitter memories would persist, and resentment between political parties would fester, prolonging efforts to transform Kilmainham into a heritage site. In the process of overcoming those hard feelings, the 1916 Rising was assigned central importance as a unifying event. In the 1960s, a heritage committee comprised of disparate political backers "agreed on the notion of preserving the jail as a monument to 'Ireland's heroic dead'" (O'Dwyer, 2010:

FIGURE 5. "The Stonebreakers' Yard." At the Kilmainham Gaol (the "Bastille of Ireland") in Dublin, a cross planted in the ground marks the spot where each Irish rebel was executed. The double doors, to the right, were opened to allow an ambulance to enter. The vehicle was transporting James Connolly, who was injured in the Rising. Unable to stand, he was shot while seated in a chair. © retrowelch 2022.

88). As a cornerstone of Irish heritage, 1916 with all of its symbolic weight would continue to narrate trouble, resistance, and ultimately Independence.

As the story goes, on Easter Monday 1916, units of the Irish Volunteers and the Irish Citizen Army seized the General Post Office and other landmarks strongly associated with the British Empire. The Rising was intended as a material *and* symbolic challenge to British rule. Greatly outnumbered by British troops, the rebels held out for nearly a week before surrendering. Hundreds of Irish men and women were rounded up and imprisoned at Kilmainham. Between May 3 and May 12, 14 of those men were executed by firing squad. Patrick Pearse, commander-in-chief of the Volunteers, was the first to be shot. The last to be executed was James Connolly of the Irish Citizen Army. In 2016, the Irish government launched an "official commemoration" of the 100-year anniversary of the 1916 Rising. Ireland's president, Michael Higgins, placed a wreath at the spot where the rebels were executed in the Stonebreakers' Yard within the Kilmainham Gaol (see figure 5). Many Irish in the South celebrate the anniversary of the events of 1916; Unionists in the North, however, remain dismissive of the Republican heritage performed in Dublin. As recently as 2016, all the major Unionist parties boycotted the commemoration.

Once again, the boundary has the symbolic capacity to define not only territory but culture as well (see McDonald, 2016).

At the Kilmainham Gaol, heritage is ritualized to memorialize political prisoners as national heroes. Displays of socio-religious objects and images reinforce an aura of transcendence and other themes of ascent. Among an assortment of thoughtfully arranged artifacts, a crucifix sculpted from three bullets looms large, a reminder of the conversion of use-value to signifying-value. It is believed to have been made by Bernard Valentine Britcher, who was imprisoned at Kilmainham in 1916, which was the year that political imprisonment and Kilmainham became nearly synonymous owing to the events of the Easter Rising. Setting the stage for a performance about the fate of the 1916 rebels, visitors are funneled into a dimly lit auditorium and seated on rows of benches. They quietly wait as the guide positions themself for a solemn moment. At that point, the former gaol becomes a theatrical space for dramatizing heritage. A slideshow is projected on a large screen as the speaker introduces some of the key actors in the 1916 Rising. The plot unfolds as the speaker talks about Joseph Plunkett. A photograph of Plunkett shows him with his fiancé, Grace Gifford. The audience is informed that as an act of mercy, Plunkett was granted permission to marry Gifford—then hours later he faced the firing squad. Suddenly, the video screen scrolls up, revealing the altar where the couple exchanged wedding vows. All the time, the group has been sitting inside a Catholic chapel. Such power of place greatly enhances the experience of heritage and memorialization. The sacred space is decorated with ornate candlesticks and other Catholic emblems, which are carefully lit to emphasize their specialness. Through its new place identity, the chapel has been *personed* with the ghosts of Plunkett and Gifford, whose images flood the room with a sense of injustice.

For continued performance of Irish heritage, the Kilmainham Gaol relies on a variety of exhibits. Curators are keen to steer visitors into a gallery titled "Last Words 1916." At the doorway, a poster maintains the narrative on the 14 executions, which "rapidly transformed the popular perception of these men into heroes in the pantheon of rebel martyrs. At a more human level, they left behind wives, children, loved ones, proud of what they had done, but broken-hearted too" (see Mac Lochlainn, 2006). In this shadowed room, heritage is staged through the cultural power of poetics and religious artifacts. Among the more compelling artifacts is a miniature replica of the altar where Plunkett and Gifford were united in the act of holy matrimony only to be torn apart by the lethality of the firing squad. The compact shrine features Gifford's scrapbook, which is opened to a page with a photograph of Plunkett and another of herself with a handwritten caption that reads "the dress worn at my wedding." A copy of the 1916 Proclamation is attached to the facing page, thus casting their loving relationship as a metaphor for national aspirations.

To reiterate, prison museums in their current form are storytelling institutions. At the Kilmainham Gaol, curators add literary elegance to the importance of 1916. "All changed, changed utterly" is a profound phrase in the poem "Easter 1916" by W. B. Yeats, who writes that in 1916, "A terrible beauty is born." Although the initial response to the Rising was "one of anger at the destruction caused to the heart of Dublin, the executions quickly changed the mood." Memorial masses and enthusiastic fundraising rallied the Irish, who began to reconsider their status in the Second City of the British Empire. Poetry, prose, and various expressions of popular culture were widely circulated, elevating the legacies of Pearse, Plunkett, Connolly, and other rebels. "From these writings emerged the impression not of reckless adventurers, but men who had sacrificed their lives patriotically for an independent Ireland." The 1916 Proclamation that was announced at the onset of the Rising gained even deeper resonance, leading to the War of Independence with all its themes of ascent.

Elsewhere in Dublin, other sacred spaces commemorate the momentous events of 1916. As a cultural pilgrimage, visitors make their way to the "Old Cemetery" (Arbour Hill), where the 14 rebels are laid to rest. Well-manicured grounds and the neighboring church reinforce its solemn purpose. The impressive monument built in 1956 pays tribute to the signatories of the Proclamation who were later executed. A curved wall of Ardbracan limestone features a gilded cross in the center. The 1916 Proclamation of the Republic is inscribed both in Irish and in English. As a reminder that this is a revered space with international reach, a placard shows a 1963 photograph of US President John Fitzgerald Kennedy standing respectfully behind a wreath placed at the memorial. He is joined by other dignitaries and high-ranking soldiers, who stand in formation. Ceremonies at Arbour Hill, however, have not always succeeded in promoting a unified vision of nationhood. In 1924, the first "official 1916 commemoration" (in 1924) was marred by poor attendance due to "objections to the Free State authority" (O'Dwyer, 2010: 15).

Even today, visitors with a keen eye will detect some tension at the Arbour Hill memorial site. Those who arrive expecting to pay their respects to the 1916 rebels from the perspective of Irish Catholics may be distracted by the presence an Anglican Church alongside a graveyard for British military personnel killed in the War of Independence. Also detracting from its sacred aura is a 30-foot containment wall with a guard tower perched on one corner. Oddly, the otherwise solemn memorial sits next to the Arbour Hill Prison—an embodiment of the profane. The fully operating prison is known for housing sex offenders. Thus, the pilgrimage to commemorate the 1916 martyrs is strained not only by the presence of the British military but also by the prison and its despised convicts. That cultural tension seems to undermine the sanctity of death. In sum, the events of the Troubles linger not only in Dublin and the South of Ireland but also and especially in Belfast and the North. As we shall see, the duality of the national border and the peace walls erected around various sections of Belfast add to the complexity of the sites of trouble.

BELFAST: CITY OF LATER TROUBLE

Northern Ireland, much like the scholarly literature describing it, must contend with complicated tensions. Brian Graham writes that "cultural artefacts, including heritage landscapes will be invested with differing and conflicting meanings by various social groups" (1996: 10; see also Crooke, 2005; Graham and McDowell, 2007). Even the expression *North of Ireland*, rather than Northern Ireland, is saturated with the Republican/Nationalist ambition for unification with the South of Ireland (McGlinchey, 2019). Correspondingly, objects, symbols, and sites are imbued with degrees of dissonance that mirror competing ethno-political identities. Flags, murals, and memorial gardens not only *belong* to certain groups but also mark their territory. Those competing social worlds lay bare the legacies of colonial and paramilitary violence. In Belfast, visitors are drawn into a unique social drama orchestrated by political tourism, an industry that relies on notions of boundaries to accentuate difference amid the Troubles (McDowell, 2008). That recognition of boundaries has two facets. First, the border separating the Northern Ireland from the South was imposed in the aftermath of the Irish War of Independence from the British state in the 1920s. During that period, Belfast was marred by sectarian violence that left 500 dead and 10,000 refugees, mostly Catholic (Lynch, 2019). Second, peace walls (or peace lines) were constructed to separate sectarian communities in Belfast in response to sectarian violence that began again in the 1960s. Both boundaries would give rise to political violence coupled with political imprisonment, perpetuating social drama preserved in myth, legend, and martyrdom (Graham and Whelan, 2007; Nisbett and Rapson, 2020).

Again, we find that the boundary as theorized by Lotman (2000, 2005), produces intense symbolic interaction. For instance, along the Loyalist side of a 30-foot peace wall, sectarian graffiti deliver foreboding messages such as "Loyalist Shankhill Rd. Supports Republican Feud" (see McAtackney, 2020; see figure 6). Passing through an imposing metal gate to the Republican side, the cultural landscape changes noticeably. Rather than Union Jacks, the Irish tricolor flies ubiquitously. The territory of heritage is reinforced by street signs written in the Irish language. Neighborhoods invite visitors into their solemn memorial gardens, where heritage is performed. The Greater Clonard Memorial Garden on Bombay Street is especially meaningful since it is located at an actual site where the Troubles were further aggravated. There, in 1969, Protestant rioters attacked and burned down the homes of Catholics. The memorial space demonstrates a transformation from political violence—the profane—to the sacred. Fresh-cut flowers underscore a living history conveyed on a sign that reads:

> This plaque is dedicated to the people of the Greater Clonard who have resisted and still resist the occupation of our country by Britain. We acknowledge with pride and sacrifices they made throughout every decade. Their names would be too numerous to mention, and their deeds of bravery and resistance are un-equalled. We, the Republican Ex-Prisoners of the Greater Clonard, salute you and your reward will only be a United Ireland.

FIGURE 6. "Peace Walls in Belfast." Barriers separating the Loyalist/Unionist communities from their Republican/Nationalist counterparts stretch for miles with restricted access. © retrowelch 2022.

The proclamation is accompanied by the coat of arms of each of the four provinces of Ireland, thus reinforcing the Republican vision of a united nation that would erase the boundary separating North and South. Above the plaque is a list of the names and faces of the Republican volunteers who perished in the struggle against British forces. Chief among them is Tom Williams, whose story is threaded through a lengthy narrative in Belfast. Standing in the memorial garden one experiences the power of place as the guide points to one of the homes on Bombay Street. It is the very house where Volunteer Williams lived in the 1940s. A sign above the front door pronounces (in Irish and English) that Williams was executed at the age of 19 at the Belfast Gaol, later known as the Crumlin Road Prison, located in a Protestant, Unionist, Loyalist section of Belfast (Welch, 2016a).

A long row of murals has become a hugely popular tourist destination in West Belfast. The colorful paintings laud the virtues of justice and equality, deliberately inscribing Irish Republicanism onto other international struggles (e.g., the plight of African Americans, American Indians, Basques, Palestinians, and South Africans). Unsurprisingly, a recurring theme is the commemoration of the hunger strikers. One jarring image superimposes the 10 hunger strikers onto the 1916 Rising, with the Proclamation prominently displayed. The same mural honors hunger strikers of earlier periods, most notably Frank Stagg, who is quoted: "I want my Memorial to be Peace with Justice." Other controversies add some edge to an otherwise upbeat series of renderings, such as a "wanted poster" of (then) British Prime Minister Margaret Thatcher "for murder and torture of Irish Prisoners." As with so many memorial sites, a duality between the profane and the sacred projects a perpetual interplay between injustice and justice (Welch, 2019).

Next to the murals is a billboard with a large photograph of the interior of the Crumlin Road Gaol—"Belfast's Infamous Prison." It serves to draw visitors to an important site where they can observe more contested heritage of Northern Ireland. That former prison offers another example of how place identity has been transformed in the realm of culture. Just as at the Kilmainham Gaol, all tours at the "Crum" are guided in groups. In contrast to the shared sense of Irish solidarity in Dublin, however, visitors seem a bit guarded about where their sympathies lie, whether Loyalist or Republican. Perhaps due to that tension, the tour guide barely mentions that the "Crum" held both Loyalist and Republican political prisoners. Curiously, the Troubles do not dominate the narrative; rather, its history as a Victorian prison is made the prevailing story. Dating back to 1841, Crumlin Road Gaol was designed by esteemed architect Sir Charles Lanyon, who based it on the radial plan of Pentonville Prison in London. Still, its legacy is heavy with hunger strikes, escapes, floggings, and riots, with the result that the "Crumlin Road Gaol is a foreboding place with a dark and disturbing past" (Souvenir Guidebook to Crumlin Road Gaol, n.d., n.p.; Greg, 2013). Of course, high-profile executions have contributed to the gaol's rugged reputation. In all, 17 men were hanged there; according to the Capital Punishment Amendment Act (1868), they were "buried in an unmarked grave, in unconsecrated ground" (Souvenir Guidebook to Crumlin Road Gaol, n.d., n.p.).

The burial site, where the bodies remain, seems more dismissive than serene. The only remnants are some initials etched into the stone wall. Those impersonal burials did not sit well with some of the communities in Belfast. Again, the story of Tom Williams looms large. In 1942, the IRA commander was convicted of murdering a police officer; later, he was executed and buried at the gaol. For decades, Republicans intensely lobbied the government to recognize Irish traditions. Eventually, the Royal Prerogative of Mercy was exercised for the case of Williams, thus remitting the part of his sentence requiring that he be buried within the walls of the prison. At the site of burials at the gaol, a pewter sign lists the name of Williams along with the others buried there. It states that the Royal Prerogative of Mercy was again exercised in 1999, allowing the bodies of Williams (and Michael Pratley) to be exhumed and reinterred elsewhere. Those efforts served to build Republican solidarity as well as aid the healing process in the aftermath of the Troubles.

More complicated narratives about the Troubles are told at the Irish Republican History Museum. The otherwise mundane building, located in an industrial yard known as Conway Mill, has been transformed into a sacred space for contemplating the plight of Irish Republicans and the victims of political violence. The exhibit is unique among the others discussed so far in that it recognizes the role of women in Irish history. "A significant feature of the commemorative landscapes that have evolved in Northern Ireland since the late 1960s relates to their highly gendered nature and, in particular, to the invisibility of women in the visual iconography of the Troubles" (Graham and Whelan, 2007: 480; see Dowler, 1998; Scarlata, 2014). Upon entering the museum, visitors are greeted by the "Republican Women's Role of Honour." Nearly twenty names of women are listed in chronological order of their death (e.g., Maura Meehan—Shot dead by the British Army on the 23rd Oct 1971. Age 31). The honor roll is decorated with a floral display, reenacting an Irish Catholic wake. "In Remembrance," the sign reads: "We also remember with pride, those women from this and past generations, who died dedicating their lives to the cause of Irish Freedom. Most of these women endured a life of severe hardship, blatant discrimination and personal suffering and in many cases years of imprisonment for their Republican beliefs (Si Eire mo Thir)." Despite the tragedies remembered at the museum, themes of ascent abound, offering visitors uplifting messages about sacrifice.

The prestige of the political prisoners is built up with layers of socio-religious symbolism. At the Irish Republican History Museum, there is no shortage of objects and images that radiate the importance of Catholicism to Irish heritage and the Republican/Nationalist cause. Celtic crosses, joined with the Irish (tricolor) flag, are displayed alongside photographs of the clergy, such as Father Raymond Murray, who served as Chaplain of Armagh Women's Prison (from 1967 until it closed in 1986). A plaque reads: "For your outstanding devotion to God and Country. Your lectures on the inhuman treatment of prisoners in Northern jails has enlightened and inspired many to secure justice and dignity for political prisoners in Ireland." That dedication signifies the reach of Irish heritage and diaspora, for it was issued by the Irish National Caucus in New York City. As is to be expected, given how profoundly the hunger strikers shaped the discourse of political imprisonment during the Troubles, the museum keeps up a steady commentary on those events. Each of the deceased hunger strikers is given considerable exposure and tribute. Photographs of them are noteworthy for their cheerful demeanors, which defy accusations that they were "dangerous terrorists." The political nature of the hunger strike is cast in mythic proportions—they are consistently portrayed as martyrs who sacrificed their lives. Many items on display demonstrate a high degree of solidarity among their supporters.

At the far end of West Belfast sits the somewhat secluded Roddy McCorley's Club. There, too, themes of ascent enhance the performance of Irish Republican heritage. Curiously, Roddy's is a *forbidden space*, since to enter one is supposed be a former political prisoner. However, the pub and the second-floor museums are an open secret, and tourists are given friendly access. Much like the Irish Republican History Museum, Roddy's Club pays tribute to the 1916 Rising, Tom Williams, and Michael Collins, whose death in 1922 is remembered in a poster featuring an image of Jesus Christ. The caption reads: "Died for Ireland . . . Another Martyr for Old Ireland." Roddy's is a reminder how even mundane places, such as an Irish bar, can serve as sacred spaces for remembrance.

"Political tourism" is how Sara McDowell describes the marketing of the Troubles in post-conflict Belfast. Such cultural commodification relies on the tangible and intangible heritage of division and hurt. Guided tours are endorsed as a form of "conflict transformation" aimed at fostering an understanding of separate communities (see McEvoy and Shirlow, 2009). Tourists willing to engage in such "conflict transformation" act as "mediators in the arena of conflict, helping to externalize the political objectives"; by doing so, they enjoy "a level of access denied to many others from the same place" (McDowell, 2008: 407). A principal reason for restricted access among Belfast residents is that the city is still segregated by boundaries—most visibly by the peace walls. McDowell goes on to describe political tourism as a vehicle for extending localized interpretations of past conflict in which disputant groups not only compete for victimhood status but also seek legitimization and power. It is believed that the experiences of political tourists are often shared with others upon their return home; personal photographs of sites and symbols serve to verify and authenticate the dissonance of heritage. With that realization, cultural stakeholders (e.g., tour guides) in Belfast, be they Republican or Loyalist, are committed to shaping a particular vision of the conflict (McDowell, 2008; Neill, 2017). From a cultural standpoint, such transformation extends beyond artifacts and sites to entire communities and societies on which acts of the profane—sectarian violence—have left deep scars. "Conflict transformation" is a conscious strategy for civic leaders committed to shedding Belfast of its reputation as the "Pariah City" due in large part to the Troubles (Neill, Fitzsimmons, and Murtagh, 1995).

Again, implications of the national border and the peace walls figure prominently in post-conflict tourism. A fleet of popular Black Taxi tours contribute to the commodification of heritage and its sites of Trouble. While crisscrossing the sectarian boundaries fortified by peace walls, drivers provide passengers details of the Troubles, paying special heed to the rival paramilitaries and their unique symbols of political, ethnic, and religious identity. As the Troubles intensified, due in large part to a contentious civil rights movement, two ideologically distinct communities became further polarized (see Dooley, 1998). While the subject requires a good deal of caution, the different groups are commonly referred to as either Protestant, Unionist, Loyalist (who might regard themselves as British), or Catholic, Nationalist, Republican (who might regard themselves as Irish) (McAtackney, 2020). Those sectarian groups—with varying degrees of commitment—continue to hold competing national aspirations. The Protestant, Unionist, Loyalist community—the majority in Northern Ireland—are aligned to maintain their connection to British sovereignty (Green, 1998). By contrast, the minority, Catholic, Nationalist, Republican people support a united Ireland. (Ellison, Pino, and Shirlow, 2013).

As famed journalist Peter Taylor writes: "The conflict is essentially about identity and allegiance. . . . The fact that those identities coincide with religion of those who wish to maintain the union with Great Britain (unionists) and those who aspire to a united Ireland (nationalists) is the legacy of history" (1997: 355).

Northern Ireland is presently governed by a power-sharing deal enshrined in the 1998 Belfast Agreement, also known as the Good Friday Agreement (see Hennessy, 2005; Shirlow and Murtagh, 2006). It is a post-conflict society where painful memories of sectarian violence remain. Curiously, as Graham and Whelan contend, the peace process "was fashioned so as to avoid creating mechanisms for addressing the legacy of the past, not least the commemoration of the fatalities of the Troubles" (2007: 476; see also McEvoy and Conway, 2004). Filling that vacuum, actors and stakeholders in the political tourism industry tend to maintain their rigid positions for purposes of performing heritage to an external audience. Because they stick to the script of the past—"exacerbating difference," critics argue—the narrative they offer becomes counterproductive since it prevents some residents from moving forward in the peace process. The dissonance of heritage is thus firmly entrenched in ways that perpetuate a social drama of protagonists and antagonists. Or, as McDowell observes:

> The "imagined" conflict needs sustenance in the construction of symbols, which remind the public that the conflict is not far away. These conflict signifiers represent continuing power struggles which symbolise contested identities and heritages and help keep the conflict ongoing. This form of tourism, particularly resonant in Republican areas, can be read, therefore, as a manifestation of the conflict by other means. (2008: 419; see Nisbett and Rapson, 2020)

Those subtle forms of tension, however, are offset by a performance that promotes harmony, thereby forging a unified front for Irish Catholics in Belfast and elsewhere. The socio-religious components of heritage—and there are many—possess the capacity to unite as well as divide. Belfast visitors gaze at competing Protestant and Catholic symbols that fueled the Troubles. In a Loyalist neighborhood bordering a Republican community, a large two-panel mural features an image of Martin Luther holding pages of his scathing denunciation of the Catholic hierarchy (see Rolston, 2003). By contrast, a tall three-columned sculpture titled "Remember/Respect/Resolution" stands nearby. Artist Lesley Cherry notes that her artwork was sponsored by the Re-imaging Communities Programme, the Shared Futures Consortium, and the Shankill Community Association. "The sculpture represents the community's willingness to embrace the future of Northern Ireland while remembering the past and respecting others' beliefs and traditions." In a deliberate attempt to alter the streetscape, the sculpture replaces a mural depicting Oliver Cromwell and the expulsion of Catholics from Ireland. While those conciliatory campaigns are genuine, residual undercurrents of cultural conflict persist between the Protestant and Catholic faithful. In Belfast, those tensions are heightened during the controversial marching season, when the Orange Order takes center stage. In 2017, the Orange Order—a conservative Protestant organization—issued a statement advising its members to stop using the phrase R.I.P. (rest in peace) because it is "un-Protestant, un-biblical and a superstition connected to Catholicism" (Collins, 2017; see also McAtackney, 2015).

In sum, McDowell explains that in Belfast, "political tourism has an obvious if, as yet, unqualified value, but this lies less in the revenue generated through the actual tours as in the externalisation of the Troubles narratives and the consequent sympathy of an external audience" (2008: 417). It is through such "conflict transformation" that the duality of boundaries exposes notions of "our" community vis-à-vis "their" community—both of which are paradoxically separated as well as united by peace walls. Correspondingly, those claims of identity are animated by social drama, spilling over into cultural transformation that converts "sites of trouble" into signifying places worthy of reflection.

CONCLUSION

"Even in the chains of despotism, Paris always preserved its intellectual independence which tyrants were forced to respect." So observed Mirabeau in the period before the French Revolution (Schama, 1990: 370). Against that Parisian backdrop, nevertheless, at rue Saint-Antoine no. 232 stood the Bastille—a fortress, prison, and legend that continues to contour how Paris is remembered. Its reputation as a Gothic dungeon, an ominous site of trouble, where political prisoners disappeared, endures to this day. Accounts of the pains of imprisonment are captured by such luminaries of the Bastille as Linguet ([1884]2015) who depicted his confinement as living in a tomb that stripped prisoners of their identity as well as their whereabouts. The walls of the Bastille—five feet thick—remained "the frontier between being and nonexistence. . . . When the prison barber was brought to him, Linguet made the grim quip that became famous: '*He* Monsieur, you wield a razor? Why don't you raze that Bastille?'" (Godechot, 1970: 95; BnF, 2010; see Bongie, 2004).

Campaigns to memorialize the sacrifice of political imprisonment by transforming profane places into sacred sites create cultural strain in Belfast. Those tensions remind us that claims of heritage evoke profound emotional states, both positive and negative (Smith, 2011, 2006). As discussed in this chapter, heritage is notoriously multivalent since it is not only a path for seeing and feeling but also a way of remembering and forgetting. As a theatre of memory, memorial sites have the capacity to regress into a contested arena of dispute and denial (Graham and Whelan, 2007). Compounded by boundaries and the peace walls, heritage is a double-edged sword that has the power to unite as well as to divide, to include as well as to exclude. In Belfast, like other post-conflict societies, community solidarity can jump the tracks, thereby activating destructive energies that lead to ostracizing, scapegoating, and "other-ing" (see Erikson, 1966; Smith and Alexander, 2005; Welch, 2006).

To recap, the "sites of trouble" in Ireland serve as places where identity and heritage are ritualized. In Dublin, the Kilmainham Gaol in its afterlife benefits from the Bastille Effect in that that site has been transformed in ways that honor the Irish rebels who were confined and executed there in 1916. Unlike the original Bastille, which was demolished in the wake of the Revolution, Kilmainham has been preserved as the "Bastille of Ireland," symbolizing the memory of Irish resistance to British occupation. By contrast, in Belfast, where heritage is contoured along the lines of the later Troubles, disputes over former political prisoners persist. The H-Blocks of the infamous Maze prison held both Loyalist and Republican prisoners. However, since it was the site of the 1981 hunger strike in which 10 Republicans died, the Maze is memorialized more by Republicans than by their Loyalist counterparts. Indeed, the site was (mostly) demolished in large part to prevent it from being transformed into a shrine to Bobby Sands and his fellow hunger strikers. In that sense, the potential for a Bastille Effect has been bottled up and tossed aside as a result of the sectarian divide. In terms of place identity, the Maze—an empty compound—remains a somewhat mundane rather than sacred space (see Graham and McDowell, 2007; Wylie, 2004).

In closing, a final word about boundaries is in order, especially given the current meaning of the border separating the North and South of Ireland. Even though the border is invisible due to British demilitarization, it continues to resonate in the political consciousness. Since 2016, volatile issues surrounding Brexit have reactivated a sense of anxiety since calls for a "soft" land border (whatever that means) are met with concerns over renewed violence. George Mitchell, the former US senator who brokered the 1998 Good Friday peace deal, has warned there could be "serious trouble ahead" if border checks were reinstated. Mitchell recalls that during the Troubles the "hard" border was steeped in the demonization of *others*. Mitchell contends that peace is often fragile, and changing attitudes between communities in Northern Ireland has taken years. Asked if a new border could prompt a return to violence, Mitchell did not equivocate: "Yes, there could be serious trouble ahead" (O'Carroll, 2018). In 2021, Northern Ireland turned 100 years old. In the days following Good Friday—if that wasn't significant enough—rioting erupted, partly as a protest against a proposed border in the Irish Sea in accordance to Brexit. Unionists fiercely reject that border since they view it as a form of cutting them off from the United Kingdom. Irony is not lost on the fact that the most violent rioting took place at the gate of one of the main peace walls in Belfast (Gladstone and Robins, 2021).

4

Sites of Condor

The Bastille was not simply a site. It was a penal institution operating within an elaborate machinery of repression where those who posed a political threat to the monarchy were subjected to a surreal ritual of arrest and confinement, without any semblance of due process. Commenting on that brazen display of power, Schama writes: "Seized without warning—usually at night—from the living world, the victim of this state abduction was then deprived of all means of communicating his existence to friends and family beyond the walls" (1990: 394; see also BnF, 2010). In more recent times, military regimes in the southern cone of Latin America would imitate the capricious authority exercised by the King of France. Memory of the dictatorships, and of the brutality inflicted on civilians regarded by the military as "subversives," has spawned a sharp awareness of those atrocities. That upsurge in memory, Nora (2002) points out, is spreading in post-conflict societies as they adjust their relationships to the past. Several forces drive this trend. First, certain groups are challenging "official" versions of history by recovering segments of the past that have been suppressed. Second, there is growing demand for signs of a past that have been confiscated. Third, the importance of heritage has taken hold among certain people interested in reevaluating their own identity.

Efforts to understand the upsurge in memory in the southern cone gain much from the significance of sitedness, which helps us sort out the nuances of space and place. Michel de Certeau (1984) posits that place is where things and people are ordered; space, by its very nature, is the use of space (see Casey, 2003). The two concepts are deeply intertwined given that former detention centers are still the precise places where atrocities occurred. In their afterlife, those sites have been strategically transformed for purposes of memorialization. Toward that end, a delicate emotional register comes into play: "memoryscapes" require that sites retain sufficient authenticity of their profane past, or its use-value, but that they do so without repelling visitors (Bilbija and Payne, 2011: Sevenko, 2004). In this chapter we explore Operation Condor—a sweeping cross-border mission to eradicate "subversives." We do so by entering former detention centers in Buenos Aires, Santiago, Asunción, and Montevideo. There we will find that the plain arbitrariness of abduction, confinement, and disappearance is a central factor in the upsurge in memory. We will also find that entire sites have been culturally transformed. As a Bastille Effect in the making, these once-polluted places are becoming metaphors for human rights activism in a post-conflict society.

CITIES OF CONDOR

In the aftermath of the 1973 coup, Chilean intelligence agents extended their power by forging a regional and international security network. On the instructions of dictator Augusto Pinochet, Manuel Contreras, director of the Chilean secret police, embarked on an anti-communist campaign, lobbying other nations for their support. In the late summer of 1975, Contreras traveled to Washington, D.C., to meet with CIA Deputy Director Vernon Walters. During that trip—the second in less than two months—Contreras pitched his plans for what would become Operation Condor. Then, on August 27, Contreras met with the Venezuelan intelligence service in Caracas. Years later, Venezuelan intelligence officer Rafael Rivas Vasquez would disclose that Contreras was "building up this grandiose scheme of a very big and powerful service that could have information—worldwide information" (Kornbluh 2013: 344). Contreras's vision of Operation Condor crystalized in October 1975 when he invited his counterparts in the southern cone to join him in Santiago (Chile) for the first inter-American conference on national intelligence. At that meeting, which was "strictly secret in nature" (Kornbluh 2013: 331, 364), the attendees arrived at a strategy for combating "subversives." From November 25 to 28, 1975, and again in June 1976, delegates from Argentina, Bolivia, Brazil, Chile, Paraguay, and Uruguay met and agreed to cooperate in a joint intelligence mission (later supported by Peru and Ecuador). Contreras, who for a time was on the CIA payroll, would gather significant backing from the Nixon administration and its intelligence agencies. Adding symbolic significance, the operation was named after Chile's national bird, the condor (Dinges 2004; McSherry 2005).

A shadowy intelligence network, Operation Condor maintained a highly centralized data bank that included computer records of abductions, detention, torture, and ultimately assassinations. The transnational reach of Condor would soon become its defining trait. Argentina was selected as the base for Sistema Condor. It has been reported, however, that the hub of that system was at the US military installation in the Panama Canal Zone (Kornbluh, 2013: 347). In one of the worst of a series of spectacular crimes, Condor agents abducted and murdered Zelmar Michelini and Hector Guiterrez Ruiz in 1976; at the time, the two Uruguayan legislators were living in exile in Buenos Aires. The following month, former Bolivian president Juan Jose Torres was assassinated in Buenos Aires. In what is often described as Operation Condor's most audacious action, former Chilean ambassador Orlando Letelier and his American colleague Ronni Moffitt were killed by a car bomb in Washington, D.C., on September 21, 1976 (Branch and Propper, 1982; Dinges and Landau, 1980). All of this lethal violence was enshrouded in black propaganda coupled with psychological warfare with the intent of convincing the wider population that the shootings and bombings were the work of leftist "subversives" engaged in a "dirty war" (Marchak, 1990; D. Taylor 1997).

It remains unclear when Operation Condor officially disbanded, if it ever did. During its peak years, 1975 to 1977, Condor agents in the southern cone murdered—or "disappeared"—hundreds of victims. Moreover, after the 1976 coup in Argentina, an estimated 15,000 exiles from neighboring countries found themselves "trapped by the increasingly coordinated, regional collaboration in abductions, torture, disappearances, and murders" (Kornbluh 2013: 417). McSherry (1999, 2005) describes Operation Condor as a parallel state that defied international law and engaged in criminal tactics to undermine constitutional institutions. In tandem with Operation Condor, other forms of state terror were being conducted before, during, and after the Condor years. So it is important to note that not all political violence in those countries can be attributed to Condor. That said, all of those dictatorships perceived a threat from so-called subversives, broadly defined as people who harbored dangerous ideas. Such people included not just armed militants but also mainstream political opponents, peaceful dissenters, and religious workers. Argentine General Jorge Videla infamously declared in 1976 that "a terrorist is not just someone with a gun or a bomb, but also someone who spreads ideas that are contrary to Western and Christian civilization" (McSherry, 2005: 1).

Clandestine detention, torture, and extermination centers were important sites for Operation Condor as well as for other forms of state repression. Decades later, many of those sites have been repurposed as storytelling institutions that issue narratives through their sitedness—a reminder that performance and spectacle continue to shape national identity in post-conflict societies (Clark and Payne, 2011; D. Taylor, 1997). In *Afterlives of Confinement: Spatial Transitions in Post-dictatorship Latin America*, Susana Draper examines former detention sites in Argentina, Chile, and Uruguay in an effort to expose the continuity of power and economic structures. Some of those sites have been repurposed as human rights memorials and museums. Others have been transformed into shopping malls that embrace neoliberal consumerism, thus masking unachieved goals. With that observation in mind, Draper furthers Huyssen's critique of the ways "memory and forgetting pervade real public space, the world of objects, and the urban world we live in" (2003: 9–10; 1995). Focusing on the "politics of amnesia," Draper refines the notion of afterlife, which "acquires the sense of a mode of experiencing the echoes of a past that is lost to history but has the potential to be heard or legible. It is a missed possibility that keeps open the promise of that which did not / could not take place" (2012: 4–5; see also Jelin, 2003; Jelin and Kaufman, 2000).

BUENOS AIRES: CITY OF RECOVERY

Remembering and forgetting figure prominently in the post-conflict heritage of Buenos Aires, especially given the immense scope of the human rights atrocities committed there. As General Iberico Saint-Jean boasted: "First we kill all the subversives; then we kill their collaborators; then . . . their sympathizers, then . . . those who remain indifferent; and finally we kill the timid" (Simpson and Bennett, 1985: 66). From that perspective, the last dictatorship in Argentina (1976 to 1983) is properly characterized as the most ruthless: while in power, it disappeared more than 30,000 civilians through a complex network of 500 clandestine detention centers (Dinges, 2004; Feitlowitz, 1998). This "dirty war" ("guerra sucia") was a military euphemism for the process of "cleansing" the nation of ideological contamination through wholesale abductions, torture, and extermination. The legacy of the dirty war has left residual scars on the Argentine psyche in ways that sensitize remembering (Suarez-Orozco, 1991). And it is often the power of place that activates such memory. One of the most notorious sites was ESMA, now known as El Centro Clandestino de Detencion, Tortura y Extermino, which was recovered from the military during the transition to democracy. Located in the wealthy suburb of Nuñez, the ESMA memorial has a brooding presence given that more than 5,000 political prisoners were held there, very few of whom survived. Its handsome neoclassical buildings are visible from the busy avenue; the iron fences that surround it are now draped with protest banners informing passersby of its profane past: "No Impunity for Genocide," "Don't Forget," and "30,000" (see Robben, 2005).

One of ESMA's main buildings, the Casino (or Officers' Club), was the central hub for planning disappearances and exterminations; it was also where prisoners were detained and tortured. While ESMA was being converted into a memorial site, more evidence was uncovered that corroborated witnesses' first-hand testimony about atrocities. Those findings are on display for the public, prompting sober reflection on state crime. Conceptually, the Casino attends to the process by which a profane site for clandestine detention is transformed into a sacred place for memorialization. Fittingly, the slogan of the Argentine human rights movement is "Memoria, Verdad y Justicia" (Memory, Truth, and Justice). ESMA has evolved into a storytelling institution that explains its brutal history and, in doing so, reflects the words of philosopher Jean Baudrillard, who warned that "forgetting the extermination is part of the extermination" (1994: 49).

The afterlives of confinement are evident in different realms, namely literature, film, and architecture. Of particular interest here is Draper's (2012) commentary on "architectural recycling." That concept captures the spatial element of a site as well as a temporal one in that it attends to the past and present simultaneously. For instance, visitors to ESMA are aware that the Casino is both a former detention, torture, and extermination center and a memorial space. The act of "recycling"

FIGURE 7. "ESMA." In Buenos Aries, ESMA was a major site for detention, torture, and extermination. Pictured is the Casino, where faces of the disappeared are arranged on the façade. © retrowelch 2022.

recedes into the background, allowing the narratives of past atrocities and current human rights campaigns to resonate together. Spatial afterlives at ESMA are also central to the analysis of Jens Andermann (2012), who untangles the debates over postmemory, secondary witnessing, and the politics of empathy. In 2004, the Argentine armed forces handed ESMA over to the City of Buenos Aires for it to begin the process of memorializing the space. The mood among human rights activists remains mixed. "The joy of having conquered a site you are beginning to populate runs parallel with the sensation that you are keeping company with the souls that have passed through here" (Ginzberg, 2008). Borrowing again from a sociology of place, the Casino has been "personed" through photographs of victims projected onto the façade, thereby enhancing its signifying-value in its current incarnation (see Bell, 1997; figure 7).

Andermann does not stray from the canon of museum studies (Bennett, 1995; Williams, 2007). Thus, he emphasizes sitedness as it enhances a sophisticated repertoire of cultural techniques for encouraging "visitors to turn into active participants of a memory performance" (2012: 82; 2007; Andermann and Arnold-de Simine, 2012). That form of museumgoing becomes an act of secondary witnessing through the deployment of an "iconography both sufficiently familiar to trigger traumatic repetition as well as prompting secondary-generation viewers to transpose their own experiences and subjectivity into the space" (Andermann, 2012: 82). To be clear, issues underlying sitedness and technique are attached to competing ambitions for ESMA. At one end of the spectrum is the testimonial perspective, which claims that the entire site is unalterable heritage. At the opposite end is the performative option. Hence, when handed over to artists and political activists, the space is symbolically "wrested from death and its executioners" (Andermann, 2012: 85). From the standpoint of the museal—or the centrist position—the site is transformed in ways that contextualize and arrange material evidence for public education and the promotion of democratic values. Among the many groups that weighed in on the repurposing of ESMA, the Association Madres de la Plaza de Mayo adopted the most anti-museal proposal. The Madres (the mothers of the disappeared) proposed that the entire site be reworked into a multifunctional center for youth culture and popular arts to commemorate their children. "We do not share the idea of a museum of horror," said Hebe de Bonafini of the Madres. "Museums are associated with death. . . . Death is for executioners, not for us" (Brodsky, 2005: 219; Di Paolantonio, 2008; Park, 2014).

In its present configuration, the vast compound of ESMA—17 acres—features testimonial, performative, and museal techniques within different buildings devoted variously to the arts, to human rights activities, and to forensic archives. The Casino is explicitly referred to as a "reconstruction" based on the testimony of survivors; thus, it is made clear to visitors that they are touring a reconstruction and not the original space. Even so, that reconstruction benefits from its sitedness, which transmits sacrality and promotes reflection. To do so, however, it has resorted to a curatorial technique, or "art of arrangement," that "recycles" the space in ways that give it shape, "illuminating a dialectical relationship between the past and present where different tenses confront rather than overwhelm each other" (Di Paolantonio, 2008: 40).

In more practical terms, the recovery of ESMA fulfills the aims of the Centre for Legal and Social Studies (CELS, an NGO affiliated with Human Rights Watch). Principally, the site has become an extension of the human rights movement, which even during the last dictatorship fought to expose the extermination. As a crime scene, ESMA provides evidence for legal teams as they prepare cases to quash the junta's efforts "to erase the physical and symbolic memory of its victims" (Andermann, 2012: 89; see also Kaiser, 2011). The spatial afterlife of ESMA possesses a temporal mode in that it links the past with the present. Placards are scattered around the Casino to remind visitors: "Here a crime against humanity was perpetrated." Indeed, curators strategically draw attention to the role of sitedness in the memorial process in ways that reveal a history of atrocities that were once concealed. In this way, the site provides a performative anchor through which visitors, as secondary witnesses, can identify with victims. That degree of emotive bonding is significant as Buenos Aires, and the nation, recover from the last dictatorship.

SANTIAGO: CITY OF RE-COLLECTING

Evidence of human rights atrocities under Operation Condor—in tandem with the Pinochet dictatorship—is harder to access in Santiago than in Buenos Aires. That is partly because sites have been deliberate demolished so as to erase all physical traces of a profane past. Still, a handful of spaces are open to the public, where objects and images have been *re-collected*—a term that refers to the actual recovery of artifacts as well as the activation of memory. Londres 38 is a former center of repression and extermination that from September 1973 to the end of 1975 held nearly 100 detainees. During that time, the building, code-named Cuartel Yucatan, was occupied by the secret police. There, DINA (Dirección de Inteligencia National) began "developing a system of forced disappearances as part of a global political framework of state terrorism" (Londres 38 brochure, n.d.). That transnational aspect of Operation Condor is evident in political posters on display at Londres 38, including one featuring Uncle Sam and Pinochet as a pawn on a chessboard (see Welch, 2020).

The curators at Londres 38 provide insights into the phenomenon of collecting and re-collecting in ways that underscore the site's cultural transformation from use-value as a detention center to signifying-value in its afterlife. A film projector displays a looping slideshow of data cards compiled by DINA to identify so-called "subversives." That information was digitized in a central data bank and distributed to neighboring military juntas; that computerized system was assisted by Tel-Ex equipment (and training) provided by the CIA (Dinges, 2004; Kornbluh, 2013; McSherry, 2005). Although the dictatorship went to great lengths to destroy evidence, a trove of 39,000 secret files was discovered at another detention site in Chile, the notorious Colonia Dignidad. At Londres 38, those files were re-collected for visitors to witness the fine detail of Operation Condor. A case in point is the profile of political prisoner Maria Elena Gonzales, about whom extensive biographical information had been collected, such as her membership in Amnesty International. Londres 38 is essentially vacant. However, as a memorial space, it has been recycled as a repository for recollection; according to a statement on one of its walls, "this void is full of memories." In the words of Collins (2011: 235), that shift from amnesia to memorialization marks an important development in "the moral economy of memory" aimed at the commemoration of space in post-Pinochet Chile.

Farther afield is Villa Grimaldi, which served as a major detention hub for DINA but now seems to have faded into the amnesia of suburban Santiago. The site was razed by the military, but in 2004 it was reconstructed as a "park for peace." To re-collect its brutal past, many of the structures have been reassembled to illustrate how the site might have looked when it functioned as Cuartel Terranova. Wooden shacks have been rebuilt to demonstrate how they were once used as cramped spaces of confinement—and torture. When the site was a prison, in one corner of the large compound there stood a water tower that was used for deten-tion. That water tower has since been rebuilt for the public to visit. The interior contains drawings by survivors, who graphically depict the ways they were forced into tiny isolation cells and subjected to electrocution. On the opposite wall hangs Pinochet's "structure of repression." The organizational chart outlines the chain of command, with Manuel Contreras, director of DINA, prominently displayed. Vis-itors are reminded that the dictatorship conducted cross-border missions under Operation Condor with the support of US intelligence agencies. Irony is not lost on the fact that Villa Grimaldi had once been an elegant social club known by its patrons as "Paradise." Its demolition left the site with mounds of colorful tiles, which artisans have re-collected—and recycled—to create sculptures, which are spread throughout the park. That shift from use-value to signifying-value made for an even greater retreat from a profane past to a sacred present. As part of the process of establishing the park's afterlife, a Catholic priest conducted an elaborate purification ritual by blessing the property with holy water (see Douglas, 1966). Still, there remains some emotive tension. Some human rights groups resisted the plan to reconstruct the water tower and the wooden cell blocks, arguing that doing so would seem "inauthentic and distract[] from the park's initial aesthetic as a place of serenity and restorative beauty" (Collins, 2011: 239).

In Santiago, perhaps one of the most surreal spaces of confinement was the National Stadium. In the early days of the coup, thousands of detainees were pro-cessed through this enormous sports facility. Between 12,000 and 20,000 Chileans and foreigners were detained in the stadium for periods ranging from two days to two months (Hite, 2004). A brochure titled "Estadio National: Memoria National" points to its global significance: citizens from 38 countries were rounded up and assigned to the bleachers, the dressing rooms, and the concourse below the stands. The Stadium still hosts major events (football matches, rock concerts), yet it is also a place of "constructing memory," which makes visiting it a somewhat jarring experience. Its afterlife as a memorial space is animated by Section 8. The dark passageway one must follow to enter that section adds to the somber tone, which is maintained by a collection of photographs recalling the mayhem of the coup, when civilians were being funneled into the stadium. The content of the pictures becomes increasingly foreboding, for they memorialize those who were detained in the stadium as well as those who disappeared—another reminder of how places remain "personed."

The transnational scope of the Pinochet regime is again evident in a poster dedicated to the Argentines placed under military arrest. Nearby, a composite of more than 20 portraits of those murdered in the stadium hangs in front of a row of candles. Their identities are revealed by name. They include Charles Horman, who was the subject of the film *Missing*. Being a US citizen did not spare Horman and his colleague Frank Teruggi from the barbaric reach of the dictatorship. Their deaths foreshadowed Condor's assassination operations elsewhere, most notably

FIGURE 8. "National Stadium." The National Stadium in Santiago held thousands of detainees in the early phase of the Pinochet dictatorship. © retrowelch 2022.

the attack on Orlando Letelier and Ronni Moffitt. Visitors exploring the previous life of the stadium are permitted to enter the bleachers, which refuse to shed their past. The original patch of seats jars with an otherwise state-of-the-art sports venue. The outdated benches are lit with candles that reinforce the message that Section 8 is a sacred space for reflection and recollection. Across the back row are the words "Un Pueblo sin Memoria es un Pueblo sin Futuro" (A people without a memory is a people without a future). Together, the memorial sites in Santiago battle the impulse to erase memory, thus pushing back against Pinochet's 1995 statement: "It is better to remain quiet and forget. That is the only thing we must do. We must forget. And that won't happen if we continue opening up lawsuits, sending people to jail. FOR-GET: That's the word. And for that to happen both sides must forget and continue with their work" (Clark and Payne, 2011: 104).

ASUNCIÓN: CITY OF TEARS

It is said that when you visit Asunción you cry twice: first when you arrive, and again when you leave (Whicker's World, 2016). While that saying is subject to personal interpretation, tears shed during the Alfredo Stroessner dictatorship (1954–89) and Operation Condor certainly help narrate the story of human rights. Toward that end, a key destination is the Museo de las Memorias. However serene it first appears, its violent past is palpable. During its years as a torture center, it processed more than 10,000 detainees. On display are devices that inflicted physical and psychological torment, including pliers for pulling out fingernails, a shock generator, and a bathtub used for waterboarding (see figure 9).

Those instruments of torture pave the way for a cultural transformation into a sacred space. The use-value of devices is neutralized, allowing their signifying-value to emerge as metaphors for suffering. To offset its profane past, the memorial has been decorated with serene artworks. Most noteworthy is a "tree of life" that was blessed and thus purified by Pope John Paul II as a means to symbolize the transition a post-dictatorship society. Elsewhere, the museum consists of a series of galleries, making it a place for learning and political commentary related to Operation Condor. A huge map of North and South America is marked in several places to identify locations of military interventions by the US government. Pre-Condor photographs of Stroessner shaking hands with US President Eisenhower in Panama are juxtaposed with a picture of Stroessner visiting Fort Sill, Oklahoma.

References to outside interests also point to the economic underpinnings of the dictatorship. A photograph of US President Ford, Vice President Rockefeller, and Henry Kissinger meeting in the White House is coupled with a document from Standard Oil. A caption takes exception to Rockefeller's visit to Latin America, positing that his mission to combat the resistance actually "hid the need to protect foreign investments." It is here that we witness some evidence of "public memory," which contains tension between the "official culture" and the "vernacular culture" (Bodnar, 1992). It is theorized that the politics of memory are managed through the power of state and its elite partners. With the downfall of the Stroessner dictatorship, his close financial ties to the US ("official culture") were laid bare, allowing memorial activists to issue a critique of Paraguay's historical past ("vernacular culture").

FIGURE 9. "Bathtub." In Asunción, the bathtub (*pileta*) used for waterboarding is on display at a former detention site currently open to the public as the Museo de las Memorias. © retrowelch 2022.

Reinforcing the ominous enigma of Operation Condor, a poster of a condor soaring over the southern cone is titled "Flights of Death." In his foreword to McSherry's *Predatory States*, former political prisoner Martin Almada recalls being interrogated by Paraguayan military operatives. Almada—a doctoral student—was charged with the crime of "intellectual terrorism" and subjected to torture. "My wife, the educator Celestina Perez, died as a consequence of the psychological tortures to which she was subjected, being forced to listen on the telephone, systematically for ten days, to my cries and screams from the torture chamber" (2005: xiii; see also 1993). After living in exile in Panama and Paris, Almada returned to Asunción to continue his human rights work. On December 22, 1992, Almada's tears of suffering turned to tears of joy when he discovered an enormous trove of documents on Operation Condor in a suburban police station. That moment is captured on camera with Almada emotionally declaring that it was like "taking the Bastille." The following day, the torture center was closed. The discarded police records, which were once used to guide thousands of detentions, have enjoyed an important afterlife: judges now rely on them to prosecute former military personnel for crimes against humanity. Among those cases was the one assembled by Spanish lawyer Baltasar Garzon against Pinochet.

The Archives of Terror are stored at the Supreme Court in Asunción, where they are available for researchers. That building has thus become another site of Operation Condor, albeit in very different way. In an eerie revelation, Almada's own arrest record (with mugshot, personal data, and fingerprints) is posted alongside those of other political prisoners from the southern cone. Formal correspondence between DINA director Contreras and Paraguayan officials further reveals the early stages of Operation Condor. It includes a 1975 letter to Pastor Coronel, who was one of the most feared torturers under the dictatorship (see Almada, 1993). After the fall of the Stroessner regime, Coronel was imprisoned on charges of torture and murder. A photograph in the Archives shows him crying while declaring his innocence. The archives unearth previously unknown details about Operation Condor, making it a tangible conduit for deciphering human rights atrocities. The afterlife of those documents is commemorated by a framed 2009 announcement from the United Nations Educational, Scientific and Cultural Organization (UNESCO) that certifies the Archives of Terror as part of the Memory of the World International Register.

In a foyer outside the Archives Center is an exhibition about the history of repression in Paraguay. It informs visitors that the collection occupies "a relevant space in the fight against collective amnesia that affects our recent and remote past." Given the practical value of the Archives, it is easy to overlook a larger conceptual element of memory. Nora reminds us that sometimes "memory is in fact a gigantic and breathtaking storehouse of a material stock of what it would be impossible for us to remember, an unlimited repertoire of what might need to be re-called" (1989: 13). Asunción, Santiago, and Buenos Aires share a common interest in using the afterlife of detention sites for transmitting memory. However, the next—and last—city to be explored, Montevideo, marks a drastic departure from this upsurge in memory.

MONTEVIDEO: CITY WITHOUT MEMORY

In her critique of penal institutions and the economics of memory in Montevideo, Victoria Ruetalo declares that the Uruguayan dictatorship (1973–85) "imposed a conscious political crusade to forget" (2008: 39). Or, what has been described as a modernizing leap in the form of a blind jump into the nation's future that negates the past (Ludmer, 1994). To further unveil that phenomenon, the Grupo de Estudios Urbanos (1983) launched the audiovisual project *Una Ciudad Sin Memoria* (A City without Memory), showing how the military regime relied on an economic logic that would meet the demands of the neoliberal city. Unlike in Santiago—and Buenos Aires and Asunción—public discourse on the dictatorship and Operation Condor as embodied in sites and architecture is difficult to extract. A minor exception is MUME (Museo de la Memoria), housed in the manor of Maximo Santos, the 19th-century dictator. MUME is not a former detention/torture center;

it does, however, provide sophisticated commentary on assassinations, forced disappearances, and political imprisonment. An exhibit on "State Terrorism" taps into Michel Foucault (1977) by interpreting how Operation Condor invented an apparatus of extreme vigilance in order to "discipline" society as a whole. "The secret intelligence . . . enabled the exchange of information between the dictatorships of Latin America's South Cone (El Cono Cur de America Latina) and the transnational repression called 'Plan Condor.'"

Consistent with Grupo de Estudios Urbanos and its insights into *Una Ciudad Sin Memoria*, two of Montevideo's main prisons used for political repression during the dictatorship have been radically transformed. In the first instance, Miguelete has been repurposed as Espacio de Arte Contemporaneo, an intriguing art museum that has embraced its panoptic heritage. A large sign on the perimeter of the property explains that the prison was built in 1880s to emulate Jeremy Bentham's design for control and vigilance. While that posting would have been a prime opportunity to connect the dots of the dictatorship and Operation Condor, it conspicuously avoids doing so. Although the containment wall facing the neighborhood does offer some edgy political street art (e.g., condemning the "extermination of the original people"), it tends to focus on the wider controversy of imprisonment. A large portrait of Foucault is situated near a mural of a caged prisoner that is captioned: "The prison is not the solution, it is the problem." That critique appears to be an extension of Foucault's (1977) contention that the prison was introduced as an answer to a crisis whose solution was actually to construct more prisons. In support of that thesis, Draper points out that the Uruguayan dictatorship in the 1970s converted a military prison (i.e., Libertad) into a penal institution—for political and common prisoners—"in an effort to improve the failure of other prisons" (2012: 212).

Fittingly, artwork at the entrance of Miguelete/Espacio de Arte Contemporaneo foreshadows the spatial transformation of another prison, Punta Carretas, into a megamall. An image shows a woman (consumer) gazing into a glitzy fashion store called "CARCEL." The piece is titled "Esto no es una carcel" (This is not a prison). Approaching Punta Carretas, visitors steeped in critical analysis will agree with Ruetalo, who summarizes the recycling: "The paranoid, bureaucratic structure, as theorized by Michel Foucault and others, suddenly became a fast-paced, neon-signed, food-chained Baudrillardian postmodern mall, an emblem for the newly democratic nation caught in globalization's zeal" (2008: 38; see figure 10). The prison and the shopping mall may seem unrelated, yet we can trace their mutual paternity back to Bentham's panopticon, which inspired developers and architects, including Alexander Haager in Los Angeles (California) and his counterpart Juan Carlos Lopez in Montevideo (see Davis, 1990; Day, 2013; Welch, 2017c). Both institutions—in form and function—embrace discipline, surveillance, and economics. Still, the transformation of Punta Carretas begs the question of how memory dissolves and forgets its past political repression, especially since a proposal to

FIGURE 10. "Shopping Mall." In Montevideo, the former prison Punta Carretas has been transformed into an upscale shopping mall. © retrowelch 2022.

convert the site into a place of public memory was rejected. "In negating the violent history of the dictatorship, Punta Carretas becomes a metaphor for the nation, a perverse and violent imposition of oblivion" (Achugar, 2000).

The tandem developments of converting Punta Carretas prison into a shopping mall and instituting impunity—both of which provide a foundation for forgetting the past—have been the subject of extensive analysis (see Ruetalo 2008). Draper (2011, 2012), for instance, offers a compelling explanation. In Montevideo, which she calls the "city of impunity," post-dictatorship politics and architecture merged in Sociedad Anónima: a corporation operated by major players in the transition to democracy, who included the Minister of the Interior, who was then juridical partner of Julio María Sanguinetti, president during the transition and Minister of Culture during the dictatorship. Sociedad Anónima, alongside the architecture team of Lopez, developed the prison into a commercial center by promoting it as a place of love. That transformation, according to Draper (2011: 134), "must be considered in conjunction with the referendum and plebiscite for the Law of Expiry which amnestied military personnel for their human rights violations during the decade of terror." Together, immunity and the shopping mall were deliberately geared toward making a country of the future, calling into question the status of the past by reconfiguring history into the present and thereby erasing memory. Especially in Montevideo, the broader legacy the dictatorship left the city was a kind of "utopia for a freedom of movement within a highly surveilled site" (Draper, 2011: 135). It is within that dystopian diagram that the shopping mall materialized as a new form of the surveillance that by then had been naturalized by the dictatorship (Ruetalo 2008).

RECAPPING THE BASTILLE EFFECT

The former sites of repression discussed in this chapter are not merely places of memory; they also serve as metaphors for human rights campaigns, suggesting a Bastille Effect in the capital cities of the southern cone. In Buenos Aires (City of Recovery), criminal charges against former military personnel have been mounting. At ESMA, the Casino remains an active crime scene where investigators continue to collect scientific data. Visitors are reminded of those ongoing tasks and are frequently cautioned not to touch the walls, which could contain forensic evidence. In late 2017, 29 former Argentine military officers were sentenced to life in prison for their involvement in the "death flights," during which detainees were thrown from aircraft into the ocean. During the five-year trial—the country's largest ever—prosecutors tried 54 defendants charged with the murder or forced disappearance of 789 victims, hearing testimony from 800 witnesses. Among those convicted was Alfredo Astiz, known as "Blond Angel of Death," who orchestrated kidnappings and systematic torture leading up to the killings. His 2017 conviction has been stacked onto a previous life sentence for crimes against humanity (Goñi, 2017). More details on the "death flights" emerged during the 2017 ESMA trials. Journalist and ESMA survivor Miriam Lewin recovered the actual aircraft, a Skyvan PA-51, belonging to its new owner in Miami (in 2011). The original 1977 flight logs of the plane remained intact, exposing the names the crew. Consequently, those pilots were convicted: Mario Daniel Arrú and Alejandro Domingo D'Agostino (Enrique José de Saint George died during the trial) (Goñi, 2017; see also Actis et al., 2006).

In Santiago (City of Re-Collection), the Museo de la Memoria y Los Derechos Humanos houses thousands of documents, images, and objects that possess a potent afterlife, thus memorializing the victims of the Pinochet dictatorship and Operation Condor. Inside a display case is a collection of jewelry made by political prisoners while incarcerated. Among those items is a white pendant in the shape of a seahorse carved from bone. Survivors recall how during their time in captivity they would be blindfolded but still able to see the floor directly below them. In the bathroom, they could see the metal covering of a drain decorated with a seahorse. Since then, the seahorse (*caballo de mar*) has been an enduring symbol of surviving the dictatorship. Extending its afterlife, the seahorse is inscribed on the windows of the archives room at the Museum. Under the dictatorship, more than 3,000 political prisoners perished, including celebrated folksinger Victor Jara. In

2018, 45 years after his murder, a judge sentenced eight retired military officers to 15 years in prison for their complicity in his death. Early in the coup, Jara was rounded up and taken to Estadio Chile in western Santiago. While he was being detained, his hands were smashed with the butt of gun; he was then shot 44 times. The stadium, in its afterlife, is named in his memory (Reuters, 2018).

The afterlife of the Archives of Terror in Asunción (City of Tears) retains a significant role in the post-Condor era by aiding research as well as providing evidence for pending international cases against perpetrators. Its founder, Martin Almada, a political prisoner who survived psychological and physical torture, continues to campaign for human rights causes and has testified at trials in Buenos Aries, Madrid, Paris, and Rome. In 2002, Almada was granted the Right Livelihood Award (the "Alternative Nobel Prize") for his outstanding courage in exposing repressors and bringing them to account. The prize committee declared that the Archives of Terror has "proved the most important collection of documents of state terror ever recorded. It is important not just for Paraguay but for the whole of Latin America and, indeed, the world" (Dinges, 2004: 241; see also Almada, 2005, 1993).

In sharp contrast to other post-Condor cities, Montevideo (City Without Memory) lags behind the campaign to hold the repressors accountable. A congressional commission attempted to launch an investigation into crimes committed by the military junta; however, the move was aborted by an airtight amnesty law ratified by a national referendum. The Expiry Law (officially known as the Law on the Expiration of the Punitive Claims of the State), passed in 1986 granted amnesty to the military involved in crimes against humanity during the dictatorship. It amounted to an ad hoc remedy to a political crisis fomented by the military, which feared prosecutions. The law—as well as the dictatorship—deeply marred Uruguay's reputation as the "Switzerland of Latin America," a nation known for its long tradition of liberal and participatory democracy. In 1989 and 2009, referendums maintained the law; in 2011, it was finally repealed (Amnesty International, 2011).

International warrants remain for many retired military officers accused of crimes against humanity; this has deterred them from traveling outside the country, since they could be arrested anywhere. That post-Condor reality is upheld by multilateral judicial agreements that continue to gain momentum as more evidence unfolds. "Those consequences are a measure, albeit imperfect, of justice. In a larger perspective there is a deep historical irony [in Operation Condor]. It once was the primary destroyer of international protections. Now two decades later its legal prosecution is the catalyst for a pioneering new era of international law" (Dinges, 2004: 246; Roht-Arriaza, 2005). Despite major advances in human rights in the wake of Operation Condor, its aftermath in the United States "is undigested history" (Dinges, 2004: 247). The lengthy paper trail unveils the complicity of US diplomats, intelligence agents, and military officers in Condor—yet there remains judicial silence. Even in the face of promising new leads contained in declassified materials, the cases of Charles Horman and Frank Terrugi are relatively dormant. Such inactivity is another reminder that the denial and amnesia surrounding Condor presents a dilemma not only in South America but in the North as well (see Cohen, 2001; Welch, 2009a).

Many former detention and torture centers in the capital cities have benefited from cultural transformation. With the force of the Bastille Effect, those sites deliver noble allegories for human rights. Similarly, Parque de la Memoria y Monumento a las Victimas del Terrorismo de Estado in Buenos Aires has established another creative forum for memorializing the victims of state terrorism. Although the park is not on a site of a previous place of confinement, its location is imbued with solemn symbolism in that it rests on the bank of the river where victims of the death flights were deposited by military agents of the last dictatorship. Perpetuating the power of memory, the park represents a "nonexistent tomb" that performs the "exorcism of forgetting" (Gates-Madsen, 2011: 159).

CONCLUSION

In *The Oxford History of the Prison*, Aryeh Neier, past Director of Human Rights Watch, contributes an insightful commentary on "Confining Dissent: The Political Prison." Setting the stage for his survey of the topic, Neier depicts the Bastille as a symbol of political imprisonment because it had been used to confine a number of well-known dissenters. Neier, like so many other scholars, reminds readers that on the day Bastille was stormed in 1789, none of the seven convicts who were freed were political prisoners. "That did not prevent the fall of that institution from coming to symbolize the triumph of liberty over tyranny" (Neier, 1995; 393). With that admission, Neier seems to recognize what is described herein as the Bastille Effect. As we shall learn over the course of this book, the Bastille continues to resonate in the popular imagination as a reminder of political repression. In contemporary times, its symbolism also reflects democratic reforms, human rights, and holding perpetrators of state crime accountable.

Neier also attends to developments in the southern cone of Latin America, correctly noting that those dictatorships used the tenets of the Cold War to justify repressive measures in an effort to stamp out "subversion." Neier draws on the persecution of Jacobo Timerman, an Argentine editor and publisher, who in 1977 was imprisoned and tortured. His status as a journalist with international credentials gave the last dictatorship pause, thus sparing his life. After a military tribunal ordered his release from prison, Timerman was placed under a bizarre form of house arrest in which government agents moved into his Buenos Aires apartment with him. Two years of political pressure from abroad culminated in his expulsion from Argentina. While in exile, his writings, most notably his book *Prisoner Without a Name, Cell Without a Number* (1981) aided the campaign against the junta. Among those moved by Timerman's autobiography was newly elected

US President Ronald Reagan. His predecessor, President James Earl Carter, had imposed an arms embargo on Argentina owing to its abysmal record on human rights. Reagan was considering lifting the ban on arms sales; however, the compelling narrative painted by Timerman prompted him to reconsider. In 1983, the last dictatorship in Argentina collapsed amid international condemnation.

Neier concludes by underscoring the impact that writings by political prisoners ultimately have on repressive governments. They provide an important literary source that serves to enlighten the general public on matters of human rights. The next section of this book, "Diagrams of Control," focuses on three crucial underpinnings of political imprisonment, namely economics, religion, and architecture. Those social and physical institutions together also shape how sites and symbols of political confinement enter the collective consciousness, as embodied in the Bastille Effect.

PART THREE

Diagrams of Control

Economic Forces

The 14th of July, 1789—what is commemorated as Bastille Day—marked a revolution that began and ended in the course of a single day. Word of the event spread quickly as "the Bastille was known and detested around the whole world. Bastille and tyranny were in every language, synonymous terms" (Michelet, [1847]2008: 11; Tilley, 1970: v). Of course, political imprisonment has always driven the dominant narrative of the Bastille; still, another force was at play, namely economics. Popular depictions of the revolt often highlight the seemingly festive mood of the crowd; Schama, however, reminds readers of the degree of desperation in France: "bread prices were reaching levels that were symptomatic not just of dearth but of famine. Conditions throughout urban France were rapidly approaching the level of a food war" (1990: 371). Compounding matters, it was suspected that the famine was not a product of climate but rather the instrument of an aristocratic cabal conspiring to eradicate the people. Among Parisians, those fears were fueled by the growing presence of German and Swiss military. Another contributor to the economic crisis was defections among French troops, who were sharing the same fate as the locals. At least one observer noted at the time: "French soldiers will never fire on the people . . . but if they should, it is better to be shot than to starve" (Schama, 1990: 376).

Economic forces not only provoke revolutions, revolts, and rebellions but also help give rise to the Bastille Effect, in that former prisons and detention centers become part of the collective memory of economic struggles. Precisely how a given site is culturally transformed depends greatly on the circumstances in which a particular conflict occurred. In this chapter we first explore La-Prison-des-Patriotes, in Montreal, where the rebellions of 1837 and 1838 have not been forgotten. On that very site, more than 1,000 Patriotes were imprisoned. Deepening the injustice, a dozen of them were executed by the British. Those momentous events parallel the 1916 Rising in Dublin, which resulted in 14 Irish rebels facing the firing squad at the Kilmainham Gaol. In each case, a failed rebellion tilted history, over the course of which a former prison was resurrected as a hallowed place for storytelling. Accordingly, La-Prison-des-Patriotes—like the "Bastille of Ireland"—has emerged as a dynamic metaphor for political struggle.

From there, we return to the southern cone of Latin America, where an extreme version of neoliberalism was instituted by the dictatorships as a "sacred" form of economic policy. In that context, the influence of the Chicago School of Economics is discussed alongside the reliance on mass detention and torture. That diagram of control aligned "economic freedom" with "political terror" in ways that ensured they would not interfere with each other (Letelier, 1976). Furthering a collective memory, several sites incorporate critiques of human rights atrocities brought about by economic upheaval. In Santiago, for example, La Casa de José Domingo Cañas has been uniquely transformed, shedding its past as a torture center so as to unleash its significance as a memorial space. Similar diagrams of control are deciphered in post-apartheid South Africa, where Robben Island, a celebrated heritage site, retains remnants of its profane political and economic history. With the benefit of a new place identity, those memorials serve as cultural vehicles in which themes of descent are rivaled by themes of ascent, thus promoting human rights.

LA-PRISON-DES-PATRIOTES

With a critical eye on the Atlantic world, prominent historians contend that the American Revolution (1776), the Dutch uprisings (of the 1780s), unrest in the Austrian Low Countries (after 1787), the French Revolution (1789), and all of the European revolutions of the 1790s constituted a single phenomenon (Godechot, 1986). Conspicuously absent from that lineage of political upheaval are Canada's rebellions of 1837 and 1838. The significance of those events has prompted another round of scholarly inquiry (Ducharme, 2007; Greer, 1995). The Atlantic Revolution is now being revisited so as to expose not only the political motives of the insurgents but also the economic forces at play. According to Donald Creighton, the rebellions in Canada were the climactic episode in a chronic struggle between "commerce and agriculture" (1956: 255). Deeply embedded in Canadian heritage, those two pillars of radical social change are contoured along competing lines of ethnicity, language, and religion, forging complex identities that persist to this day.

As discussed in previous chapters, that contested heritage has been channeled through former prisons to express particular interpretations of the conflict. In Montreal, the city's oldest prison, Pied-du-Courant, has been transformed into an elaborate exhibition space named La-Prison-des-Patriotes (see figure 11). From the standpoint of building a narrative, it is a curious place. On the one hand, it casts the British as the central authority with all their political and economic clout, thus marginalizing the non-British people in Lower Canada who fought the establishment. On the other hand, the museum places itself at the center of authority as it narrates those conflicts, and in doing so delivers messages that could be interpreted from a divergent point of view.

FIGURE 11. "Pied-du-Courant." In Montreal, the former prison, Pied-du-Courant, has been transformed into an exhibition space named La Prison-des-Patriotes. © retrowelch 2022.

La-Prison-des-Patriotes carefully dissects the rebellions of 1837 and 1838, drawing close attention to the very site where more than 1,300 Patriotes were imprisoned. To emphasize its profane history, the curators remind us that 12 of those Patriotes were hanged by the British military. La-Prison-des-Patriotes—the "lieu de memoire des rebellions"—echoes Nora's (1989) idea that memory is attached to places. The brochure invites visitors to "discover" and "relive" a moment in history that is "indelibly stamped on Quebec's collective memory, and let yourself be transported by the Patriotes' spirit of freedom and democracy." The site strives to connect with those who were executed, quoting the eloquence of Chevalier de Lorimier: "I die without regret. In insurrection and independence I desired nothing but the good of my country. My views and actions were sincere and were not stained with any of the crimes that dishonor humanity and are only too common in the tumult of unleashed passions" (La-Prison-des-Patriotes, n.d.). Those personal testimonies serve to "person" the place with the ghosts of Patriotes: the site has undergone a cultural transformation as a memorial while also issuing an allegory about the ascent of democratic values.

Reflecting on the rebellions, La-Prison-des-Patriotes establishes itself as a unique voice for Canadian history, in large part because the displays are written almost entirely in French. Thus, visitors who are not equipped to interpret lengthy passages of text are likely to find themselves outside the conversation on the meaning of the rebellions. Lacking as it does any bilingual crossover, the message is clear: the exhibition solely represents the perspectives and heritage of the French

Canadians, or Québécois. For visitors possessing some basic familiarity with the French language, however, the tour is worthwhile and informative as it attempts to set the record straight—whatever that might be.

As a storytelling institution, the museum assumes the position of authority, relying on a series of lengthy posters to establish its narrative. Arranged in chronological order, the exhibition navigates visitors down a *walk through time* (see Bennett, 1995; Williams, 2007). The curatorial narrative at La-Prison-des-Patriotes is quite didactic, especially with respect to the underlying economic threads of the rebellions. For example, one such lesson is titled "Colonial Economy of Lower Canada" (now known as Quebec):

> Local economy depends on the size of the metropolis and imperial policies. The [British] Empire encouraged the importation of products of its colonies—in the case of Lower Canada there are endless wood products and grains—which benefits its markets because of preferential customs rates. But, membership of the Empire has to affect a specialization of economic development of the colony and a closing of other possible markets. In the 1830s, the economic link of the Empire gave rise to important debates.

To heighten their scholarly tone, the curators—as local experts—rely on other experts to authenticate the narrative. Among the key sources is renowned author Alexis de Tocqueville, who visited Lower Canada in 1831. "The wealthy classes for the most part belong to the English race. Although French was almost the universally spoken language, most of the newspapers, posters, and up to the signboards of French merchants are in English. The commercial enterprises are almost all in their hands. It is truly the ruling class in Canada."

The passage includes this key statement: "This finding, the newspaper *The Irish Vindicator* of Montreal has already done before in 1830." That final sentence acknowledges a presence of the Irish in Lower Canada without any further explanation; yet the direction of the narrative remains almost exclusively on the experience of the French Canadians. Hence, messages are likely to undergo some tension, as other non-British ethnic groups in Lower Canada are reading the narrative differently. For instance, historical scholarship is steeped in Irish contributions to Lower Canada, including its politics, economics, and heritage. As Maureen Slattery points out, Irish Catholics in Lower Canada were a "double-minority in a majority French Catholic Church and a dominant English Protestant society" (1997: 33). Despite being pushed to the margins on both sides of the power play between the French Catholic Church and English Protestant society, Irish Catholic leaders in Lower Canada remained very much part of the French Canadian resistance to British hegemony—economic and otherwise (Bowen, 1988; O'Gallagher, 1988; Wilson, 1989).

Allen Greer weighs into the discussion, suggesting that a comparative approach to the rebellions (of 1837 and 1838) benefits from lessons in Ireland, for it demonstrates how the Irish had been marginalized by the British state elsewhere. He writes: "Ireland provides a particularly striking parallel in many respects, and the Patriotes were well aware of this connection; Papineau was proud to be known as the 'O'Connell of Canada'" (Greer, 1995: 6, 10). Here curators embrace themes of ascent as the narrative introduces Louis-Joseph Papineau as a central leader in the Patriote movement. Papineau had taken inspiration from Daniel O'Connell, known as The Liberator (or The Emancipator) for his success in securing the rights of Irish Catholics in Great Britain in the first half of the 19th century. In the years leading up to the rebellions, the print media circulated written messages to readers on the margins of a British-controlled state. Among those sources was *The Irish Vindicator*, later known simply as *The Vindicator*. The influential newspaper was edited by Dr. Edmund Bailey O'Callaghan, a bilingual Irishman, member of the Patriot party, and "Papineau's right-hand man in the Lower Canadian Legislative Assembly" (Slattery, 1997: 29; Verney, 1994). Papineau recruited O'Callaghan in part because of his personal—and political—contacts with O'Connell. Papineau courted Irish Catholics since they provided the swing vote in Lower Canada. As a regular feature of *The Irish Vindicator* (in 1833), O'Callaghan reprinted O'Connell's "Letters to the Irish People," thus underscoring the Patriotes' affinity with the Irish cause. In the wake of the 1837 rebellion, Papineau and O'Callaghan escaped together across the American border (Slattery, 1997; 1980).

Returning to the theme of economics, La-Prison-des-Patriotes celebrates the rise of the People's Bank as a counterweight to the Bank of Montreal, which engaged in discriminatory lending practices against French Canadians and supporters of the Patriote party. Tensions between the French (alongside the Irish) members of the Assembly and the British business elite spilled over into parliamentary maneuvers to exert pressure on the government. "The Assembly makes use of its ultimate weapon by refusing to vote on the subsidies under the principle no taxation without representation. The government can then allow no public expenditure, and the management of the State is paralyzed." Along the way a set of grievances, in the form of the 92 Resolutions, reached London as a petition to the King, the House of Lords, and the House of Commons. That petition opposed the policy of surrendering territory to speculators in Crown land; the Assembly also "denounced the discrimination" in the granting of public posts to officials of British origin, who outnumbered those of French origin 157 to 45. The Assembly reminded the British Parliament that the majority of the people of Lower Canada were of French origin and that their use of the "French Language, has become for the colonial authorities a pretext of insult, of exclusion, of inferiority policy and separation of rights and interests."

Those linguistic tensions compounded a contested heritage, and La-Prison-des-Patriotes is quick to point out that those at margins of society were being kept there through the degrading social practices of the British elite. The exhibit goes further, pointing to the ironies of British control that failed to establish order and indeed incited rebellion. From the standpoint of cultural sociology, punishments are intended to symbolize a sense of legitimate authority that strives to promote civilization. On the flip side, injustice looms as its shadow (Smith 2008). By 1837, economic, political, and ethnic strife had reached critical mass as British administrators imposed martial law, initiating a "process of repression of a magnitude previously unknown. . . . The guarantee of individual freedoms and the protection against arbitrary arrests are immediately suspended." By the end of the year, the Patriotes' armed defense had been repressed by British forces and more than 500 people had been arrested and taken to prison, where most of them would remain until June 1838. Soon after that, administrators of the colony proclaimed a new martial law and the suspension of *habeas corpus*.

The number of arrests reached 800, and a military tribunal was established to judge the prisoners. Fourteen trials were held in 1838 and 1839. Louis T. Drummond, an attorney of Irish descent, and Aaron Philip Hart, a Jewish lawyer, served as defense council. Their legal intervention proved insufficient. Of the 108 defendants, nine were acquitted and 99 were condemned to death; 12 were hanged, 58 were deported to Australia, and two were banished. The remaining 27 defendants were released on bail (see Dunning, 2009). La-Prison-des-Patriotes provides a sacred space for memorialization and reflection by reminding us of these personal tragedies. "Among the twelve hanged in Bas-Canada, seven are married. They leave behind 26 children, a large number of infants. Three other children were born in the weeks following the hanging of their father." *The Irish Vindicator* reported that in solidarity, young people of Montreal formed a permanent political association whose name, the Sons of Freedom, was borrowed from the American revolutionaries. Embracing themes of ascent in the face of adversity, the fraternal organization adopted a strident republican orientation in its manifesto.

Michel Ducharme digests the Rebellions of 1837 and 1838 as the "last chapter of the Atlantic Revolution, a chapter that did not end happily for Canadian republicans" (2007: 420). In that vein, La-Prison-des-Patriotes concludes its *walk through time* by pondering the failed Patriote rebellion, which has resonated "through generations of Quebecers who are seeking to understand what really happened . . . [as well as current] debates on the balance of power in the political institutions, on the sharing of wealth in society and on the assertion of identities in the common State of citizens." Along those lines, the curators concede that the performance of heritage is indeed contested since a reconstruction of history does not always benefit from all possible angles. Thus, many questions remain unanswered. In telling its story, the museum ends with a note of noticeable ambiguity. "In this case, we would like to remind you of two things: that the views of the witnesses of the time vary, and that among the current historians, the divergence of points of view persist." That lack of closure seems to leave visitors with a sense of unresolved differences, which undermine an otherwise virtuous defense of the eternal good. In this way, La-Prison-des-Patriotes, unlike the Kilmainham Gaol, seems to stop short of entrenching a full-fledged Bastille Effect (see Flander et al.,2016).

LOS CHICAGO BOYS

A revolution of a different kind began in the 1950s at the University of Chicago's Economics Department, whose tightly knit faction of conservative professors would shape a new cross-national identity known as the Chicago School of Economics. They aspired to establish a school of thought so recognizable that their prized students would proudly declare themselves "the Chicago Boys." Together, they "represented a revolutionary bulwark against the dominant 'statist' thinking of the day" (Klein, 2007: 57). Leading this academic mission aimed at revolutionizing economics was the charismatic Milton Friedman (1962), whose catchphrase was simple: unbridled laissez-faire. The Chicago Boys were taught the tenets of neoliberalism and the power of the market; indeed, they were inculcated to accept its theory as "a sacred feature of the system" rather than just a scholarly hypothesis (Knight, 1932: 455). "The core of such sacred Chicago teachings was that the economic forces of supply, demand, inflation and unemployment were like the forces of nature, fixed and unchanging. In the truly free market imagined in Chicago classes and texts, these forces existed in perfect equilibrium, supply communicating with demand the way the moon pulls the tides . . . an Eden of plentiful employment, boundless creativity and zero inflation" (Klein, 2007: 61). Or at least, so the story goes.

Initially confined to basement workshops in the social science building, the Chicago Boys seized upon a rare opportunity to experiment on an entire nation, whose economy would serve as their laboratory. On September 11, 1973, General Augusto Pinochet launched a devastating coup d'état that altered the history of Chile, with spillover effects on the entire region. Inducing "states of shock . . . the bloody birth of the counterrevolution" dismantled the progressive policies of President Salvador Allende (Klein, 2007: 92). Before proceeding with greater details about the Pinochet dictatorship and its alliance with the Chicago Boys, some theoretical consideration is in order to help us sift through the political—and human rights—casualties of the Chilean economy. As a guidepost, we turn to Foucault, whose interest in notions of power pivots on how it is exercised, especially since it involves distinct domains of knowledge (or *savoirs*). That "know-how" (technique, or *techne*) becomes the underlying rationale for government practices. Moreover, those constructs also prepare the ground for what Foucault calls the spaces of security (2007: 11; see also Dilts and Harcourt, 2008; Harcourt, 2011).

Indeed, space and security are tightly coupled, while allowing pathways through which various forms (*multiplicities*) of power flow. Somewhat schematically, Foucault explains: "Sovereignty is exercised within the borders of a territory, discipline is exercised on the bodies of individuals, and security is exercised over a whole population" (2007: 11). Sovereignty, security, and discipline figured prominently in the Chilean coup: the military dictatorship quickly restructured economics through brazen campaigns of state-sponsored terror that were not limited to detention, torture, and murder. To refine our understanding of this, let us establish a few more distinctions between discipline and security: "Discipline is essentially centripetal. . . . It isolates a space. Discipline concentrates, focuses, and encloses. . . . Discipline regulates everything. Discipline allows nothing to escape. The apparatuses of security . . . are centrifugal. Security involves organizing . . . allowing the development of ever-wider circuits" (Foucault, 2007: 44–45). With those notions in mind, one can associate discipline with detention and torture while security segues into matters of the economy and the financial performance of the state (see Welch, 2008, 2010a).

Those conceptual distinctions improve our understanding of diagrams of control and sharpen our capacity to recognize momentous shifts in history. It is believed that in Santiago on the day of the coup, while fighter jets bombed the La Moneda, the presidential palace, Allende took his own life rather than surrender to Pinochet. State terror swiftly ensued: more than 13,000 civilians were rounded up and taken to detention centers set up at the National Stadium and other sites scattered throughout the country. At Pinochet's direction, brutal conditions of confinement were exacerbated by the routine abuse and torture of carefully targeted victims. Among them was Orlando Letelier, an economist who had just returned to Chile from his ambassadorship in Washington, D.C. On the day of the coup, Letelier was ambushed by soldiers toting submachine guns. After being detained in Santiago, he was banished to Dawson Island in the Strait of Magellan, in the far south of the country—Pinochet's version of a Siberian labor camp (Dinges and Landau, 1980; Guzmán, 1993).

The coup cleared the slate for a total overhaul of political institutions and the economy. This paved the way for Los Chicago Boys, who had completed their studies with Friedman and Harberger. Pinochet assigned these newly minted economists to senior advisory slots within the military junta, authorizing them to institute the laissez-faire principles contained in their 189-page report referred to as "el ladrillo" (the brick; see Valdes, 1995). As the official economic document, *el ladrillo* would defy other logics. Critiques of it, or even any sensible alternatives to it, would be regarded as dangerous—vaguely subversive or Marxist—and contained by military force. As a result, those diagrams of control would make room for massive economic re-engineering alongside repression and crimes against humanity.

Meanwhile, dissenters pressed their plans to revive democratic platforms. After a year of confinement—and torture—Letelier was released on the condition that he leave Chile. In 1975, Letelier joined the Institute for Policy Studies in Washington, D.C., where his resistance to the Chilean junta gained international support. His scathing rebuke of the new economic order was starkly titled "The 'Chicago Boys' in Chile: Economic Freedom's Awful Toll" (Letelier, 1976). From the outset, Letelier singled out US financial officials (i.e., William Simon, Secretary of the Treasury; Robert McNamara, President of the World Bank) for providing economic aid to Pinochet. He criticized them for condoning a diagram of control in which "economic freedom" and "political terror" seemed to reside in the same social system without touching each other. Letelier also pointed out that the CIA had funneled funds to the Chicago Boys, who in turn administered Friedman's "shock treatment" of the Chilean economy (e.g., a drastic reduction in government spending on social programs). Their pure free market policy would bring about extreme inequality and indeed exacerbate it.

With the keen eye of an economist, Letelier (1976) posted economic indicators demonstrating the collateral damage inflicted by Los Chicago Boys and *el ladrillo*. "The inhuman conditions under which a high percentage of the Chilean population lives is reflected most dramatically by substantial increases in malnutrition, infant mortality and the appearance of thousands of beggars on the streets of Chilean cities." Letelier stressed that the concentration of wealth was not the marginal outcome of a difficult situation; rather, it was the very basis of Pinochet's social project. And to complete that project, the economic plan had to be enforced "by the killing of thousands, the establishment of concentration camps all over the country, the jailing of more than 100,000 persons in three years, the closing of trade unions and neighborhood organizations, and the prohibition of all political activities and all forms of free expression" (Letelier, 1976). Los Chicago Boys' strategy entailed repression of the masses and "economic freedom" for a small, privileged group. Those two imperatives operated with an "inner harmony"—two sides of the same coin. Andre Gunder Funk (1976), a dissident Chicago Boy, contributed to the wider critique by issuing his own commentary, titled *Economic Genocide in Chile* (see also Friedman, 1982).

Letelier would pay dearly for his sustained condemnation of Pinochet and Los Chicago Boys. Less than two weeks after his essay was published, on September 10, 1976, Chilean authorities revoked his nationality. Eleven days later, on September 21, 1976, agents for Operation Condor assassinated Letelier (and his US colleague Ronni Moffitt) with a car bomb on Embassy Row in Washington, D.C. For those murders, the Chilean courts, in 1993, convicted Manuel Contreras, former chief of Chilean intelligence, along with Brigadier Pedro Espinoza and Michael Townley, a US expatriate (Branch and Propper, 1982; Dinges and Landau, 1980).

Pinochet was now a global pariah, the embodiment of a truly profane regime. Over time, the human rights movement would mount a formidable attack that would shift history away from the disorder of injustice and toward upright accountability. Facing intense international—and even US—pressure, Pinochet grudgingly stepped aside, allowing Chile to transition back to democracy in the late 1980s. But his problems were just beginning. In 1998, he was placed under house arrest in London for crimes against humanity committed in Chile; he was eventually released (on medical grounds) and returned to Santiago in 2000. Later that year, he was indicted on kidnapping charges related to state violence in the course of the coup (e.g., the Caravan of Death). Once again, on medical grounds, the Chilean Supreme Court dismissed those indictments. Another round of charges for human rights atrocities, in 2004 and 2005, kept Pinochet in the frame for prosecutors, and in 2006 he was sentenced to house arrest for the kidnapping and murder of two of Allende's bodyguards. Days later, on December 10, 2006, Pinochet died. Although he avoided convictions on an array of criminal charges, his legacy continues to be stained not only by state terror but also by evidence of an elaborate money-laundering scheme involving US banks that defrauded the Chilean financial system of millions of dollars (Kornbluh, 2013; Roht-Arriaza, 2005).

In Santiago, at the Museo de la Memoria y Los Derechos Humanos, a special exhibit in 2017 curated by the investigative journalist Peter Kornbluh examined Pinochet's "Secretos de Estad" (State Secrets). The archives were brought to light following a sweeping declassification order by President Clinton. The exhibit contains multiple examples of how the coup was aided by US elites. To reenact a conversation that then President Nixon had with Henry Kissinger (then National Security Advisor) in 1970, a telephone placed on a pedestal is accompanied by a transcript. Verbatim, it informs visitors that Nixon and Kissinger opposed President Allende's progressive policies. The White House was prepared to sabotage Chilean labor, production, and the distribution of goods—as Nixon put it, to "make the economy scream" (Kornbluh, 2013: 17, 83).

In *The Shock Doctrine: The Rise of Disaster Capitalism*, Naomi Klein takes aim at Pinochet, Los Chicago Boys, and the use of political force to dismantle an economy that had been regulated by Allende. As inflation, unemployment, and the cost of basics such as bread spun wildly out of control, Los Chicago Boys refused to reconsider their laissez-faire assumptions; rather, they insisted that the problems were caused by insufficient strictness. "The economy had failed to correct itself and return to harmonious balance because there were still 'distortions' left over from nearly a half-century of government interference. For the experiment to work, Pinochet had to strip these distortions away—more cuts, more privatization, more speed." Or in the words of Friedman (1982), the Chilean economy must undergo "shock treatment" (Klein, 2007: 97, 98).

La Casa de José Domingo Cañas, in a residential neighborhood in Santiago, is another reminder of the interplay between figurative and literal shock treatment. The former detention/torture center has been repurposed as a memorial space. Much as happened with Villa Grimaldi, the property was demolished, leaving exposed foundations that curators have since marked so as to transpose visitors onto a different place and time. "Sala de Tortura" (torture room) is now an empty plot on which a metal bed frame rests: a cue to its previous life. Known as "the hole," that room was used for a sadistic electrocution technique called "la parrilla" (cooking grill) (see Feitlowitz, 1998). The site is enclosed by walls covered with murals, most notably a painting of a vulture with wings colored with the US flag, an obvious reference to Operation Condor (McSherry, 2005; see figure 12).

Violence, repression, and economic chaos were not confined to Chile. Los Chicago Boys had a comparable impact on neighboring Argentina, where similar diagrams of control emboldened strict disciplinary and security measures. In Parque de la Memoria Monumento a Las Victimas del Terrorismo de Stado in Buenos

FIGURE 12. "La Casa Cañas." At Casa de José Domingo Cañas (Santiago, Chile), a mural featuring a vulture with a US flag is captioned: "La paz era una Paloma y alrededor los buitres oveja negra" (Peace was a dove and around the black sheep vultures). © retrowelch 2022.

Aires, human rights activists pay their respects to the victims of state terrorism but also condemn economic injustice. In doing so, they throw critical light on the reckless financial policies imposed by the military junta following the 1976 coup d'état. Along the promenade, a group of artists (Grupo de Arte Callejero) have installed Carteles de la Memoria (Memory Signs) that inject the visual language of traffic signs with the synthetic power of images. A sign featuring a tank with a peso/dollar symbol signifies the relationship between the last dictatorship and the concentration of capital in the oligarchy. A similar posting shows a graph illustrating the booming foreign debt incurred during the junta; names of US financial institutions are encrypted into the art (e.g., Boston Bank). Another sign targets the International Monetary Fund and the World Bank, which syphoned Argentine capital across borders according to the principles of neoliberalism. The words "se vende" (for sale) are superimposed on emblems of public utilities (e.g., transport, telecommunications, postal services) to convey the cynical logic of privatization, which creates greater profits for corporate entities at the expense of Argentine consumers.

At the time, investigative writers sought to amplify the resistance to the Argentine dictatorship and its economic platform, among them Rodolfo Walsh—a literary dynamo born to third-generation Irish immigrants. On the one-year anniversary of the military Junta, Walsh issued his "Open Letter from a Writer to the Military Junta" (1977). The lengthy essay is regarded as a passionate strike at the brutality of the repressors. Much like Letelier, Walsh recognized that human rights atrocities run parallel to economic exploitation. In tandem, these "introduce[ed] Argentine society to the most profound terror it has ever known":

> Fifteen thousand missing, ten thousand prisoners, four thousand dead, tens of thousands in exile: these are the raw numbers of this terror.
>
> Since the ordinary jails were filled to the brim, you created virtual concentration camps in the main garrisons of the country which judges, lawyers, journalists, and international observers, are all forbidden to enter. The military secrecy of what goes on inside, which you cite as a requirement for the purposes of investigation, means that the majority of the arrests turn into kidnappings that in turn allow for torture without limits and execution without trial

Walsh, skilled at cracking espionage codes, is best-known for intercepting a CIA telex that blew the cover off the US invasion of the Bay of Pigs in Cuba (Klein, 2007: 115). His letter to the junta was signed on March 24, 1977, then delivered through a system of clandestine channels, eventually reaching foreign press offices. Walsh told his wife (Lilia): "I want to let those fuckers know that I'm still alive and still writing." The following day, Walsh was attacked by a team of soldiers with orders from Admiral Massera to "bring the fucking bastard back alive, he's mine." As the story goes, Walsh, who embraced the motto "It isn't a crime to talk; getting arrested is the crime," produced a weapon and began shooting. The military returned fire and threw his wounded body in a car bound for ESMA, where he was pronounced dead on arrival. It is believed that Walsh's body was burned and dumped in a river (McCaughan, 2002: 284–90; Klein, 2007: 117–19).

Walsh accurately predicted that "the Argentine people's resistance for more than twenty years will not disappear but will instead be aggravated by the memory of the havoc that has been wreaked and by the revelation of the atrocities that have been committed." At a memorial space at ESMA, his letter is displayed in front of the Casino (the former detention, torture, and extermination center), where his words enter the collective consciousness of human rights activism and economic justice. Walsh's criticism of brutal labor practices still resonates. In 1977, Walsh railed: "By freezing salaries with the butts of your rifles while prices rise at bayonet point, abolishing every form of collective protest. . . . And when the workers have wanted to protest, you have called them subversives and kidnapped entire delegations of union representatives who sometimes turned up dead, and other times did not turn up at all."

Human rights atrocities as they intersect with economic crimes continue to be investigated in Argentina. In 2018, two ex–Ford Motor executives were convicted on charges of kidnapping and torturing workers employed in an auto plant located just outside Buenos Aires. Pedro Muller and Hector Sibila were sentenced to 10 and 12 years respectively. Their trial marks the first time officials from a foreign company have been held criminally liable for state violence. The company acted in a coordinated manner with the military, and testimony demonstrated that "executives provided the military with lists, addresses and photo IDs of workers they wanted arrested and even provided space for an illegal detention centre at the plant where the abductees could be interrogated" (Goñi, 2018). Supporters of the plaintiffs declared that Ford was an example of civilian-military state terrorism operations. "The majority were kidnapped right off the assembly line. . . . They were taken by rifle-toting military officers and paraded before the other workers so they could see what happened to their union representatives. This created an atmosphere of terror in the workplace that prevented any wage or working condition complaints" (Goñi, 2018). A lawyer for the plaintiffs said that the victims were considering suing Ford Motor Company in the US since it "is clear that Ford Motor Company had control of the Argentinian subsidiary during the 70s" (Goñi, 2018).

POST-APARTHEID PARADOX

Similar diagrams of control are critiqued elsewhere, including in Cape Town, where key sites memorialize political prisoners. Above all, the maximum security prison at Robben Island has a reputation as a Bastille of sorts. There, a steady flow of international tourists board crowded ferries to journey across the harbor to see where anti-apartheid activists were confined. Of course, the real draw is the prison cell that held Nelson Mandela. The pilgrimage reaches its climax as visitors stare through the iron bars into an empty cell furnished only with a sleeping mat, a night stand, and a rubbish bin (Welch, 2015: 226; 2012). The cell has undergone a cultural transformation, having abandoned its use-value as a profane place of confinement. In its current incarnation, the prison cell—with all its signifying-value—speaks to the power of the anti-apartheid movement that prevailed over injustice. Imagining Mandela sleeping on his mat serves to "person" the space, allowing visitors to sympathize with his pains of imprisonment. Still, with its themes of ascent, the tour is uplifting: Robben Island projects an impressive Bastille Effect, emerging as a metaphor for a democratic nation. Lending the experience added authenticity, former political prisoners serve as tour guides to narrate a collective story about the struggle for freedom.

Beyond Mandela's prison cell, Robben Island offers more lessons on political imprisonment during the apartheid era. Minivans transport tourists around the island so that they can examine other aspects of the prison regime, including remnants of manual labor. The lime quarry, for instance, retains special meaning: that former worksite is where Mandela and other political prisoners toiled in the African heat. As a form of resistance, the prisoners, emboldened by their solidarity, looked toward the future. The tour guide points to an enclosure at the quarry where political prisoners huddled during their breaks. That otherwise cramped space became known as "the university," for that is where Mandela and his comrades shared their visions of a new South Africa, portending the demise of its racist regime (Mandela, 1994). Yet visitors are not told about the complexities of social change, particularly with respect to macroeconomics (see Ramsamy, 2016).

In 1990, after 27 years as a political prisoner, Mandela was released. After a rapid succession of events, he emerged as the President of South Africa in 1994. History, especially economic history, was just beginning. Although Mandela and his political party, the African National Congress (ANC), held high hopes for progressive economic transformation, other factors and forces would change the course of the country's financial affairs. Drawing on harsh lessons from the southern cone of Latin America, Klein (2007) recognizes a similar pattern of economic shock. While the ANC kept its eye on the prize—electoral politics—the old apartheid bosses within the de Klerk government watched for economic spoils. During negotiations, those financial rewards would be secured in the fine print of the deal. In line with the Washington Consensus model, supposedly impartial experts would dictate central bank policy and trade policy, besides making arcane inroads into the IMF and the World Bank.

Vishnu Padayachee, one of the few classically trained economists in the ANC, conceded: "By the time the draft was complete . . . it was a new ball game. . . . We were caught completely off guard" (Klein, 2007: 253–54). From his studies in the US, Padayachee was well aware of the Chicago Boys and their strategies for central banks, which were to be run as "sovereign republics within states out of reach of the meddling hands of elected lawmakers" (254). That version of power was being embedded in the new South African economy and administered by the same men who had run it under apartheid (i.e., Chris Stals, Derek Keyes). Such a deceitful maneuver is identical to the way Argentine finance ministers for the military junta managed to get their jobs back when the country transitioned to democracy (McSherry, 2005).

Despite all the enthusiasm and fanfare of a post-apartheid society, it turns out that the original economic operations remained at the core of the state. The national budget was consumed by debt passed on by the apartheid government. Human rights activist Rassool Snyman realized sadly that "they never freed us. They only took the chain from around our neck and put it on our ankles" (Klein, 2007: 257; see also Gumede, 2005). Under the weight of debt, the government was pressured to privatize services and to comply with the demands of foreign investors. Mounting inflation and unemployment were met with cuts to basic housing and food allowances, further shocking the economy and its citizens. Meanwhile South Africa's Truth and Reconciliation Commission grappled with such horrors as torture and disappearances. One of the commission's jurors, Yasmin Sooka, regrets that more attention wasn't paid to the economic crimes of the apartheid system. Echoing Rodolfo Walsh as well as Orlando Letelier's critique of the "inner harmony" between torture and free market economics, Sooka said she would have done it differently. "I would devote only *one* hearing to torture because I think when you focus on torture and you don't look at what it was serving, that's when you start to do a revision of the real history" (Klein, 2007: 267; see also Marais, 2001).

CONCLUSION

Viewed from abroad, the Bastille had a long-standing reputation as a place of arbitrary confinement. In Paris, however, that fortress prison was just part of a larger network of institutions designed to hold political prisoners, including the Conciergerie, the Grand Chatelet, and the Petite Chatelet (BnF, 2010: 29–31). The Chateau de Vincennes is associated with the Bastille in more ways than one. It was rumored that the Bastille and the chateau—on the edge of the city—were connected by an underground passage (Schama, 1990: 411). Today, visitors to "the keep"—the former prison—at the Chateau de Vincennes are informed by a sign that tells them: "In the second half of the 18th century, Vincennes became a symbol of royal despotism. Some prisoners here were victims of royal *lettre de cachet* (ordering imprisonment without trial). They were imprisoned, like Diderot in 1749, for writings deemed subversive." On display is an original printing of the book *La Theorie de l'Impot* (The Theory of Taxation). Its author, Mirabeau ([1760] 2010), caused such a stir that the king ordered that he be detained in Vincennes for eight days before being exiled. According to a storyboard posted at Vincennes, Mirabeau, an economist, launched a "new economic thought, speaking with frankness that attracted numerous votes to him. . . . In particular, he took a stand against the *fermiers generaux* [who farmed out the right to collect taxes], severely criticized the fiscal regime of the day and set out the conditions necessary for fair taxation." Mirabeau's writings are admired for their understanding of the importance of *economic justice*, which earned him the nickname "the friend of man."

The Bastille Effect incorporates critiques of economic forces within a wider apparatus of control. At La-Prison-des-Patriotes, curators narrate the contested heritage of Quebec as contoured by commerce and agriculture, culminating in violent rebellions. In the collective memory, that profane past is subject to virtuous transformation in that it recasts the Patriotes as heroic martyrs. The actual site of their execution has been converted into a memorial space, thereby expunging its malevolence. In the southern cone of Latin America, disciplinary power—with all of its centripetal forces—was imposed on the victims of the dictatorships through detention and torture. Similar forms of disciplinary power were unleashed on the economy in ways that delivered dividends to the financial elites while subjecting the people to unforgivable misery. Even in its demolished ruins, La Casa de José Domingo Cañas continues to project scathing condemnation of military repression, which relied on foreign investment. As with other memorials studied here, curators rely on the power of place to convey the significance of sited-ness as a metaphor for transcendent justice. Indeed, Robben Island has been designated a world heritage site due in large part to its capacity to inspire support for human rights. In the following chapters, relevant cultural developments are examined within other diagrams of control, namely religion and architecture.

6

Catholic Nuances

In Paris, the Conciergerie, a palace that had been the seat of royal power dating back to the sixth century, was repurposed to serve as a jail during the Revolutionary Tribunal (BnF, 2010). Having undergone another transformation, the site is currently a tourist destination where visitors descend into its dungeon to view the (reconstructed) holding cell of Queen Marie-Antoinette. It is there that she spent her last days before execution. The ghostly space is "personed" with a mannequin of the Queen dressed in a black veil and seated before a crucifix. Apart from that dramatic display, the scholarly narrative of the Conciergerie chronicles the grim events surrounding the Reign of Terror. In the years following the fall of the monarchy, thousands of civilians were put to death under a capricious judicial system aimed at identifying "counter-revolutionary" threats. Attention is directed at the broad sweep of the Committee for Public Safety, which through its Law of Suspects "ordered the arrest of anyone presumed to be an enemy of the Revolution or confessed to being so" (Conciergerie, n.d.). Former holding cells expose their profane past. Between 1793 and 1794, more than 2,700 people appeared before the tribunal, and then carted off to the guillotine in groups of 12. A sparsely lit room lists the names of those who perished under the Terror. With its new place identity, the solemn space performs memory.

In its afterlife as a place for learning history, the Conciergerie offers rich details on political imprisonment during the revolutionary period. Its exhibition, however, seem careful to avoid some of the more controversial events that fueled the Terror, among them the September Massacres of 1792. At the time, there was growing fear that foreign and royalist militias were plotting to invade Paris; their plan was to open the prisons and recruit inmates to join them. In reaction to that fear, violence spread throughout the city's prisons and the number of brutal killings quickly mounted to more than 1,400 (Tackett, 2011). It is estimated that more than half the prison population was summarily executed, with more than 1,000 murdered in the span of 20 hours. Victims of that wave of slaughter included not only political prisoners but also common criminals as well as women and children.

A defining trait of the September Massacres was the deliberate targeting of priests. In 1790, the Civil Constitution of the Clergy was passed to subordinate the Catholic Church in France to the French government, thereby requiring priests to pledge their allegiance to the Revolution. Even clergy who had complied with the Civil Constitution were not spared casualties inflicted by knives, axes, hatchets, sabers, and in at least one incident, a carpenter's saw. Historians for decades have debated the underlying threads of this mass hysteria (Caron, 1935; see also Bluche, 1986; Schama, 1990). Etienne Bericourt captured the spectacle of death in a drawing titled *Transporting Corpses during the Revolution*, currently housed at the Musée de la Ville de Paris, Musée Carnavalet. The graphic image shows officials supervising a gleeful work crew disposing of naked corpses and severed heads. Among the patriots in attendance is one of "le vainquer de la Bastille" recognizable by his emblematic helmet (Schama, 1990: 637–38).

In this chapter, the nuance of Catholicism as it manifests itself in political imprisonment is carefully considered in several historical—and cultural—moments. Correspondingly, thought is given to the manner in which sites and symbols express memory of religious identity. We begin in Montreal, where La-Prison-des-Patriotes reflects on the emergence of both political and penal power. Discussion expands to how Catholic institutions contended with the Protestant establishment. This "Political Catholicism" is followed "Contrasts in Catholicism," as were apparent in Buenos Aires, where progressive offshoots of religious activism were eradicated by reactionary forces with the complicity of the Argentine Catholic Church. Those atrocities suggest a duality of purity and danger (see Douglass, 1966). Elsewhere in the southern cone of Latin America, the Catholic hierarchy in Santiago strongly defied the Pinochet regime, going so far as to establish the Vicariate of Solidarity, which provided social and legal services to the families of political prisoners. Performances of Catholicism are also interpreted with regard to Northern Ireland, where the hunger strike of 1981 raised the stakes for faith and morality. Altogether, socio-religious developments in Montreal, the southern cone, and Northern Ireland open critical space to contemplate diagrams of control and the resistance they produce. The back-and-forth between justice and injustice is reinforced by more impulsive remedies to restore order and contain disorder. Of course, what constitutes those binaries is often contested, making Catholicism under these circumstances very much a nuanced phenomenon.

POLITICAL CATHOLICISM

The prison officially named Au Pied-du-Courant served not only the City of Montreal but the entire district as well, and as discussed in previous chapters its role in the rebellions of 1837 and 1838 is central to its story. Curiously, a storyboard within the transformed space since renamed La-Prison-des-Patriotes explains that the prison was "baptized" as Au Pied-du-Courant because it was on the banks

of a river and at the foot of the Sainte-Marie stream. Any further religious references at La-Prison-des-Patriotes are conspicuously absent: the narrative maintains
a strict secular perspective on the controversies in Lower Canada. Two exceptions
are worth noting. In the first instance, a poster tracks the influence of British
investors, which prompted anxiety among French Canadians, who worried about
the Protestant direction the territory was taking. Second, a portrait of Jean-Jacques
Lartigue, Bishop of Montreal, is prominently displayed. However, the accompany-
ing biographical sketch (in French) seems more than a little disparaging:

> Jean-Jacques Lartigue is a cousin of Louis-Joseph Papineau. . . . Appointed bishop in
> 1821, his relations with the Canadian Party are relatively cordial at the beginning of
> his episcopate. But at the time of the publication of the two mandates against rebel-
> lions, he has become one of the greatest opponents of the Patriotes and Papineau.

Visitors to La-Prison-des-Patriotes who arrive expecting more discussion than
this of the role played by institutional religion may well be disappointed, or
perhaps perplexed given the wealth of historical records on the subject. Michel
Ducharme, in his characterization of the "Last Chapter of the Atlantic Revolution," reminds us that French Canadians and the Patriotes adhered to highly
vetted sources of inspiration. Those "colonial republicans" sought respectability,
credibility, and legitimacy. As a consequence, their role models were the Americans—and to a lesser extent the Irish—both of whom had waged war on the British. "Rousseauian-style rhetoric about the social contract was widely used, especially in Lower Canada, but its author was rarely mentioned or quoted extensively,
nor were other French republicans. The painful memory of the Terror and the
ultimate failure of the Revolution, heralded by the Restoration, led the Lower and
Upper Canadian republicans to turn to Anglo-American references" (Ducharme,
2007: 420).

Religious tensions, to be sure, were deeply entrenched in Lower Canada, especially in the run-up to the rebellions. French Canada was still a Catholic and conservative society that bristled at the democratic, anticlerical, and revolutionary
instincts of the Patriote movement. In the eyes of traditional historiographers, the
rebels possessed some admirable qualities but were destined to fail. "They lost
because they had to lose; they were not simply overwhelmed by superior force,
they were justly chastised by the god of History" (Greer, 1995: 3). The nuances of
"political Catholicism" are insightfully sorted out by Maureen Slattery (1997), who
delves into the strands that wove together the Catholic Churches in Quebec and
Ireland. As noted in the previous chapter, Papineau, alongside his trusted patriot
O'Callaghan, greatly admired Daniel O'Connell, who had secured the political—
and religious—freedoms of the Irish people. But even though O'Connell's campaign had the backing of the liberal Catholic Church in Ireland, O'Callaghan and
his editorials in *The Irish Vindicator* failed to draw similar support from the conservative Catholic Church in Lower Canada.

Slattery explains that the Catholic Church in Lower Canada played a sharply
different role than it did in Ireland. After 1791, the French Catholic Church

in Lower Canada was rewarded by the British government for remaining politically neutral. The benefits of this were clear given that the governor held a veto over the appointments of newly ordained priests. Moreover, the local Catholic Church "retained its land and aristocratic privileges gained during the ancient regime. . . . [Hence] it saw no advantage in supporting the liberalism of its French Catholic petite bourgeoisie, much less of an Irish-Catholic editor" (Slattery, 1997: 34). As a result, the French Catholic clergy occupied a fixed position in Lower Canada, where the feudal society of the *ancien régime* had long endured. Unsurprisingly, when the Patriote party officially formed in 1834, its platform was rejected by the local Catholic Church, which viewed "democracy as a machine producing mass atheism" (Wallot, 1973; translated in Slattery, 2007: 34). The French Canadian clergy served valuable disciplinary functions. Priests promoted a doctrine of submission to lawful authority and reminded their congregations of the "good government" they enjoyed under British rule (Dickinson and Young, 1993: 160). O'Callaghan was undeterred, and in his writings he even resorted to biblical devices by comparing Lower Canada to Egypt during the Plague of the locusts. He also repeated a common metaphor adopted by certain Irish Catholics who identified themselves as a "chosen people in exile from their natural rights" (de Paor, 1985: 160).

Given the socio-religious context of Lower Canada, it is understandable why the exhibit at La-Prison-des-Patriotes adopts an unswerving commitment to secularism. While the former prison marks the site of political imprisonment—and execution—it also performs heritage in a style that honors the memory and ideals of the Patriotes. Ducharme (2007) describes the Patriotes as a movement that transcended institutional religion. Put simply, the republican framework in the 1830s was built on virtue   a quality imbued with political liberty, not necessarily individual rights or civil liberties. Echoing a call to arms made during other rebellions of the Atlantic Revolution, Ducharme interprets virtue as having three meanings:

> First, a virtuous citizen was a citizen who was independent socially and economically: this independence was the best guarantee that he could not be corrupted and that he would be independent politically.
> Secondly, to be virtuous implied an ethic of simplicity and frugality.
> Thirdly, virtue meant the willingness of a citizen to defend the common good instead of his own personal interests; in this sense, virtue meant patriotism. (2007: 426)

In sum, it is suggested that Canadian rebels envisioned a virtuous society. Departing from classical liberals, they were not demanding more civil freedom or even more autonomy from the state. To reverse the diagram of control, the Patriotes sought to "control the state" (Ducharme, 2007: 426; see also Greer, 1995, 1993). Moving from issues contained in "political Catholicism" to more nuanced "contrasts in Catholicism," we detect tension not between religious groups but within an otherwise shared institutional faith.

CONTRASTS IN CATHOLICISM

The last dictatorship in Argentina was established along contrasting visions of Catholicism. Polarizing those binary opposites, the authoritarian military leaders directed violence against progressive religious workers for their "dangerous" views of theology. Admiral Ruben Chamorro announced: "They will not confuse us either with their titles or their ecclesiastical robes, nor with their cunning and speculative behavior. An infinite minority cannot be allowed to continue upsetting the minds of our youths, teaching them foreign ideas and converting them into social critics, with an interpretation cunningly distorted of what Christian doctrine is. All this is subversive" (Andersen, 1993: 184). The transformation of ESMA from a rather mundane naval academy to a profane place of violence is described by Julio Cesar Urien, who was expelled by the Marines in 1974 for opposing the repressive model. In 2010, he testified in the ESMA Trial Case 1270 (May 8). "At the Naval School an excerpt of the movie *The Battle of Algiers* is played. It shows how the French colonial army throws the National Liberation Front from Algeria into disarray in the cities by a sequence of abduction, torture, and missing." The Argentine junta replicated the French "dirty war" in Algeria, instituting similar tactics while relying on the complicity of the Argentine Catholic Church. Urien's 2010 testimony confirmed that the military bishop was present during the viewing of the film *The Battle of Algiers* to offer moral support, thus inverting notions of purity and danger (see Robin, 2003).

In pursuit of ideological support to legitimize its power, the junta turned to the hierarchy of Argentine church for spiritual guidance. Admiral Emilio Massera and General Jorge Videla were personally close to Archbishop Adolfo Tortolo, chief vicar of the armed forces, who offered his blessings for the coup and praised the junta for its "clean and efficient action" (Andersen, 1993: 184). Similarly, Monsignor Victorio Bonamin, another military vicar, recognized a primordial struggle between the sacred and the profane, declaring that "the army is purifying the dirtiness in our country" (Andersen, 1993: 184: see Lernoux, 1985). Clerical support for state violence was not confined to rhetoric. Among the findings of the 2017 ESMA trial is clear evidence that Church officials participated in the hiding of detainees from international human rights inspectors. A photograph at ESMA shows the island of "El Silencio" in the Argentine Delta. The caption states that the island had belonged to the Catholic Church, which sold it to the navy to serve as a clandestine detention and torture center; moreover, detainees were relocated to the island from ESMA in 1979 to conceal them from legal monitors.

Exhibits at ESMA go to great lengths to trace the indoctrination of the Argentine armed forces. Since the 1930s, a poster explains, a "authoritarian, Catholic and nationalist" right-wing perspective had guided military training in tandem with "Nazi and Fascist" ideologies fueled by "anti-Semitism and anti-Communism." The military regarded itself as the "moral reservoir" of society that would protect the nation from its enemies; by the 1950s the Cold War had institutionalized that worldview. The influence of France and the United States accelerated those political developments. As France stretched out its colonial wars in Algeria and Indochina, Argentine military leaders shared a quest to eradicate communism and defend a "free and Christian world." They also believed that the "enemy" was not in a distant land; rather, even more ominously, it festered as a "subversive" force within Argentina itself. Students, intellectuals, and trade unionists were all under suspicion, for they embraced "dangerous" interpretations of political power. To combat all of this, military expertise were recruited from abroad. French generals arrived in Argentina to teach cadets the tactics of nonconventional war, including "clandestine murders, infiltration, plundering, psychological actions and dirty press campaigns." On display at ESMA is the 1960 France–Argentina Agreement that documents the mission to train the Argentine army and "provide technical assistance" for the nonconventional doctrine. Providing that apparatus a veneer of legitimacy, local ecclesiastical—and secular—authorities opened a branch of the French organization called the Catholic City (see Ranalletti, 2010; Robben, 2005; Verbitsky, 2006).

As part of a wider campaign to enlighten Argentines and visitors to Buenos Aires about the Church's complicity in human rights abuses, an art installation at the Parque de la Memoria y Monumento a las Victimas del Terrorismo de Estado takes aim at "Iglesia Complice." The lengthy commentary on Church complicity insists that while many priests and nuns were committed to social justice, the Church leadership sided with the junta, which claimed to be carrying out detentions and genocide in the "del nombre de Dios" (the name of God). A key method of extermination was the death flights. As noted in chapter 4, detainees at ESMA would be injected with a sedative, transported to the nearby airport, and loaded onto military aircraft. Once airborne, victims were pushed to their deaths into the sea. It is known that Major Luis María Mendia sought approval from the ecclesiastical authorities to authorize the death flights as a Christian and humanitarian practice (see Andersen, 1993; Morello, 2019). Journalist Jacobo Timerman (1998), who himself was abducted but who survived, reported that Admiral Emilio Massera had told him that the use of firing squads was unacceptable because the pope would oppose such forms of violence.

As they returned from the death flights, some pilots were plainly traumatized; as a form of intervention, chaplains consoled them with biblical parables. In doing so, the priests reaffirmed that the military was justified in using violence to eradicate the threat of the profane, for in doing so it was defending the eternal good (see Katz, 1988). At ESMA, human rights organizers recognize the importance of sitedness—the power of place—for promoting remembrance. They have planted a sign where the original chapel, Capilla Stella Maris, once stood. It informs visitors that in its previous incarnation the building housed the chaplains who participated in the genocidal dictatorship and its state terror by comforting the marines for their criminal actions. In 2007, naval authorities demolished the chapel before human rights organizers could recover the site, thus ridding the compound of its profane past. Physical and cultural transformation would give the site a new place identity. There, a new building has been constructed for ecumenical prayer, bringing the site back to its original sacred purpose. It is named after Patrick Rice, an Irish priest who relocated to Buenos Aries to assist the poor and the families of the disappeared. Due to his missionary work, which supposedly was driven by "dangerous ideas," Rice was kidnapped by the military junta in 1976, then detained and tortured at ESMA. The Irish government and other religious groups lobbied successfully for his release, and he was deported. Rice returned to Buenos Aires 1984. Having since left the priesthood, he married Fatima Cabrera, who had also been detained and tortured by the military. Together they continued their human rights advocacy until his fatal heart attack in 2010 (*Irish Times*, 2010) In 2012, the President of Ireland, Michael Daniel Higgins, visited "Espacio Patrick Rice" and, embracing themes of heroic ascent, dedicated it to Rice and others who had fought for "Memoria, Verdad y Justicia."

Other exhibits at ESMA promote memory and human rights while condemning the last dictatorship. Centro Cultural Memoria Haroldo Conti is named after an Argentine intellectual and author who was disappeared by the military junta on May 5, 1976. To commemorate Conti, that date is known as the "Day of the Buenos Aires Province Writer"; it celebrates the courage to circulate writings that portrayed the junta as unjust. The center sponsors an array of cultural activities. A large banner titled "Obispo Angelelli" introduces visitors to the career of Bishop Enrique Angelelli. Nearby, a montage of photographs commemorate the assassination "of a Bishop who wanted a free and fraternal world." News clips recount that in 1976 Angelelli was murdered by the junta, which then concocted the story that he had died in a car accident. His death remains deeply divisive within the Argentine Catholic Church; even so, well-publicized events have been dedicated to Angelelli. In 1986, US Senator Edward Kennedy traveled to Argentina to memorialize Angelelli as well as the tens of thousands of people who had been disappeared. His pilgrimage restored the sacred while paving the way for a transition to democracy (Andersen, 1993).

In 2006, Argentine president Nestor Kirchner called for a national day of mourning for the religious workers who were victims of state terrorism. In 2014, after decades of prosecution, the former commander of the Third Army Corps, Luciano Benjamin Menéndez, and Luis Estrella, at the time head of the air force base and torture center at El Chamical, were sentenced to life in prison for the murder of Angelelli (Andersen, 1993). The following year, Pope Francis, who had served as the Archbishop of Buenos Aires, joined others in supporting the canonization of Angelelli. Despite those pronouncements, many among Argentina's church hierarchy accepted the military's version of Angelelli's death. Among them was Cardinal Juan Carlos Aramburu, who consistently denied any complicity with the junta. Moreover, Aramburu brazenly dismissed revelations of the forced disappearances, common graves with unidentified bodies, and other human rights abuses. In his 2004 obituary, he is remembered for turning a blind eye to Argentina's last dictatorship (Vidal, 2004). At ESMA, an exhibition hall sponsored by the Families of the Disappeared and Political Detainees is signed "Edificio: 30,000 Companeros Presentes." There, an extensive collection of political posters rekindles another memory of Cardinal Aramburu, who is condemned as a "Minister of Genocide."

Also at ESMA, matters of detention, torture, and extermination are diffused through accounts of state violence against religious workers. Survivors testified that the lack of hygiene compounded the dehumanization. Rare opportunities to shower were met with caution, since detainees risked being beaten, humiliated, and abused. Yet the bathroom was also a privileged space where detainees could have a moment of human contact. Sometimes they were able to speak to one another, or at least look silently at one another. During the trials of former military officers, many of the disappeared were identified by survivors. Ana Maria Marti told the court: "There was a woman seriously beaten, with a shocking look, in grey shirt and white blouse or similar color, [who] whispered . . . 'what's your name?' I said my name and asked 'and you, what's your name? and she replied 'I'm Alice Domon.' I knew Alice asked a lot of people what their names were, and I knew she thought she was going to be freed and wanted to know the names to declare that we were there" (2010).

The memory of Alice Domon and her colleague Leonie Duquet, two French nuns who relocated to Argentina to conduct missionary work and support families in search of their missing relatives, is encountered in several locations within the memorial space. In an area designated as "the fishbowl," a display describes the media operations at ESMA. The military established an elaborate propaganda apparatus to misinform the public about abductions and disappearances: mainstream media outlets contributed directly or indirectly. In "the fishbowl," a team of abducted writers were forced to prepare press statements for the junta. Shown is a photograph of Domon and Duquet that was taken in the basement of the Casino on December 14, 1977. Days later, the image was sent to the French press along with a fabricated story that the nuns were involved with the Montoneros, left-wing guerrillas. In fact, they had been kidnapped by military operatives and detained at ESMA, where they were tortured and then placed on the death flights. The junta mocked the extermination of Domon and Duquet, referring to them as "the Flying Nuns" (after a popular television program). The tour guide at ESMA adds a curious twist to the kidnapping of Domon and Duquet. Directing attention to the propaganda piece containing the photographs of Domon and Duquet, the guide points to the banner of the Montoneros. Argentines familiar with the Montoneros would detect a mistake in the military's message: the insignia appears as a circle rather than as an oval. Apparently at the demand of the military propaganda

FIGURE 13. "The French Nuns." Upon their detention at ESMA, Alice Domon and Leonie Duquet were photographed. Their images along with a concocted story about their involvement in a paramilitary group, Montoneros, was released to the press. © retrowelch 2022.

machine, mainstream news outlets did not refute the contrived story. Photographs of the French nuns serve to "person" the place of memory at ESMA (see figure 13).

In the San Cristobal neighborhood of Buenos Aires, the story of state violence against religious workers resonates at the Iglesia Santa Cruz. In the late 1880s, Santa Cruz was a social and religious community of Irish immigrants ("Los Irish Porteños"), and during the turbulent 1970s the parish became known for its human rights activism. The solemn courtyard offers visitors an opportunity to deepen their understanding of local heritage. A large banner, "Detenidos—desaparecidos de la Iglesia Santa Cruz," displays the photographs of 12 activists who were abducted, detained, and disappeared between December 8 and 10, 1977. Four storyboards focus on the sequence of those events. Text explains that the military coup, in 1976, used violence and terror to establish a neoliberal Argentine economy designed to concentrate wealth in the hands of the few. Wide-scale detention was eventually met by opposition, especially by the mothers and families of the vanished, who demanded to know the whereabouts of their relatives. On December 10, 1977, to commemorate the Universal Declaration of Human Rights, they released a statement titled "For a Christmas in peace. We only ask for the truth."

Alfredo Astiz (the "Blonde Angel of Death") infiltrated the group at Iglesia Santa Cruz by pretending to be a brother of one of the disappeared. In a brazenly profane attack on a sacred place, Astiz and a military task group from ESMA raided the church on December 8 and carried out kidnappings there and elsewhere until December 10. The detainees, who became known as the "Santa Cruz 12," included Alice Domon and Leonie Duquet, founders of the Madres de Plaza de Mayo (Esther Ballestrino, Mary Ponce, and Azucena Villaflor), and several other activists. All of them were all transported to ESMA and later sent on death flights. The bodies of Ballestrino, Ponce, Villaflor, and Duquet (as well as activist Angela Auad) washed ashore, and in 2005 they were positively identified by a forensic team. Their remains are interred in the courtyard at Santa Cruz. The body of Domon has yet to be recovered (Goñi, 2017). In 1990, Astiz was condemned in absentia by a Paris court for the murder of the Domon and Duquet. In Buenos Aires in 2011 and 2017, he was convicted of crimes against humanity. During his sentencing in 2011, Astiz remained defiant, laughing in the face of Judge Daniel Obligado. With nationalist fervor, he pinned a ribbon with the blue and white colors of the Argentine flag to his coat lapel. In his closing words, he accused the court of being "accomplices of foreign colonialism" by finding him guilty of murder (Goñi, 2011; see also D. Taylor, 1997).

As another reminder of the extent of clerical involvement in state violence, Father Christian Federico von Wernich, a former chaplain of the Buenos Aires Province Police, was convicted in 2007 of complicity in seven murders, 42 kidnappings, and 32 instances of torture. He was sentenced to life imprisonment. During the trial, Reverend Rubén Capitanio was called as a witness. Capitanio "condemned the Roman Catholic Church's 'complicity' in atrocities during the Dirty

War,"' saying: "There are some that think that this trial is an attack on the church, and I want to say that this is a service to the church. This is helping us search for the truth" (Barrionuevo, 2007). That same year, the City of Buenos Aires declared Iglesia Santa Cruz a historical site in memory of the "Mothers, Families, and Militants who fought for Human Rights."

Presidential politics continue to inflame the controversies over the last dictatorship, a reminder of the enduring forces of the justice vis-à-vis injustice. Past Argentine president Cristina Fernandez de Kirchner, a champion of human rights, consistently cites 30,000 as the widely accepted number of those who were disappeared. Past president Mauricio Macri, however, often suggests that the number is closer to 9,000 (based on a much earlier, and inconclusive, count). His use of the term "dirty war," bristles human rights advocates, for whom it chimes with "denialist thinking, which holds there was no genocide—only an internal battle between the dictatorship and terrorists" (Goñi, 2016). Argentine historian Mario Ranalletti, who studies dictatorship denial groups, adds: "They consider military repression was a good and morally unquestionable act. To them the cold war was a religious war" (Goñi, 2016; Ranalletti, 2010). Macri, whose neoliberal economic policies stifled the poor (and the middle class), also took a swipe at Pope Francis by donating a sum with 666 embedded in a 16,666,000-peso contribution to an educational foundation (Goñi, 2016). Given the offensive reference to Satan, the pope returned the gift, perhaps another sign of lingering tensions in Catholicism over notions of danger and purity (Douglas, 1966).

CATHOLIC ACTION

In Santiago, Plaza Padre Juan Alsina at Puente Bulnes memorializes victims of the Pinochet dictatorship, most notably the priest who was executed at the site on September 19, 1973. Father Alsina relocated from Spain to Chile to serve its impoverished people, an outward sign of his commitment to the eternal good. At the height of the coup, the military took him into custody, then transported him to the bridge, Puente Bulnes, where Nelson Bañado, an 18-year old soldier, riddled his body with a submachine gun bullets. Bañado later confessed and provided unnerving details of the assassination. In a scenario reenacted on murals at the memorial, Alsina refused a blindfold. Instead, he instructed Bañado to shoot him in the front because "I want to see you to give you forgiveness." Bañado stood trial and was convicted. Overcome by guilt, he later committed suicide, compounding tragedy with tragedy as cyclical violence (*Nation* [Chile], 2007). The memorial at the Plaza is "personed" not only by renderings of Alsina but also with photographs of victims of state violence (see figure 14).

In Chile, as in Argentina, violence against religious workers occurred, albeit not on the same scale. Moreover, in sharp contrast to the Argentine Catholic Church, the Chilean religious hierarchy took action against the dictatorship.

FIGURE 14. "Plaza Padre Juan Alsina at Puente Bulnes." In Santiago, Plaza Padre Juan Alsina at Puente Bulnes preserves the memory of the victims of state violence with murals that include the famous words of Father Alsina. © retrowelch 2022.

The internationally recognized Vicaría de la Solidaridad (Vicariate of Solidarity) resonates in Chileans' collective memory, due in large part to its commitment to human rights, which would endure throughout the Pinochet years. The organization was founded in 1973 as the Committee of Cooperation for Peace in Chile (Comité Pro Paz), but Pinochet demanded that the group cease its legal work on the fabricated claim that it was being used by subversives. Cardinal Raúl Silva Henríquez seemed to comply but in fact soon reorganized the agency in 1976 under the Chilean Catholic Church and Archdiocese of Santiago. In this way, activists thwarted the military's efforts to disrupt their social and legal services on behalf of the disappeared. As an extra measure of insulation from the dictatorship, secret passages connected the vicariate to the adjacent cathedral. At Museo de la Memoria y Los Derechos Humanos in Santiago, an extensive exhibit chronicles the vicariate's activism. It features a larger-than-life photograph of Cardinal Silva, who emerged as "a constant thorn in the Government's side" (Kinzer, 1983). Photographs also show the vicariate's crowded law office, where long queues of families are filing *habeas corpus* petitions for political prisoners.

Among the more visible symbols of the vicariate are the *arpilleras* (meaning items of burlap or sackcloth). Those patchworks of brightly colored folk art provided emotional outlets for women who were coping with their anguish over missing relatives. The vicariate sponsored workshops so that participants could work together, engage in political discussions, and build solidarity. *Arpilleras* also generated income for families while raising consciousness for the vicariate's human rights campaign (Adams, 2000). The Museo de la Memoria y Los Derechos Humanos displays and catalogues an array of *arpilleras* as cultural artifacts of civilian life under military rule. Unsurprisingly, much of the needlework is decidedly political, including scenes depicting protests, candlelight vigils for executed political prisoners, and demonstrators being watercannoned by a police. *Arpilleras* also disseminate memories of the victims of the dictatorship. As a gift, Eliana Horta, a Chilean-born nurse, gave one titled "Andres de La Victoria" to a former priest and a former nun. It "honors the memory of a missionary who, while serving the poor in the shantytown of La Victoria, was shot and killed by the military. With stark symbolism, the image shows two holes where the bullets entered the house, and a cross and heart show where the priest was standing. Outside, a kneeling woman lights a candle, while two men stand with their arms raised, a sign of protest in Chile" (Robinson, 1989).

The vicariate promoted its role in defending the community's cherished values by publishing a biweekly magazine aptly titled *Solidaridad*. Articles fused evangelical sermons with statistics on unemployment and malnutrition. Throughout its mission, the vicariate found inspiration in the gospels aimed at protecting the world, most significantly the parable of the Good Samaritan in St. Luke. Still, its nondenominational work served people of all faiths, and it did not expect anything in return, becoming a "frontier" ministry that supported grassroots social justice. Despite years of harassment by the dictatorship, the agency amassed records of more than 19,000 cases of human rights violations. The collection is regarded as "the best administered and most complete private human rights archive in the country" (Collins, 2011: 256). Naomi Roht-Arriaza, in *The Pinochet Effect*, concurs: "Those files, carefully guarded over the years at the Vicaria de la Solidaridad, would prove a treasure trove of information when political conditions changed" (2005: 70). After Chile returned to democratic rule, attorneys relied on those documents when drafting lawsuits; so did truth commissions investigating the assassinations of Pinochet's opponents (i.e., Schneider, Prats, Leighton, Letelier) (Dinges and Landau, 1980: 215–17).

PERFORMING CATHOLICISM

In this final section, attention is turned to Ireland, where Catholicism is performed as a ritual to memorialize political prisoners. The collection of paramilitary and religious artifacts at Roddy McCorley's Club in West Belfast contributes to its post-conflict heritage. That same collection opens a window onto how Catholicism is presented as a tribute to the 1981 hunger strike in the H Blocks of the Maze prison.

A visual montage contains still shots and published reviews from the "multi award winning film HUNGER," in which Bobby Sands (played by Michael Fassbender) is given hagiographic treatment. "Positively riveting, an artistic masterpiece . . . a harrowing, poetic film"—*Time Out New York.* "Both horrifying and, strange to say, beautiful"—A. O. Scott, *New York Times* (see McQueen, 2008). In displaying those movie reviews, curators are tapping into their use-value *and* their signifying-value, adding greater weight to the cultural importance of *Hunger.* With even more authenticity, a framed copy of *The Irish News* captures the historical moment with this bold headline: "Sands Dies on Day 66 of Fast in the Maze." Those words seem to stress a certain degree of Catholic reverence for Sands's death, in that a fast is a religious act of faith. Toward that end, stills from the film show the half-naked—and starved—bodies of Sands and fellow hunger strikers as they protest their conditions of confinement.

Two other images from that film demonstrate the distinct manner in which Catholicism is performed between the political prisoners and the clergy. First is a scene depicting a Sunday Mass, in which the priest goes through the motions of the sacraments while the hunger strikers mill about the chapel talking incessantly in an effort to get the latest news on the Troubles. A second photograph shows a defining moment involving Sands and the chaplain as they debate the political and religious merits of the hunger strike. The sharp and witty conversation soon escalates into an intense standoff, with Sands arguing that the political prisoners feel abandoned by the local church. These tensions within a nuanced Catholicism, however, are offset by a performance that ultimately advances themes of ascent, thus forging a unified front for Irish Catholics in Northern Ireland and elsewhere. Indeed, as a performance of power, the hunger strike became a tactic that showcased to the world that prisoners could resist state-sponsored brutality. By outmaneuvering their captors, Republican prisoners culturally reconstructed the Maze as "a theatre of political allegory" (Feldman, 1991: 148; see also Campbell, McKeown, and O'Hagan, 1998; Sands, 1998).

The film *Hunger* and related images displayed at McCorley's Club offer visitors a snapshot of the complex series of events that led up to the hunger strikes. Whereas those matters will also be discussed in later chapters, at this stage, a socio-historical approach offers a layered point of view. David Beresford's *Ten Dead Men: The Story of the 1981 Irish Hunger Strike* is a book with not just one story, but many. That book's structure is simple: ten chapters numbered without titles. Ten stories about each of the hunger strikers who died. Since each main character is surrounded by other characters, their stories diverge into overlapping scenarios that move full circle until the performance is complete. Sands, the first to die, emerged as an iconic figure that would foreshadow nine more deaths. The story of Sands is that of a prisoner who immersed himself in the eloquence of poetry, which allowed him to perform his commitment to the struggle with carefully chosen words. By comparison, the others were rather ordinary young men working mundane jobs—

a draper's assistant, a mechanic, an upholsterer, and a milkman. Still, they were all bound together to drive the British occupiers out of Northern Ireland.

In the preface to his book, Beresford is credited for being peculiarly suited for the task of sorting out the many strands of stories recorded as "comms"—the secret communications from prisoners written on tiny pieces of tissue paper and smuggled out of the Maze. While assembling the various stories, Beresford detected an innate sense of colonial trouble since he himself was an outsider. He was neither English nor Irish; rather, he was born in South Africa and raised in Rhodesia, another part of a defunct British Empire where discrimination was administered through brutality. Beresford understood how seemingly minor details held major meaning. Early on, IRA inmates were considered prisoners of war, which among other things allowed them wear their own clothes. In 1976, the prison policy then changed, requiring them to wear the uniforms of common criminals. This met fierce resistance. "The symbolism was enormous: the H-Blocks rang with songs against Britain's attempt to 'brand Ireland's fight 800 years of crime'. . . . The wraiths of these ten men bear immutable witness" (Maas, 1987: xi-xii).

Among their weapons was the hunger strike, so polarizing it would divide not only supporters and politicians but also the Catholic clergy. In *Last Weapons: Hunger Strikes and Fasts in the British Empire, 1890–1948*, Kevin Grant reminds us that "the hunger strike and the fast are reflective experiences, performances of death in which we see ourselves" (2019: 1; see also Bargu, 2014). In Ireland, by ancient Celtic custom, hunger strikes have been regarded as legitimate forms of public protest. A debtor, for example, who complains that his debt is unjust can invoke the *troscead*, the practice of fasting, upon another. The debtor sits outside the home of his debt holder and refuses to eat until the debt is forgiven. The fast shames the debt holder, and furthermore, the debt can be enforced by the Brehon Law, according to which the debtor can be reimbursed twice the amount owed (Grant, 2019). That legend had been internalized by Irish prisoners, who performed hunger strikes as a sacred ritual. Republican Ernie O'Malley, imprisoned in 1923, wrote to a friend saying that his prison experience and hunger strike intensified his Catholic faith (English, 1998). The socio-religious foundations of hunger strikes are evident not only in individual acts but also in collective performances. "In Ireland, female and male Republicans represented the hunger strike in explicit terms of Catholicism, binding themselves in a shared sacrifice" (Grant, 2019: 19).

Among the witnesses of the 1981 Irish hunger strike were members of the Catholic clergy, most notably Cardinal Tomás Ó Fiaich, officially known as the Prince of the Roman Catholic Church, 112th successor to St. Patrick in the See of Armagh, Primate of All Ireland. His home village, Crossmaglen, has significant purchase in the Irish political directory, for it was known as a place that had long been troublesome for the authorities. In earlier times, the village had hosted rowdy festivals that attracted "undesirables." In 1922, the partition made the village an even thornier problem for the British state, for it was now one of the southernmost towns of the

North. The South Armagh countryside with its winding lanes, ghostly terrain, and proximity to the border provided safe haven for the IRA, bolstering its reputation as bandit country. The partition divided not only Ireland but also the Armagh diocese, geographically as well as politically. Ó Fiaich, a Republican, stressed harmony and professed the motto "Brothers in Unity," taken from the 113th Psalm. Nonetheless, due to a publicized comment in which he seemed to advocate a British withdrawal from Ireland, Ó Fiaich was maligned as the "Chaplain-in-Chief of the IRA"—at least from the perspective of Protestant Loyalists (Beresford, 1987).

In 1978, Ó Fiaich visited the Long Kesh/Maze prison for the first time. Republican prisoners received him with respect, a signal of their high morale as a paramilitary. By the time Ó Fiaich returned for a second visit, resistance to the brutality and inhumane conditions was well under way. Most notable was the "dirty protest" (also known as the "no-wash protest"). The controversy stemmed from the rule that prisoners were required to wear a uniform, as previously noted. The Republican prisoners refused because the uniform would signify that they were common criminals without political status. Instead, they covered themselves with blankets and towels. When the prisoners visited the toilets located down the corridor, the guards violently strip-searched them:

> It was all just to fuck guys about trying to break them. We says no problem, keep fucking us about and we'll not use the toilets; so we stopped using the toilets, just used a slop bowl in the cell . . . [then] we'll just put the shit in the corner . . . The screws would have [to] come in and all the shit and urine [w]as in the corner. They lifted your blankets fucked it into the corner and walked the shite all over your blanket . . . So the only effective way of combating that was to spread it on the walls. (Feldman, 1991: 167–68)

In cultural terms, the "dirty protest" was driven by a duality of pollution and courage. On behalf of the prisoners, Ó Fiaich drafted a lengthy statement that criticized the penal regime as unjust. Political status was central to the complaint: the Cardinal noted that the prisoners seemed to prefer "death rather than submit to being classified as criminals." Ó Fiaich continued: "Anyone with the least knowledge of Irish history knows how deeply rooted this attitude is in our country's past" (Beresford, 1987: 140). The Northern Ireland Office stressed that those confined at the Maze were not political prisoners but rather criminals who were totally responsible for the situation in which they had found themselves.

High-ranking church leaders—Presbyterians and Anglicans as well as Catholics—publicly denounced Ó Fiaich. Undeterred, Ó Fiaich appealed to the Vatican, but on the day he delivered his report, Pope Paul VI died. Soon after, his successor, Pope John Paul I, also died—33 days after assuming office. By at least one account, John Paul I was reading Ó Fiaich's report the night before he died. Those events were compounded by political upheaval: the Labour government in Britain collapsed in 1979, ushering in a more strident Thatcher administration. The following year, Ó Fiaich went back to the Maze, where he met Loyalist leader Gusty Spence. The encounter did not go unnoticed. It symbolized a meeting between "the folk hero of a gang of sectarian killers and the man who represented the 'Red Whore of Rome.'" Apparently, the two refused to clash, and Spence, himself fluent in Irish, bade the Cardinal "caed mile failte" (a thousand welcomes) (Beresford, 1987: 142).

Amid the commotion, the hunger strike would play out, and so too would deeper religious questions about death. For the Catholic Church, the hunger strike strained relations within its ranks as well as with the British state as Ó Fiaich and other priests tried to persuade the Thatcher cabinet to compromise. Such a negotiation would avert a theological predicament regarding whether the hunger strike constituted suicide and an act of violence, a distressing issue within Catholic morality. In some parishes, pastoral letters were read during mass repudiating the hunger strike. Along the way, Thatcher maintained her criminalization policy, ignoring advice on how she could avert a looming political crisis. When Sands died, Thatcher received a scathing telegram from the Four Horsemen, powerful leaders of the Irish-American community: Senator Ted Kennedy, Senator Daniel Moynihan, Speaker of the House Tip O'Neill, and New York Governor Hugh Carey. For all his performance as an influential Catholic, Ó Fiaich could not change the course of history and the fate of ten dead men. The notion that a hunger strike constitutes a performance of death still resonates. From at least one point of view, the Irish prisoners had engaged in their own form of *troscead* by fasting upon another. That ancient Celtic ritual transcends political and theological entanglements by embracing a commitment to a higher order of justice. Due to the complex meaning of sacrifice—and martyrdom—greater cultural observations are set to unfold in forthcoming chapters.

CONCLUSION

As noted early in this chapter, the 1792 September Massacres in Parisian prisons consumed more than 1,000 victims, among them priests and seminarians. Scholars continue to reflect on the various causes of that "justified violence," such as the roles of rumor, fear, and anxiety, but one thing is clear: in its aftermath "a great many people came to look on the Massacres in a new light and express their shock and horror over what happened" (Tacket, 2011: 64; see also Caron, 1935; Bluche, 1986; Schama, 1990). Similarly, when dictatorships in the southern cone dissolved under the force of democratic movements, state terror was staunchly condemned. In *The Catholic Church and Argentina's Dirty War*, Jesuit sociologist Gustavo Morello examines the nuances of the faith. With the Second Vatican Council, Catholicism entered into a dialogue with modernity. Progressive Catholics understood such "religious transformation as a cultural characteristic," while more conservative members of the Church "perceived the changes as a corruption of the divine" (Morello, 2019: 181). Morello writes that those internal conflicts within Catholicism represented different forms of relating to the sacred and would ultimately determine the ways in which political life was conceived.

The Argentine junta and its Catholic supporters "believed that the only way to preserve faith was to conserve power" (Morello, 2019: 181). As the nation transitioned to democracy, that power shifted dramatically, giving rise to the memory of political prisoners, religious workers, and other victims of state repression. By engaging in modern institutions, progressive Catholics practiced their political life through enduring human rights campaigns evident in legislation and the prosecutions of perpetrators. Alongside those important developments were cultural rituals that speak to the nuances of Catholicism. In Santiago, for instance, two former detention and torture centers, Villa Grimaldi and the National Stadium, underwent an elaborate ceremony in which a priest—an agent of the deity—performed a spiritual cleansing. Those sites were thus purified of past sins and repurposed as a memorials that would speak to the prevailing sentiment "Nunca Más" (Never Again). Those sacred rituals are just one form of cultural expression that attempts to eradicate residue of the profane while embracing the sacred. To be sure, the authoritarian use of religion is just one example of the diagrams of control. In the next chapter, we discuss architecture as another form of domination aimed at political prisoners and the population at large.

7

Architectural Designs

The Bastille emerged as a potent expression of the French monarchy, which chose to deliver "a show of force, in order not to have to use force" (Godechot, 1970: 86). Like other prisons in the Paris network of confinement, such as Saint-Lazare and the Conciergerie, the Bastille was recognized for its unique architecture, which was bolstered by a bad reputation. It had been built in medieval times not as a prison but as a citadel. In fact, the word *bastille*, or *bastide*, means fortress (BnF, 2010). The Bastille's transformation from castle to prison was ridiculed during the reign of Louis XIV by poet Claude Le Petit, who was executed in 1662 for writing licentious verse. With notable disdain for the Bastille, he wrote: "What's the use of this old wall in a ditch? . . . this unmanned castle, which is no use as a fortress, but tries to be a prison!" (Godechot, 1970: 87). Despite that barb, the Bastille stood the test of time, due in large part to its imposing structure. Blueprints of the Bastille accurately specify its elaborate design, floorplan, and architectural ambition (BnF, 2010: 21). The rectangular layout was surrounded by massive walls 100 feet high. Eight round towers were suitably named, including the Liberté, and select prisoners were free to walk about the inner courtyards, which were decorated with ornate Doric doorways. The entrance to the Bastille was guarded by two drawbridges over a moat filled with water from the Seine. Perhaps as an outward sign of the Bastille's slow decay, the moat was dry by time it was stormed in 1789.

In the popular imagination, the Bastille endures as a subject of artist Hubert Robert, whose painting of its demolition remains a defining image of the prison. Pictures, posters, and postcards continue to depict the Bastille as a magnificent projection of royal power. But it is important to separate fact from fiction: Robert took artistic license to make the Bastille appear even taller than it actually was—thus giving the structure a "Babylonian eminence" (Schama, 1990: 389; see figure 15).

Robert's rendering of the Bastille was greatly influenced by his visual mentor Giovanni Battista Piranesi, whose *carceri d'invenzione* (imaginary prisons) entered the subconscious madness of the prison labyrinth. "Certainly, the elevation of the

FIGURE 15. "Hubert's painting of the demolition of the Bastille." A popular postcard in Paris celebrates the painting of the Bastille by Robert Hubert. © retrowelch 2022.

Bastille in his painting, with tiny figures scampering jubilantly over its battlements, suggests an immense Gothic castle of darkness and secrecy, a place into which men would disappear without warning and never again see the light of day until their bones were disinterred by revolutionary excavators" (Schama, 1990: 389). Robert's Romantic aesthetics contributed to the seemingly virtuous Revolution, yet he would be arrested and imprisoned in 1793, and narrowly missed the guillotine due to an error in the processing of the condemned (see Bailey, 2016; Catala, 2013).

This chapter explores the architectural designs of institutions holding political prisoners by attending to the logic of their original plans as well as to their afterlives. As we survey numerous former sites of political imprisonment—and later memorialization—evidence of the Bastille Effect allows us to appreciate how place is remembered, reinvented, and repurposed for public experience. Those physical and cultural transformations speak to the manner in which the previous purposes of prisons and detention centers are eclipsed by symbols of defunct political regimes, emerging as metaphors for democratic reform. Toward that end, two architectural motifs are explored. Discussion begins with a critical examination of *panopticism*, especially the visual power that the surveillance produces over its subjects. Next, we offer a close look at the phenomenon of *illusion* whereby certain sites were deliberately modified to distract and deceive inspectors in search of evidence of human rights violations. As diagrams of control, those expressions of architecture were aimed not only at those confined but also at the wider population kept under the watchful eye of the authorities.

POWER OF PANOPTICS

The work of Jeremy Bentham (1748–1832) is an important element of any sophisticated commentary on crime, punishment, and social control (Bentham, [1787]1995). In the 1770s, Bentham proposed a solution to the English penal crisis, which had been compounded by horrific prison conditions. With futuristic flair, he unveiled plans for the *ultimate penitentiary*, to be known as the panopticon, from the Greek, meaning "everything" and "a place of sight" (Welch, 2011a, 2011b). Bentham's inspiration for the design is traced primarily to reformer John Howard, who had inspected many prisons in the British Isles, including Ireland. Also known as the "inspection house," the panopticon departed from standard designs by placing an indoor guard tower in the center of the floor plan and surrounding it with several circular tiers of cells. The layout maximized surveillance, providing guards inside the tower with a complete and continuous view of the prisoners confined to their individual cells. Adding a theatrical element, each cell was fitted with an exterior window, which allowed natural light to illuminate the space from behind. Perhaps the most insightful critique of the panopticon was issued by Foucault, who in *Discipline and Punish* examines the subtleties of social control that distinguish the panopticon from other penal institutions. He reveals how the panopticon couples geometry with economics, thereby refining the mechanics of social control. In other words, the circular design of the institution would render the prison population more visible, making the entire institution more efficient since fewer guards would be needed to implement adequate supervision (see Alford, 2000).

Foucault maintains that the key to prisoner control is constant inspection through two forms of power. First, panoptic power is visible, and second, it is unverifiable. "Visible: the inmate will constantly have before his eyes the tall outline of the central tower from which he is spied upon. Unverifiable: the inmate must never know whether he is being looked at any one moment: but he must be sure that he may always be so" (Foucault, 1977: 201; 1996). Due to the omniscient—God-like—presence of the guard tower, prisoners could never be sure when they were being observed. Foucault notes that the target of social control is not so much the convict's body. Instead, it is the prisoner's consciousness, because continuous surveillance establishes a permanent presence in the mind. "Hence, the major effect of the Panopticon: to induce in the inmate a state of conscious and permanent visibility that assures the automatic functioning of power" (Foucault, 1979: 201). It is that dystopian function that prompted author Aldous Huxley to deride the panopticon as a "totalitarian housing project" (Johnston, 1978: 20). Although the plans to construct a panopticon were seriously considered by some Members of Parliament, it never won complete approval in England. Elsewhere, similar circular prisons were built in Holland, Spain, and the Isle of Pines off the coast of Cuba. In America, the design of the panopticon was modified, at the Virginia Penitentiary, the Western Penitentiary (Pittsburgh), and, later, Stateville Correctional Center (Joliet). Panopticism continues to permeate penal architecture in various forms as a means to enhance visibility and control over the prison population (see Jacobs, 1977).

The Kilmainham Gaol stands out for its unique Victorian design, which draws heavily on panopticism and the power it produces. Inside, the use of architectural space reinforces the transmission of heritage as visitors are escorted to the East Wing. Creating a moment of suspense, the tour guide pauses patiently for all members of the group to gather at the entrance. The large door to the East Wing is kept shut as the guide says a few well-chosen words about the power of Victorian prison design. Then suddenly he flings open the door and visitors are immersed in the grandeur of a spectacular atrium. It has been said: "Architecture matters because it lasts, of course. It matters because it is big, and it shapes the landscape of our everyday lives. But beyond that, it also matters because, more than any other cultural form, it is a means of setting the historical record straight" (Sudjic, 2006: 23). The East Wing does not disappoint. With Victorian authority, it delivers a sensation of power and awe. The guide does not interfere with visitors' absorption of the architectural splendor, allowing them to practice space and mill around without any specific itinerary (see McConville, 1995; figure 16).

Spatial effects are further complemented by curatorial statements that tutor tourists about the architectural significance of Kilmainham. A poster titled "The Victorian Prison" establishes a scholarly—and nationalist—tone, first in Irish followed by English:

> The Victorian age was the great age of prison design and construction. At no time before or since have so many new prisons been built. As late as the 1970s, over 40% of the prisons in use in Great Britain and Ireland had been built during Victoria's reign (1837–1901). The Victorians placed great faith in the power of prison to reform offenders, and regarded prison architecture and design as critical to the process.

Like other Victorian prisons, Kilmainham was modeled after Pentonville penitentiary in London. The plan was well ahead of its time, eliminating corridors, installing catwalks, and illuminating the entire vaulted space with a skylight. A placard continues the narration: "This design combined separate confinement with the greatest possible level of inspection by prison staff, in a manner that echoes Bentham's *Panopticon* ('all-seeing eye')."

Because political imprisonment was so tremendously significant to Kilmainham's purpose, it became "the most secure county prison in the Kingdom," according to a poster. Moreover, by recognizing select political prisoners, Kilmainham—in

FIGURE 16. "The Atrium of Kilmainham." At Kilmainham prison in Dublin, visitors are invited to explore the Victorian architecture. © retrowelch 2022.

its afterlife—performs heritage in ways that connect important historical events. Eamon de Valera is among those Irish luminaries featured in the exhibit. Upon his arrest in the 1916 Rising, "de Valera would have been the fifteenth man executed at Kilmainham had he not been saved by his America citizenship." De Valera joined the anti-treaty side of the civil war and was subsequently imprisoned, becoming the last prisoner at Kilmainham in 1924. De Valera was later elected as the Irish *taoiseach* (prime minister) and then as President of Ireland (Visitor's Guide, n.d.; see also O'Dwyer, 2010).

In Belfast, Victorian prison architecture is commemorated at the Crumlin Road Gaol, which held both Loyalist and Republican political prisoners until 1996. As noted earlier, the recent conflict does not dominate the narrative. A single placard simply states: "As the prison population exploded due to the start of The Troubles and also the introduction of internment (arrest without trial) in August, 1971, it was common to find up to four prisoners to a single cell." Attention swiftly turns away from political prisoners and toward the institution—its lack of sanitation (and use of chamber pots) as well as its overcrowding, in that more than 1,400 prisoners were held in a prison designed to hold between 500 and 550. Overall, a leading narrative on the Crum is its status within the Victorian tradition. Dating back to 1841, the institution was designed by esteemed architect Sir Charles Lanyon, who based it on the radial plan of Pentonville prison (London).

Much like at Kilmainham, steel and glass predominate the interior design besides maintaining the thrust of Victorianism as an imperial project (see McConville, 1995). Tour guides at the Crum attempt to follow a script on Victorian architecture, but controversies over the Troubles inevitably surface. Directly across the street on Crumlin Road is a Victorian-style courthouse, also designed by Lanyon. The building has regrettably fallen into decay, but in earlier times, its symbolic presence shaped the history of the Troubles, for it was there that political prisoners—most of them associated with the Provisional IRA—stood trial before being sentenced. Adding a subterranean intrigue, the courthouse and the Crum are connected by a dark tunnel into which visitors are escorted. Halfway through the passageway, the guide stops and points to the ceiling, which was reinforced with extra cement to prevent its collapse in case the IRA detonated a car bomb directly above on Crumlin Road (see *Souvenir Guidebook to Crumlin Road Gaol*, n.d.; Greg, 2013).

Other architectural modifications speak to the significance of the Troubles. While touring the prison yard, the subject of escapes gets ample treatment, since Republican prisoners had earned a reputation for dramatic "breakouts" as far back as the 1920s (see McEvoy, 2001). More recent escapes from the Crum are now part of Republican legend, including the nine "Kangaroos" who scaled the wall in 1971. To reduce the risk of escape, and the subsequent humiliation of prison authorities, the perimeter wall was retrofitted with a protruding metal barrier that deformed the original design. Other politically tinged accounts have shaped the heritage of the Crum, most notably the fate of the Suffragettes. In the run-up to the First World War, women agitating for the right to vote were imprisoned in the A-Wing. The Suffragette movement was marked by bomb threats and hunger strikes, prompting a novel response by prison staff. Instead of force-feeding the suffragettes, they were temporarily released until their health was restored, then rearrested and returned to the Crum. "In this way, the government sought to prevent the Suffragettes gaining martyr status" (*Souvenir Guidebook to Crumlin Road Gaol*, n.d.; Grant, 2019). Against that logic, the Suffragettes are currently honored at the "Crum" by placing a mannequin—dressed in a period costume—behind a large Victorian window pane in the vestibule (see Grant, 2019).

In South Africa, many former penitentiaries have been transformed so as to celebrate political prisoners for their role in dismantling apartheid, the racist apparatus that brutally separated Blacks from Whites until the early 1990s. Chief among those sites is Robben Island off the coast of Cape Town, where Nelson Mandela was imprisoned for 27 years before emerging as the President of South Africa (Mandela, 1994; Welch, 2015). In Johannesburg, tourists are invited to visit the Old Fort, Number Four, and the Women's Jail, where the power of panoptics is visually displayed. The interior provides a classic example of Victorian design in which form and function create a unique blend of semiotics and architecture. As Robin Evans so insightfully recalls in *The Fabrication of Virtue: English Prison Architecture, 1750–1840*, "[prison] architecture, once the emblem of social order, was now one of its fundamental instruments" (1982: back cover; see also Bender, 1987).

The Women's Jail is a departure from the traditional neo-Gothic fortress of the neighboring Old Fort in that it embraces panopticism, which puts more emphasis on its interior than its exterior. As a consequence, internal messages on confinement are more nuanced, fusing the religious with the rational so as to promote prisoner reform. Deferring to Beccaria and other enlightened thinkers, John Howard conceded: "We have too much adopted the gothic mode of correction by rigorous severity, which often hardens the heart; while many foreigners pursue the more rational plan of softening the mind in order to [encourage] its amendment" (Bender, 1987: 22, 261). As they stand at the epicenter of the atrium at the Women's Jail, visitors get a sense of the power contained in the space, which once functioned as a command center for the guards. There, they experience the jail's semio-technology, in particular the concentric geometry that dictates both its design and its purpose. According to Evans, circular architecture can be traced from the temple to the chapel, to the roundhouse theatre, to the model penitentiary. "In the temple, the circle was used for its symbolic panorama of architecture, sculpture and painting to be contemplated by the observer. In the prison, however, the properties of the circle were employed otherwise, establishing the authority of the gaoler by displaying not the architecture and its decoration, but the inmates and their activities" (Evans, 1982: 414; Welch, 2015).

To reiterate, panopticism unites geometry with economics by relying a circular design to reduce the number of guards need to provide adequate supervision. It also projects a sense of morality by imitating Christian beliefs in an all-knowing God so as to promote personal reform. In fact, Bentham ([1787]1995) cited the 139th Psalm in positing that the invisible guard in the central tower performed an executive power analogous to that of an omniscient deity who could see everything at all times. A poster in the Women's Jail quotes Bentham's reasoning: "Rather than confine prisoners to medieval dungeons, he said they should be under constant surveillance by the all seeing eye of prison authorities." Thus panoptics materialized through the radial plan, with corridors connecting to a circular gallery supported by classical columns. Tall, vaulted windows flood the interior space with natural light. Much like the guards who once patrolled the jail, visitors practice surveillance by standing at the epicenter and gazing down each hallway. Its appealing form, however, deceitfully hides its main function. Audrey Brown, Director of Research at the Women's Jail, explains:

> Unlike the men's section, which does not conceal its primary purpose, this space beguiles the eye and misleads the mind. The light-filled atrium and the cells radiating off it conceal the very essence of a jail—punishment and subjugation. The architecture of the Women's Jail might be more subtle than that of a male prison in terms of power and control, but it is just as violent.

A brochure reinforces the mission of the former prison as a place of learning: "Built in 1909, the grace of this Victorian brick building obscures the pain and humiliation suffered by the many women detained within it. The Jail held black and white women in separate sections. The infamous murderess, Daisy de Melker was held here, as were prominent political prisoners Winnie Madikizela-Mandela and Albertina Sisula." With respect to its afterlife animated by signifying-value, curators add that "the building has been transformed into a temporary exhibition that honors the contribution of women in the struggle for freedom in South Africa" (Constitution Hill, Visitor's Brochure; see also Segal, 2006). In that sense, the entire institution serves as a metaphor for a new society in which women are recognized for their political contributions.

In a suburban district of Seoul (South Korea), the Seodaemun Prison History Hall has also shed its profane history; in its current incarnation, it is now a place of memory. As a symbol of oppression and terror, it "preserves and displays Seodaemun Prison signifying the suffering and pain of Koreans during the modern period" (Seodaemun Prison History Hall, English version brochure). As a living memorial, the site honors independence and pro-democracy activists who were jailed, tortured, and martyred (Seodaemun Prison History Hall, 2010). Seodaemun prison was opened in 1908 during the Japanese occupation to imprison members of a growing Korean resistance. A poster contains an image of the City Gate (at Street no. 101 of Hyeonjeo-dong) at the edge of the prison. The caption reads: "Japanese imperialists installed a large-size prison around that area as a tool for ruling the colony." By the 1930s, the prison had been expanded to accommodate a huge influx of Korean political prisoners. Indeed, the "Japanese imperialists" established so many prisons in the main cities on the Korean peninsula that it transformed the country into one enormous prison. A map dotted with prisons sites illustrates the massive scope of the colonial project (Welch, 2015).

With its neo-Gothic façade joined by three watchtowers, the Seodaemun prison conforms to the radial plan (i.e., spoke and hub). Visitors are able to recognize the economy and strength of the circular diagram as they enter the Central Prison Building. A sign describes its architectural form and function: "This 2-story central building was built in 1923 as a way to connect the 10th-11th-12th jails for effective surveillance along with office works and ideological persuasion." Deep inside the institution sits the "Monitoring Location of Warder": an elevated wooden platform fitted with a large desk and chair. An open gate invites visitors to step into the station to practice surveillance and gaze down the long corridor of cells. Compared to the panopticon, the optics of the radial plan are compromised since the supervision of prisons is linear-intermittent rather than circular-continuous; thus, the guard must walk the length of the tier to peer inside each cell (Welch, 2011b). To compensate for that extra task, the cell blocks at Seodaemun are equipped with a "PAE TONG." That simple device allows prisoners to get the attention of the guard by pushing a stick out from their cell, to within view of the guard seated in the monitor booth.

Like other modern prisons, the interior of Seodaemun was constructed with thick walls separating the cells not only for security reasons but also to prevent political prisoners from communicating with one another. Curators reveal how prisoners circumvented the design by staging mannequins on both sides of the cell wall as they sent tapping messages similar to Morse code. Meanwhile, outside in the prison yard, Japanese guards maintained a strict regime to separate Korean political prisoners. Conspicuously present is a circular exercise yard inspired by Benthamite architecture. Known as a "Gyeokbyeokjang," the semicircular brick structure is arranged with pie-chart symmetry containing ten separate slices. An observation platform is situated at the hub, where the guard has a complete and uninterrupted view of each prisoner confined to a wedge stretching 15 meters. There, visitors can position themselves as the inspector to experience the power of panoptics; conversely, they are allowed to enter one of the individual yards to gain the perspective of a prisoner. The exercise facility was designed to maximize monitoring; the individual compartments prevented the prisoners from communicating with one another. The authentic sitedness of the "Gyeokbyeokjang" is complemented by a photograph that verifies its profane past (Welch, 2015).

A tour of the institution is more than just a survey of its architecture. The exhibit celebrates the resistance as a successful pro-democracy movement, thus embracing a unique version of a Bastille Effect. After 36 years of hardship, Korea was liberated in 1945. Later, under Korean rule, the prison was repurposed to hold pro-democracy activists who challenged the despotic regime. "Seodaemun Prison was a symbol of the 80-year journey to freedom. Now, the site has been reborn and Seodaemun Prison History Hall, echo[es] to the world the invaluable importance of freedom and peace" (Seodaemun Prison History Hall, English version brochure, n.d.). Just as Nora (1989) suggests that memory is attached to places,

Seodaemun prison is remembered as "The Place of Independence and Democracy" (Seodaemun Prison History Hall, 2010).

As discussed earlier, the former prison in Montevideo known as Miguelete enjoys an afterlife as a space for contemporary art. Visitors are encouraged to explore the exterior as well as the interior of the institution; in doing so, they come to appreciate its architecture, which was inspired by Bentham and critiqued by Foucault. Vintage photographs posted around the compound demonstrate the power of optics, highlighting the awesome radial plan with its central hub towering over prisoners in the yard. A placard titled "Panoptico" honors the architect Juan Alberto Capurro who designed Miguelete, stating that the central watchtower "generated in the prisoners the certainty of being watched." Taking a more activist tone, the containment wall of the prison is scrawled with graffiti suggesting a general awareness of surveillance: "The Big Brother observes us from the Foucaultian panopticon."

As a final example of the power of optics, we return to the National Stadium in Santiago to consider how panopticism merges with spectacle – a dramatic event displayed to a mass audience. While Foucault delves into the disciplinary power of the panopticon, Guy Debord (1967) proposes that the spectacle is yet another instrument for dehumanizing subjects. To reiterate, upwards of 20,000 prisoners were processed through the National Stadium in the early stages of the 1973 military coup. Journalists captured the surreal nature of the *penal stadium*, where armed soldiers in the infield observed prisoners confined to the bleachers. In response, prisoners internalized the gaze not only of the soldiers but also of the authoritarian Pinochet regime. Those photographs are scattered throughout the memorial site of the National Stadium as visitors—secondary witnesses—grasp the enormity of state repression.

ILLUSIONS OF ARCHITECTURE

Panopticism, simply put, gains power by allowing everything to be seen. Conversely, illusion refines power by prompting viewers to see something else, thereby concealing the truth and evidence of human rights atrocities. In *Disappearing Acts: Spectacles of Gender and Nationalism in Argentina's "Dirty War,"* Diana Taylor deciphers how the military dictatorship performed power and projected authoritarian control over civil society. She also draws on Guy Debord (1967), who critiqued a society of spectacles that locks individuals into an economy of looks and looking. As a locus and mechanism of repression, spectacles forge certain impressions even while erasing other images from public view. Toward that end, *Disappearing Acts* remains focused on how the military junta used the spectacle to produce a form of power that manipulated the population "and render[ed] it passive and blind though the theatrical control of the visual sphere" (1997: 222; see also Andermann 2012; Brown, 2009).

In Buenos Aires, the Casino located at the ESMA compound offers visitors lessons on the spectacle as well as illusion. Under the direction of the curators, those secondary witnesses are subjected to a unique form of temporal performance that allows them to view the past and present simultaneously (Clark and Payne, 2011). That split consciousness enables them to grasp that the Casino is both a former clandestine detention site and a memorial space. By design, visitors come to understand how evidence of repression was initially concealed, then subsequently revealed. The tour guide points to key features of infrastructure that were modified in an effort to mislead the 1979 Inter-American Commission for Human Rights. Those inspectors were responding to the testimony of survivors who had found refuge abroad. Since detainees were hooded during their captivity, they had to describe their surroundings by tracking their movements (e.g., walking down stairs) along with recognizable sounds (e.g., the noise of an elevator). Anticipating the inspection, the junta plotted to throw the commission off the trail by removing sections of the main staircase in the Casino and boarding up the elevator. As a result, inspectors might (mistakenly) conclude that the testimony of the survivors did not match the physical layout of the Casino. Such inconsistencies might then raise questions about the accuracy—or veracity—of the survivors. However, in 2010, while ESMA was undergoing its transition to a memorial space, evidence was uncovered that corroborated the survivors' testimony.

Both the renovated staircase and the elevator shaft are displayed for visitors to view, thereby dissolving the illusion. Some brief text repeats testimony by survivors and in doing so facilitates the performance of space: "I was taken down the stairs, I also counted the steps, I did it to entertain myself, but I had the feeling that there was a lift (elevator) somewhere as an engine could be heard" (Vasquez, 2010). Visitors are encouraged to gaze at the modified railing of the staircase, which appears to bend in the direction of a lower level (which does not now exist). Evidence of the elevator can be found at two locations in the building. In the basement, a section of a wall has been cut open, creating a window into which visitors can see the springs of the shaft; it is deliberately illuminated to intensify the act of visual absorption. Correspondingly, a wall upstairs has a slightly different shade of paint. Upon closer inspection, visitors—*spectators*—can see that it is here that the doors of the elevator had been removed and replaced with sheet rock. To reinforce a performance of space, scripted statements are posted: "We went down to that Basement by the lift which was very noisy, there was also a door that made a big noise when we left the Basement, they were like locks made of thick metal sheet" (Soffiantini, 2010).

As another act of illusion, a bathroom on the first floor of the Casino has its door wide open for visitors to look inside. That compartment represents another ruse by the military. The bathroom was installed after a telephone booth was removed in order to deceive the inspection team. The telephone booth was well-known to the survivors since upon their detention they were forced to call their family and say they were fine. In some instances, they asked for money or property to be transferred to the military. Andrea Bello (2010) recalls: "I was told that I would be able to phone home on condition that I would not tell them I was a prisoner. I phone home, my mother answered she was shocked and asked 'What happened? We have been looking for you for four months. They took everything in your house. And I said, 'Well mum don't worry, everything is all right,' I was trying to calm her down, she was really distressed." Suddenly, Bello breaks the illusion: "My mum pressured me and I said: 'I'm detained' and they hang up, of course."

The buildings at EMSA were originally a mundane naval training academy and were not designed to be soundproof. Consequently, when the compound was repurposed as a clandestine detention, torture, and extermination center, it could not completely conceal the junta's repression. Since the survivors were hooded during their captivity, they had to describe their surroundings by sounds they heard from the outside. Their testimonies corroborated claims that ESMA was indeed a site that did exist, thus bolstering the legal claims against the military. An initial task faced by investigators was to find the precise location of the clandestine site. With the aid of testimonies describing certain noises, the secret detention center was eventually revealed. Several survivors reported hearing car engines on a nearby street (i.e., Del Libertador Avenue), trains on a nearby railway (i.e., the Belgrano Norte Line), and planes taking off and landing at a nearby airport (i.e., Buenos Aires City Airport). Survivors also recalled hearing children from the nearby school (i.e., the Raggio school) and football fans chanting for their favorite teams (i.e., River Plate and Defensores de Belgrano Clubs). Confirming the location of clandestine site, Carlos Loza testified: "We immediately identified the place. Firstly, we were oriented because of the movement of planes and trains. . . . We looked and we identified the place as the Navy Mechanics School" (Loza, 2010).

Other survivors recalled what they heard during the 1978 World Cup, which was held in Argentina that year (despite international condemnation). When a goal was scored, they could hear fans cheer through a television being watched by the repressors, and seconds later they could hear the actual crowd. So they knew that ESMA was very close to stadium. So that visitors understand the importance of these discoveries, curators put on display a darkened room hauntingly lit by the glow from a television set. The room represents what the repressors routinely did while on duty, and in doing so, it reminds visitors of the banality of their atrocities.

The strategic use of sonics enhances the performance of space at ESMA. Most conspicuously, video monitors are scattered around the interior of the Casino, allowing visitors to spectate and listen to the court testimony of survivors. Touring the actual site being described adds to the dynamics of cultural transformation: a profane space (where atrocities were committed) becomes a sacred space (where tragedy is memorialized). As mentioned earlier, the "fishbowl" (*pecera*) is located in the attic (*capucha* or hood) of the Casino. Visitors are invited to step into that restricted space, where select detainees were subjected to a form of forced labor, known as "recovery process," aimed at altering their political ideology. "[Captain Jorge 'Tigre'] Acosta, a man of great cleverness baptizes it and said: 'this is a recovery process.' . . . The Tasks Group members called themselves 'the Sorbonne of the anti-subversion: We do not only destroy, we reconvert enemies.' That was their vision" (Gras, 2010). The "fishbowl" (then and now) consists of a row of tiny cubicles where detainees were kept under constant surveillance by CCTV. Graciela Daleo comments on the degree of panopticism: "The Fishbowl . . . had those acrylic panels that allowed them to see us from anyplace, it was partly made of hardboard and transparent panels to the ceiling. But over the time, in fact, I gave it another meaning: we, the same as fish in a fishbowl looked like normal people that were leading a normal life, but the same as fish when they are in a fishbowl, they are not in the sea, they are imprisoned, but to the outsider it looks as if they were normal fish. Well, we were that" (Daleo, 2010; see also Feitlowitz, 1998).

The "fishbowl" was central to media operations: prisoners were kept busy writing press releases and translating newspaper articles for the junta. Curators transport visitors into the "fishbowl" by navigating them through the cubicles covered with newspaper clippings. Audio speakers fill the room with sound of typewriters, thereby replicating a surreal workplace that was concealed deep inside a military compound. The strategic use of sounds is a common performative technique in memorial spaces, for it further activates the power of place.

The illusion produced by transforming urban buildings into clandestine detention centers has been exposed at numerous other sites in Buenos Aires. In the residential neighborhood of Floresta can still be found the inconspicuous Automotores Orletti. In its original incarnation, the mundane place was used as an automotive repair shop. Under the last dictatorship, Orletti was repurposed as a hidden site for political confinement. As a major hub for Operation Condor, Orletti, codenamed "El Jardin" (The Garden), held upwards of 300 detainees not only from Argentina but also from Bolivia, Brazil, Chile, Cuba, Paraguay, and Uruguay (between May and November 1976). Numerous posters and storyboards outline the role of Orletti in the cross-border operations of Condor. On a closed door, a sign designates the room as an office that housed repressors from Uruguay and Chile who carried out interrogations and torture on detainees specifically targeted by those countries (see Timerman, [1981]1998). A sign above the entrance reminds the community that Orletti has a new place identity committed to memory and the promotion of human rights.

The spatial afterlives of Orletti underwent several transitions. When agents from Operation Condor abandoned the building, it resumed its function as an automotive shop, then in a strange twist of events the space was used as a sweatshop for "slave" labor from Bolivia. In fact, it was the detection of the sweatshop that led to the discovery that it had previously been used as a clandestine detention center. In its current form, the memorial space does not attempt to shed much of its past life. Especially compared to the sanitized space of ESMA, Orletti still looks like an auto shop cluttered with equipment and tools. Pictures of the disappeared (identified by nationality) are arranged across a wall. Nearby mugshots of the repressors are captioned as genocidal criminals, thus conveying a sense of justice. Storytelling institutions, such as memorial spaces, often rely on performance as a curatorial technique (Casey, 2003; Williams, 2007). Likewise, the tour of Orletti concludes with a dramatic tale of escape in which detainees seized a weapon from a dozing guard and literally shot their way out. The scene is re-created by a guide, who activates the electronic gate so that visitors can see the bullet holes punctured the metal curtain. The spatial afterlife of Orletti is properly grounded in its tragic history: plaques located outside explicitly link the site to Operation Condor (see Sorbille, 2008).

The recovery project aimed at shattering the illusion of architecture—and "normalcy" under the last dictatorship—unfolds at other former detention sites in Buenos Aires, including "Olimpo," where many political prisoners were transferred before their extermination. Formerly an automotive depot for the federal police, the clandestine center was repurposed by the military to hold detainees (from August 1978 until January 1979). Military personnel code-named the center "Olimpo" in perverse homage to the Greek gods. While detainees were being tortured, guards bragged that they had the power over life and death (Sorbille, 2008: 118). The initiative to recover the site stemmed from a local battle for memory on behalf of the victims. The site now serves as a community center offering lectures, workshops, and various human rights activities (Welch, 2020b).

Much of the compound was demolished by the military in an effort to erase its profane past, but there remain the skeletal frames of the detention buildings surrounded by a fortified containment wall separating "Olimpo" from the residential neighborhood (see Lopez, 2013). For several square blocks, the afterlife of the site is animated by political murals condemning the last dictatorship, including a stencil that reads "NN"—symbolizing the mass graves where victims with "no names" were buried. Murals and graffiti add texture to a residential neighborhood whose residents still grapple with the memory of that particular site. Striking the proper emotional register is profoundly important in establishing a memorial space. As Draper correctly points out, Olimpo, ESMA, and many other sites avoid the trap of promoting some sort of morbid fascination with torture. Draper goes on to describe those sites as having a complex and open persona: entering the compound, visitors are likely to find "themselves confronted with very incompleteness that characterizes these ruinous spaces" (2011: 143).

A mysterious site known as Virrey Cevallos provides a final example of the illusions of architecture embedded in former detention centers in Buenos Aires. During the last dictatorship, the townhouse was hidden in plain sight along an unassuming street just blocks from Congress. Virrey Cevallos, currently an "Espacio Para La Memoria," was previously used by the air force, police, and other intelligence agencies to hold numerous kidnap victims, though the precise number of those held captive there has not been determined. As a memorial space, Virrey Cevallos contains sparse commentary from ex-detainees, who were often hooded during their confinement. Survivors recall that the small cubbyholes deprived them of natural light and proper ventilation. Curators navigate visitors by orienting them to the period when it operated as a clandestine site. A floor plan showing rooms is labeled: "You are here . . . Cells where the kidnapped remain." On the mezzanine level, visitors peer through an opening in a wall located over the staircase where guards monitored the comings and goings of military personnel. For a detention site intended to remain clandestine, Virrey Cevallos was noticeably noisy: survivors described the blaring sounds from vehicles delivering the kidnapped. Residents next door later testified hearing cries for help from detainees being tortured during interrogation sessions. At the time, however, they were too frightened to report such violence, adding to the illusion of normalcy (see Feitlowitz, 1998). When the nation transitioned to democracy, the building remained vacant and unnoticed until 2003, when a group of residents—"Vicinos de San Cristobal Contra La Impunidad"—seized the property as part of a broader campaign to condemn state terrorism. Soon after, they lobbied successfully to protect Virrey Cevallos as a historic site offering public seminars on human rights ("Vierry Cevallos"). With the power of place, those physical and cultural transformations offers local evidence of a Bastille Effect.

CONCLUSION

At the outset, we were introduced to Hubert Robert, whose painting of the Bastille relied on stark visual techniques to create the illusion of larger-than-life monarchical power. Such fascination with the Bastille extended to other artists who re-created the prison's exterior as well as its vast interior. Since those images predate photography—which otherwise might authenticate the architectural designs—viewers tend to give the artist the benefit of the doubt. In doing so, the audience relies on the artist's version of the Bastille. At BnF (Bibliotheque national de France) in Paris, an exhibition on the Bastille (2010–2011) displayed an array of related artworks, including "La Bastille vue par un artiste" (The Bastille Seen by the Artist). The artist in question was Jean Honoré Fragonar whose sketches of the Bastille possess a style strikingly similar to that of Giovanni Battista Piranesi (BnF, 2010: 148–50). Recall that Robert was also inspired by Piranesi's "imaginary prisons" (*carceri d'invenzione*), which delved into the illusion of architecture to deliver a deep psychological effect on his viewers.

As conveyed through the tours at Kilmainham, the Women's Jail, and the National Stadium, the psychological impact of panopticism is carefully managed so as to enhance visual power over political prisoners. Much like the artists who projected their vision of the Bastille, authorities rely on prison architecture to penetrate consciousness by erecting surveillance systems. Bentham and Foucault frequently draw attention to the God-like power contained in notions of the omniscient deity. That diagram of control benefits from other secular interpretations as well. For instance, the panopticon was founded during the Enlightenment as part of a quest to instill order and control through observation, symbolizing what Virilio (1994) called the utopian vision machine. Visitors at the former prisons discussed here experience not only the space that once held political prisoners but also the broader power of panoptics. On display, the illusions of architecture found in the modification of the Casino at ESMA speak to the power of the last dictatorship as it attempted to throw human rights inspectors off the trail.

The memorialization of former prisons in Buenos Aires constitutes a recovery project aimed at dismantling the illusion of architecture—and "normalcy"—under the last dictatorship. As noted, many residents in Buenos Aires were at least subconsciously aware that certain buildings were being used by the junta to commit state crimes. Amid the "dirty war," psychoanalyst Juan Carlos Kusnetzoff introduced the concept of "percepticide" to suggest that "the perceptual organs, too, soon became a causality of the engulfing terror" (1986: 95; Suarez-Orozco, 1991: 942). Through the "failure to recognize," denial is among the first coping mechanisms to be activated in response to death (Vaillant, 1986: 128). As the number of disappearances reached critical mass, Argentines developed "a passion for ignorance" (Corradi, 1987: 119) coupled with "conscious and unconscious strategies for knowing what not to know about events in their immediate environment" (Suarez-Orozco, 1991: 469). To reverse the psychological effects of the last dictatorship, human rights groups use the afterlives of detention sites to heal the collective wounds of the nation. In the chapters that follow, critical attention is turned to the technologies of power aimed at transforming the mind (through propaganda), the body (through torture), and society at large (through genocide).

PART FOUR

Technologies of Power

8

Censorship and Propaganda

Transform the Mind

The maintenance of order in Paris under the *ancien régime* was highly bureaucratic, not to mention arbitrary and ultimately ineffective. Among those in charge, the Lieutenant of Police served many functions, most notably controlling of the streets, public safety, and the press. During the reign of Louis XVI, those prerogatives had been greatly expanded. Royal enforcers targeted Parisian society by dispersing prohibited meetings, including those of trade guilds that might be involved in "seditious" activity. "The *ancien régime* did not only keep watch over the actions of the people of Paris, it tried to control their thoughts too" (Godechot, 1970: 74). Newspapers and books, especially those critical of the regime, were targets of a vast apparatus of inspectors. Indeed, censorship had emerged as a key mechanism of control. Ironically, the banning of certain books only enhanced their worth. Confiscated works were ordered to be burned; in practice, however, the authorities would perform a fraudulent ritual—or spectacle—by publicly incinerating one or two copies; the rest of the bonfire was made up old papers and rubbish. Interestingly, many banned books that had avoided the flames were stored in the cellar of the Bastille and over time allowed to drift back into clandestine circulation, where they enjoyed a value of 10 times their original price (Godechot, 1970). Several prominent political and philosophical works entered the black market of the banned, including Voltaire's *Siecle de Louis XVI* and Rousseau's *Emile*. Voltaire, and many other authors (e.g., Diderot, Morellet), were arrested and sentenced to prison. "Mirabeau and de Sade were also imprisoned, but not for offenses under the press laws. These arrests provided the *philosophes* with a martyr's halo" (Godechot, 1970: 77; BnF, 2010).

Along with the Bastille, the Château de Vincennes on the edge of Paris, now a historic site, was well-known for its famous prisoners, who were subjected to the arbitrary punishment of the monarchy. Visitors today are drawn to the chateau's

Gothic design and invited to enter its former prison, which has been transformed into place for learning and exploring. A brochure titled "Witness to France's history" explains that "the keep, or donjon, is an architectural feat and the expression of remarkable political determination. . . . Standing 50 metres high, it is the tallest medieval keep in France . . . protected by a wall and a deep moat, . . . You can climb the oldest preserved example an outwork stairway." Postings provide a history of the institution. "In the second half of the 18th century, Vincennes became, together with the Bastille, a symbol of royal despotism. Some prisoners here were victims of royal *letter de cachet* (ordering imprisonment without trial). They were imprisoned, like [Denis] Diderot in 1749, for writings deemed subversive." Original printings of Diderot's books are displayed in a glass case accompanied by captions that offer more information on censored literature:

> Diderot's *Lettre sur les aveugles* à *l'usage de ceux voyent* [trans Essay on Blindness], published on 9 June 1749, led to his being imprisoned for two years, accused of spreading materialistic propaganda. . . . This work marks his passage from deism to atheist materialism, displayed for all to read: 'It is important not to take hemlock for parsley, but in no way believe or not believe in God.'

This chapter sifts through the reliance on political imprisonment for suppressing writings, speeches, and other forms of communication. Censorship and propaganda are twinned phenomena: authoritarian regimes invest heavily in policies and practices for determining what can—and cannot—be seen, heard, and said. In *Escape to Prison* (Welch, 2015) those technologies of power have been examined in South Korea under the Japanese occupation as well as in South Africa during apartheid. Here similar developments are explored in Argentina during the last dictatorship and Northern Ireland amid the Troubles. Setting the stage for a critical look at those repressive measures, we return to the significance of performance, *percepticide*, and spectacle. Censorship and propaganda aim to transform the mind and thereby shape how citizens think. As a counterweight, many former prisons and detention centers, with a new place identity, have been repurposed to enlighten visitors with inspiring messages about the importance of the free flow of ideas in a democratic society.

PERFORMANCE, PERCEPTICIDE, SPECTACLE

To reiterate, Taylor's *Disappearing Acts* considers how the last dictatorship performed power and projected authoritarian control over civil society. The public spectacle emerged as a locus and mechanism that both forged and erased images of national and gender identity. In a very Debordian manner, during the "dirty war," everyone was performing. "Everyone was trying to look the part that offered them security and relatively invisibility (if they wanted to stay out of the fray) or access and information (if they were somehow involved)" (D. Taylor, 1997: 109). Much like Kubiak (1987, 1989), Taylor applies performance theory from the perspective of the humanities, comparative literature, and theatrical critique. In a similar vein, the notion of performance enjoys a long tradition in sociology dating back to the work of Kenneth Burke (1945), who inspired Erving Goffman (1959) to develop a multilayered paradigm known as dramaturgical analysis. Such an approach applies the theatre (rather intuitively) as a metaphor for comprehending society, in which members play various roles through the use of stages, scripts, props, and the like. Dramaturgy remains a dynamic vehicle for interpreting the last dictatorship in Argentina, given that the junta went to great lengths to *stage* terror.

With respect to the sociological implications of dramaturgy, Goffman (1959) introduces the simple idea that individuals occupy both a *front stage* (visible to the audience) and a *back stage* (invisible to the audience). While very much conceived as a micro-sociology, dramaturgical analysis is amenable to the macro-performances of groups as well as states. The "dirty war" in Argentina operated on the *front stage* with spectacles of abductions in broad daylight to instill an aura of intimidation. Military personnel also carried out detention, torture, and extermination on the *back stage* at clandestine centers. Through its use of those hidden sites the junta engaged in what Goffman calls *mystification*, in that it concealed lurid details from the general population as well as international human rights monitors. From the standpoint of dramaturgical sociology, mystification stems from a related phenomenon, namely secrecy. Goffman (1959) identified many forms of secrecy maintained by individuals and groups. *Dark secrets*, as the term implies, contain damaging information about performers that might otherwise contradict their public image. The Argentine dictatorship, indeed, held many dark secrets surrounding crimes against humanity and genocide.

The military, through the use of specialized teams, also relied on *strategic secrets* that were intended to control the audience, such as by prompting civilians to realize they were under surveillance. *Inside secrets* were shared only with certain military teammates who could be trusted with sensitive information, thus enhancing a degree of bonding that protected those secrets. Even today, when former military officers are facing prosecution, many refuse to divulge knowledge that could be used to convict their colleagues. Occasionally, the former military also disclosed *open secrets* by claiming that their acts—however repressive—were justified to protect the nation from "subversion." Goffman (1959) also distinguishes between different *roles* people acquire to manage and manipulate information. During the last dictatorship, task groups would recruit certain detainees to serve as informers and spotters, who might even accompany the team during abductions. Some of those cooperative detainees were viewed by the military as having the potential to "recover" from their subversive ideology and ultimately be released from

FIGURE 17. "Abduction." A poster at memorial sites in Buenos Aires features a famous photograph (by Pablo Lasansky) capturing a moment of abduction. © retrowelch 2022.

confinement. Others, however, were exploited for their inside information and subsequently murdered (Park, 2014; Timmerman, [1981]1998)).

As described in the previous chapter, psychoanalyst Juan Carlos Kusnetzoff (1986) observed evidence of *percepticide* during Argentina's last dictatorship. Due to intense trauma, civilians tended to crowd out and ignore atrocities occurring within their visual field (see Suarez-Orozco, 1991). Even when kidnappings by military agents took place in full view, they often went unnoticed, for many witnesses suffered from denial as a prominent coping mechanism, allowing them to pretend that everything was normal (Feitlowitz, 1998). At many memorial sites in Buenos Aires, a jarring reminder of state terror is captured in a well-circulated picture: the action photograph shows soldier abducting a young man while a woman seated in a restaurant tucks her head into her hands in an effort to avoid looking at the brazen assault (see D. Taylor, 1997: 123–24; figure 17).

Taylor's (1997) coupling of spectacle and disappearance underscores the significance of sociological dramaturgy, in particular Goffman's (1959) interpretation of the *front* and *back stages*. Along those lines of inquiry, *percepticide* contributes to a deeper analysis of performance by throwing critical light on the perceptual process that consigns the obviously visible (*front stage*) to a seemingly invisible void (*back stage*). Manipulating the front *and* back stages would become an important tactic for the military. In the immediate aftermath of the coup (March 24, 1976), the junta declared "No Public Spectacles," temporarily banning events from theatre to horse racing. The exception was football—or soccer—which would later be orchestrated as an international spectacle during the 1978 World Cup in Argentina. "The idea was not to seize power—they had already done that. Now, they wanted to usurp space formerly associated with civil society" (D. Taylor, 1997: 60). In its place, the military would strategically perform its own drama, exercising what Foucault (1979: 200) termed "lateral invisibility." That is, through the spectacle, the military would project an awesome threat: hereafter, *all* Argentines (*spectators*) were vulnerable to state terror.

The "dirty war" had profound cultural and psychosocial implications, especially since the military instituted various forms of censorship, blacklisting, and the not so subtle management of what Goffman would regard as *scripts* and *performances*, literally and figuratively. Theatrical plays, television programs, newspaper articles were subject to content control; by junta decree, "stories had to have happy endings." Prohibitions—euphemistically referred to "guidelines"—governed cultural content, the junta having declared that the "dirty war" was not only about weapons but also about "ideological penetration" at the hands (and minds) of "subversives" (D. Taylor, 1997: 11; see also Suarez-Orozco, 1991). The same decree demanded that "nothing should diminish the image of the guardians of order [or illustrate] any deterioration in the image of parents, or justify the rebellion of their children" (Avellaneda, 1986: 155; D. Taylor, 1997: 11, 268).

This disciplinary power had a panoptic effect insofar as Argentines internalized the military's gaze by censoring themselves (see Foucault, 1979, 1986). The sense of an omniscient deity loomed over civil society to the extent that people began burning any literature that might violate the "guidelines." Diana Raznovich, an Argentine playwright, confessed: "The prohibitions made fascists out of all of us, we were on the lookout for anything that could be construed as 'subversive' in our possessions. . . . [I remember] burning even my Jewish cookbook" (D. Taylor, 1997: 12). The former detention, torture, and extermination site, Olimpo, has been transformed from a profane place of violence into a vibrant place for celebrating free thought. There, visitors contemplate the extent of censorship under the last dictatorship. On display is a small collection of banned books authored by Jose Murillo, Juan Domingo Peron, and Karl Marx. That modest example of "dangerous reading," signals a broader recognition of censorship during the military junta.

In *Public Pages: Reading along the Latin American Streetscape*, Marcy Schwartz (2018) meditates on the power of repression as well as the resistance it creates. Those "books that bite" are now available in libraries established at Olimpo and other former detention centers in Argentina. Rather than entering the commodified "memory market" of published testimonials, those collections "celebrate the end of censorship by transforming that experience into public reading spaces and events" (Schwartz, 2018: 193: see also Bilbija and Payne, 2011). By displaying previously invisible, silenced, and hidden books, these libraries have once again put objects into circulation; metaphorically, the resurrected libraries symbolize the reappearance of those persons who were disappeared (Invernizzi and Gociol, 2003; Park, 2014). That process, what Taylor (1997) calls "acts of transfer," preserves rather than erases. As a form of cultural resistance, libraries of banned books inject life into spaces that once practiced torture and death. The library at Olimpo, Biblioteca Publica y Popular Carlos Fuentealba, is named not for a victim of the junta but for a teacher and labor activist killed by police during a union protest in 2007. "Dedicating the library in his memory exemplifies the center's interest in human rights in general, beyond the context of the dictatorship" (Schwartz, 2018: 204).

Strangely, detainees at Olimpo actually read forbidden books while in captivity. Those works had been confiscated during house raids and stored at the detention center, where detainees gathered them and distributed them on a cart. One survivor recalled: "How could there be library in a dungeon? . . . [ironically, the secret library formed] a bridge to our dreams" (Cerruti, 2010: 65). The junta's surveillance of reading is documented in the more than 4,000 volumes contained in the collection at Olimpo, which began as an exhibit titled "The Return of the Banned" and is currently called "Banned under State Terrorism." The community center offers a forum for critical thinking, a reminder that "reading can be a practice of resistance," especially since the regime's attack on the arts and culture was as calculating as its reliance on detention and extermination (Schwartz, 2018: 204).

By way of Debord, Taylor remains focused on how the spectacle was used by the military junta to produce a form of theatrical power that manipulated the population, rendering it passive and visually impaired (1997: 222; see Andermann, 2012). Interestingly, football (soccer) was exempt from the junta's suspension of all public events; in fact, an important football match was played on the very day of the coup. While the sport has long been understood as a mechanism for building social solidarity—especially as a masculine expression of bonding—the military strategically deployed the allure of football to improve its image within Argentine society and beyond. That spectacle culminated in the 1978 World Cup. For years, the military had been working behind the scenes (*back stage*) with international football promoters. The event would enhance national identity and pride among Argentines, and in a Goffmanesque manner it would also provide a badly needed political "make-over" for the dictatorship (see Suarez-Orozco, 1982).

With the number of disappearances surging, the junta mounted a public relations campaign by directing the media to release articles blaming human rights abuses on the incompetence of President "Isabelita" Perón, who was in office at the time of the coup. In doing so, the military insisted that its intervention was rational and justified, aimed at placing the nation back on the right track. The generals went so far as to invite former US Secretary of State Henry Kissinger to sit with the military dignitaries so as to lend some legitimacy to the event. Elsewhere,

Kissinger and other Nixon and Ford insiders were condemned for their complicity in *dark secrets* of the Argentine junta and other Operation Condor dictatorships (Chile, Paraguay, Uruguay) (Dinges, 2004, McSherry, 2008; Welch, 2020b). The spectacle of the final World Cup match was closely monitored by a heavy military and police presence to ensure that the event proceeded without any disruptions. Taylor offers a distinct Debordian take on the spectacle, adding that the security measures staged a "complex net of 'looks' as spectators watched and were watched, [and] submitted to visual controls of surveillance" (1997: 113). The outcome of the 1978 World Cup—the Argentines took the cup—proved that spectacles possess a unique cultural power to unite citizens, even in the face of widescale crimes against humanity.

Given the social and political significance of the 1978 World Cup, it is unsurprising that the event is closely scrutinized in several exhibition spaces at ESMA. In the former "fishbowl" in the attic of the Casino, an elaborate set of *scripts* and *props* critically narrates the spectacle and its effects on those held in captivity. It is here that the World Cup is again *performed*. To maximize that performance, storyboards are translated into English for the benefit of a larger audience. A placard informs visitors that the proposal to host the World Cup had been ratified in (June) 1976 under the direction of the military, in particular Admiral Emilio Massera, who organized the championship as a "political instrument of the dictatorship to get social support" and "accumulate power." Plans for the World Cup, however, faced stiff opposition from the global community. In France, a committee was formed to organize a boycott of the games; as it gained momentum, its activism spread to other European nations. Its slogan, "No Football in Between the Concentration Camps," is accompanied by an image of Argentine General Videla superimposed on that of Hitler.

For added grounding at the Casino, European protests are authenticated through a series of international news clips and photographs condemning the last dictatorship. In response to these, the junta reinvigorated its public relations efforts by attacking "foreign" opponents as "anti-Argentine" and as bent on unleashing "unpatriotic" sentiment. Curators at ESMA quote Graciela Daleo, who testified in the 2010 trial. She reports that when the Argentine team won the World Cup, all military personnel were celebrating in ESMA. Captain Acosta shouted "We won, we won," and began shaking hands with the male prisoners and kissing the women. In a rare break in *percepticide*, Daleo thought to herself, "If they won, we lost." That revelation within a larger performance, or *spectacle of resistance*, reveals a dramatic technique of temporality by which "lived time makes space for the assimilation of historical time" (Bishop, 2014: 565). Through the use of theatrical cues, curators at ESMA have transformed a formerly profane place that, in its current incarnation, inspires visitors to reflect on a sense of historical consciousness contained in the memorial space they temporarily inhabit.

MEDIA OPERATIONS AND THE FISHBOWL

Moving beyond the wider parameters of performance, percepticide, and the spectacle, it is important to examine some of the political maneuvers that were occurring behind the scenes. In the wake of the coup, media operations were in full swing. On exhibit inside the "fishbowl" at ESMA, detailed notecards describe the junta's campaign to improve its image, especially in the face of incriminating evidence. Under the direction of Admiral Emilio Massera, the armed forces took control of the Ministry of Social Welfare and the Chancellery, then established the Direction of Media and the General Directorate for Press and Broadcasting. Its purpose was to coordinate "propaganda actions" abroad and send out information that could discredit charges of human rights violations. Interestingly, the Navy's Center for Press and Information (Centro Piloto) was based in the Argentine Embassy in Paris, from where it channeled messages throughout much of Western Europe.

That agency was more than a propaganda tool. Massera also used it to "infiltrate" and spy on exile organizations. Members of the Tasks Group at ESMA were dispatched to Centro Piloto de Paris, including Captain Alfredo Astiz (the Blond Angel of Death). Among their targets was Elena Holmberg, a career civil servant for the Foreign Service assigned to the Argentine Embassy in Paris. When Holmberg objected to the Centro Piloto, she was removed from her post and sent back to Argentina. In 1978, Holmberg was abducted by the Task Group; her body was recovered floating in the Lujan River of El Tigre Mendez (see Mendes Carreras and Villagran San Millan, 1982). Meanwhile, Massera retired from the navy in 1978 and deployed the media machine (with several newspapers) to rehabilitate his image in an effort to appear presidential, even claiming to be a moderate member of the junta and an advocate of democracy. After announcing his candidacy, Massera campaigned for the Party for Social Democracy until 1983, when he was detained on charges of participating in the disappearance of businessman Fernando Branca. Massera, as a result of his arrest, was disqualified for the elections.

As noted previously, media operations were accelerated inside ESMA's "fishbowl" (*percera*), where detainees prepared articles and press briefings favoring the military. Moreover, media outlets cooperated with the junta by knowingly disseminating false information. In a bizarre media event, Norma Esther Arrostito (aka Gaby) was abducted by the Task Group (in 1976). The army swiftly released a press statement declaring that Arrostito had been fatally shot while refusing to surrender. To bolster its case, the Task Force set up a sham armed confrontation and built a fake crime scene with blood of the same type as Arrostito. All the while, Arrostito was being held in isolation at ESMA, where she would be tortured for nearly two years. The Task Group bragged of her capture and even showed her to military leaders as a "War Trophy." In 1978, Arrostito was murdered by the Task Group. With growing frequency, the junta's media operations issued news stories that portrayed detainees as people "killed in battle." "These reports were published every day and were part of the political propaganda the regime used to create the ghost of fear and violence."

Reconstructing incidents of shootouts was just one aspect of the junta's media apparatus. To reiterate, the 1978 World Cup stands as perhaps the most highly crafted event during the last dictatorship. To stage that global spectacle, however, required years of maneuvers behind the scenes. Posters and storyboards inside the "fishbowl" chronicle those developments. The campaign to host the 1978 World Cup was launched in 1973 and then fast-tracked in 1976 by Admiral Massera and Captain Carlos Lacoste, who had strong contacts in international football (he would serve as vice president of FIFA in 1980). "The Navy and Massera used it to accumulate power. A great deal of the population massively supported it and celebrated the triumph as a national victory." Along the way, the regime pushed back hard against human rights activists opposing the event, in particular the French-based collective "Boycott against Soccer World Cup in Argentina." In yet another peculiar move by the military, Lisandro Raul Cubas, a detainee at ESMA, was issued new clothes and media credentials to attend what is described as a "surreal press conference" at the 1978 World Cup. A photograph of Cubas appeared in the newspaper *La Nación* (3 May), showing him (alongside his undercover captors) transcribing the words of Cesar Luis Menotti, the coach of the Argentine team. Apparently, Cubas had been tasked to prompt a favorable statement about the military by coach Menotti that could be circulated in other news outlets.

SIGNS OF TROUBLE

Matters of censorship and propaganda—as dual tactics—surface in other societies, especially those mired in conflict. In Northern Ireland during the later Troubles, British authorities went to great lengths to silence opposition groups, activists, and rival paramilitaries. Not without controversy, Home Secretary Douglas Hurd imposed media restrictions on the voices of political opponents, most notably members of Sinn Fein who expressed their support for the Republican movement. As a form of state censorship, the Broadcasting Ban of 1988 had the full backing of Prime Minister Margaret Thatcher, who declared: "Democracies must find a way to starve the terrorists and hijackers of the oxygen of publicity on which they depend" (Cottle, 1997: 283). The restrictions went beyond news reporting, applying to television dramas, documentaries, and talk shows. Much like Paul McCartney and Wings, whose 1972 song "Give Ireland Back to the Irish" was banned in the UK, the Irish rock band, The Pogues, was also targeted. Their lyrics in "Streets of Sorrow/Birmingham Six" were barred for criticizing the British response to terrorism. That song defended Irish prisoners (including the Guilford 4) who were later exonerated after being convicted on bombing charges (*Pittsburgh Post-Gazette*,

1988). In resisting the Broadcasting Ban of 1988, news executives found creative ways to defy censorship, such as overdubbing voices of controversial figures (e.g., Gerry Adams and Martin McGuinness of Sinn Fein). Under intense pressure by journalists and free speech advocates, the ban was eventually lifted in 1994.

Mass media scholars paid close attention to the manner in which news was relayed during the Troubles. Mainstream reports typically focused on the violence committed by the IRA while downplaying the brutality of the British army, who were at times portrayed as "a rather superior kind of Boy Scout Troop" (Cottle, 1997: 285; see also Moloney, 1991). In the midst of the conflict, both sides waged a "propaganda war" during which claims and counterclaims took turns in a flurry of partisan publicity. Liz Curtis explains: "The British public is generally allowed to see only the worst of the 'enemy's side and best of their own. As a result, cause and effect become topsy-turvy—IRA violence comes to appear the alpha and omega of the problem, and Britain's historical and contemporary responsibility is obscured" (1984: 275–76; 1991; see also Taylor, 1986).

Faced with media regulation, banning, and censorship, political activists in Northern Ireland energized another popular form of communication: street art. Those public expressions thrived due in large part to their capacity to fuse use-value in conveying political messages with signifying-value in promoting political culture. Throughout much of the urban space, murals promoted both the Loyalist and Republican causes while also commemorating those who had perished in paramilitary and colonial violence. Correspondingly, the harsh experience of political imprisonment—and censorship—inspired muralists to take up arms in the arts. Republican Gerard Kelly developed his "revolutionary art" while serving time for a "politically related offence" (Rolston, 1992: vi). Kelly, known as "mo chara" [Irish for "my friend"], recalls:

> Prison was supposed to be a breakers' yard for republicans. You were stripped of your dignity, your clothes, anything that showed your identity. You were allowed to paint hankies (handkerchiefs) of the Pope, the Virgin Mary, Mickey Mouse and things like that. They censored everything. Anything with "Long Kesh" on it or "H Blocks," anything like that was not allowed. (Rolston, 1992: vi)

Under the watchful eye of the prison guards—known as "screws"—Kelly immersed himself in Irish mythology. Upon his release, he fused his interest in Celtic traditions with the Troubles by painting murals of Gerry Adams, the 1981 hunger strikers, and the eight IRA men killed by the SAS in Loughgall. Describing his artwork, Kelly says: "I don't like the word 'propaganda,' because propaganda seems to be telling half-truths. . . . People would stand and look at a mural before they would read a paper. Also it gives the people of the immediate area a sense of pride" (Rolston, 1992: vii). Bill Rolston's series of books *Drawing Support* reflects on the social and symbolic significance of murals. "In a war such as the one in progress in the North of Ireland," murals play a vital role in political education in the local community; indeed, "murals thus have a crucial role in the battle for the hearts and minds of people. . . . They are an effective form of propaganda" (Rolston, 1992: viii; 1998, 2003, 2013). Rolston adds that allies of paramilitaries rely on murals—as well as pamphlets and posters—to offset the propaganda of the British state that dominates the main channels of mass media. Against those barriers, images contained in murals become windows that allow onlookers to see a different political and cultural world.

The "propaganda war" during the Troubles went beyond broadcasting. Much like competing Loyalist and Republican murals, political posters remind us that many overlapping social worlds cannot escape their inherent contradictions, since, according to Lotman (2000), they are unequal yet unified as well as asymmetrical and uniform. As discussed in previous chapters, the boundary sharply divides cultural and territorial space between "our" internal space that is "my own," "safe," and "harmoniously organized" from "their" external space, which is "hostile, dangerous, and chaotic" (131). Just like murals, political posters animate streetscapes where heritage is contested. By way of use-value, political posters deliver pointed messages about the Troubles. And with added signifying-value, the Irish Republican and Nationalist movements inject vivid symbolism into their campaigns, condemning the Royal Ulster Constabulary, supporting hunger strikers, and calling for the unification of Ireland. Relying on an array of techniques, those *signs of trouble* are aimed at generating solidarity in the face of adversity, thereby adding to what Graham recognizes as "the contested interpretation of heritage" (1996: 10).

Political posters in Northern Ireland benefit from a duality of use-value and signifying-value. In the context of the Troubles, the word sign operates in two fundamental ways. First, it is an object that is meant to be publicly displayed. Second, it is something that symbolically stands for something else. The Irish Republican History Museum, a place of learning in Belfast, boasts a vast collection of political posters (see also Welch, 2019). Those material artifacts, in their previous incarnation, added to the "propaganda war" from the Republican standpoint. In their afterlives, however, archived posters are testament to the importance of preserving the past while connecting it to the present. In the museum, political posters contain cultural residue from a period of intense conflict, and their preservation stabilizes collective memory while resisting its erasure. Those particular *signs of trouble* are kept in a series of albums of original posters dating back to the 1960s. As Carrabine correctly points out, "archival practices have a significant bearing on how meanings are organized" (2014: 134). The range of subject matter reaches deep into the history of the Troubles; it includes resistance and sacrifice, women as warriors, and great escapes. In that context, issues pertaining to occupation and brutality are worth examining, especially as they resonate in the "propaganda war."

Barbed wire is among the recurring motifs used to convey the message that the Irish Catholic community is under occupation by a foreign power. One poster, for instance, shows a prisoner behind barbed wire at the Long Kesh internment camp. It should be noted that Long Kesh is not only a contested site in the events of the Troubles but also a significant source for political and cultural dispute. In the early

1970s, Long Kesh held hundreds of detainees, and most of them were Republican/ Nationalist. In the wake of "Operation Demetrius"—a sweeping round-up—many of those detainees were interned without trial (McEvoy, 2001; Taylor, 2001). Years later, Long Kesh was replaced by Her Majesty's Prison Maze (or "H Blocks"—due to the shape of the design). Still, political prisoners continued to call the entire prison compound Long Kesh (or "the Kesh"), while the British authorities referred to it as "The Maze." After the prison was closed in 2000, rival political groups and stakeholders debated plans for the site. Republicans organizations (e.g., Sinn Fein) advocated the development of an International Centre for Conflict Transformation. Loyalists proposed that the compound be bulldozed, since it would prevent the contested site of heritage from being transformed into place of pilgrimage and a "shrine" to the IRA and its leader, Bobby Sands, who died there on while a hunger strike (Kindynis and Garrett, 2015; Neill, 2017). Eventually, "the Kesh"—or "the Maze"—was quietly demolished except for a "representative sample" of the prison (e.g., a cell block, a guard tower, and the medical unit) (Graham and McDowell, 2007; McAtackney, 2014; Wylie, 2004). To reiterate, the physical erasure of the Maze was driven, in part, to undermine any cultural potential for a Bastille Effect.

Returning to the significance of barbed wire, the illustration shows a guard tower looming over the prisoner's shoulder as he looks left. A caption states: "irish republican p.o.w.'s tortured and denied political status." Above is a picture of members of the Royal Ulster Constabulary. One officer of the unit is armed with an assault weapon. Another subtitle reads: "british army and ruc murders and torturers go scot free" (see figure 18).

The RUC's policing practices were (are) so controversial that it was disbanded, paving the way for the Police Service of Northern Ireland (PSNI) in 2001. Political parties swiftly weighed into the debate with contrasting responses. The Social Democrat and Labour Party (SDLP, a moderate Nationalist organization) backed the PSNI from its inception; however, Sinn Fein (a Republican party) withheld its support (Hearty, 2014). Numerous posters in the archive capture the tone of that opposition to police reform, including one with a large photograph of an officer in riot gear aiming an assault rifle at the audience, thus ensnaring political tourists in the social drama of the Troubles. The text blends methods of "naming names" with official reportage alongside Hollywood (action) movie promotion. At the top of poster, three politicians are listed: David Trimble, Ronnie Flanagan, and Tony Blair, with the statement "These men are after your hearts and minds." In report style it continues. "They want you to join a paramilitary force that:

> Stands condemned by the UN and Amnesty
> Engages in collusion with loyalist death squads
> Uses plastic bullets to kill children
> Is not supported by the nationalists and republicans

With detectable degrees of ridicule and sarcasm, the poster's headline reads "Coming Soon PSNI—the shocking sequel to the RUC. . . . Only the name has been

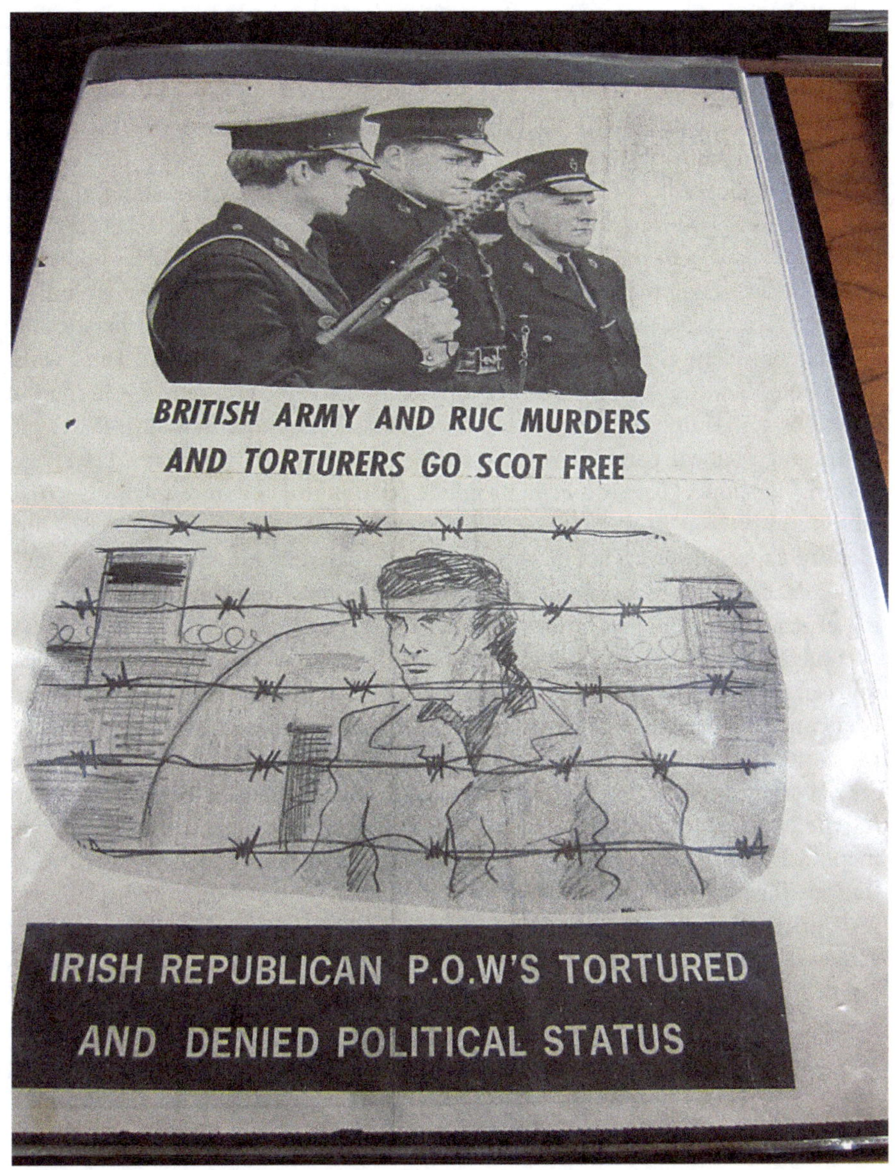

FIGURE 18. "British Army." A poster archived at the Irish Republican History Museum combines themes of brutality and political imprisonment. © retrowelch 2022.

changed." Critics of the PSNI continue to characterize its practices as "political policing" against those "left behind" through covert policing and misuse of anti-terrorism legislation. Sinn Fein issued a bolder condemnation by referring to the PSNI as a continuation of colonial policing by a "British police force still referred to as the 'the RUC'" (*Saoirse*, 2013: Hearty, 2014: 1053). The residual effects of the brutality of the RUC have been located in the everyday experiences of the Republicans, who view its members as a force of the "state oppressors" (Ellison and O'Reilly, 2008; see also Ellison and O'Rawe, 2010).

Unsurprisingly in a cultural world of dissonant heritage, *assault* is a theme that is repeated in many posters. Among the more inventive techniques is the reworking of the topography of Great Britain and Ireland in which the island of Great Britain is morphed into an officer in riot gear with a club striking Ireland. Again, that theme speaks to the "memory politics" of a divided society in ways that rely on the meanings of maps to express the Republican/Nationalist vision of a united Ireland (Hearty, 2014). Through repetition, a standard technique in persuasion, the map of Ireland is drawn without a partition separating the North. Thus, without a boundary, the notion of unity is visually conveyed. Moreover, the map of Ireland is superimposed with the letters "S F", as a reminder that Sinn Fein is an all-Ireland political party as well as a major stakeholder in contested heritage. Shoring up support for Sinn Fein, its public relations office commonly prints Irish words and phrases in ways that evoke a strong sense of ancestral belonging and identity, especially since language is a form of shared symbolism (Burke, 1966). Similarly, cultural observers recognize that "difference" has considerable signifying purchase, for it allows ethnic groups to distinguish themselves from colonial occupiers (Gregory, 2004; Said, 1993). As noted previously with respect to political tourism in Belfast, there is the tendency to "exacerbate difference" in the drama over contested heritage in Northern Ireland (McDowell, 2008)

As the peace process urges communities in Northern Ireland to enter a new era of openness, more disclosures are emerging about what actually occurred during the Troubles (McAtackney, 2013, 2014; McGlinchey, 2019). In a revealing comment, a former British intelligence officer conceded that while the British won the "intelligence war," the IRA won the "propaganda war" (Spy in the IRA, 2017; see Curtis, 1984). By that remark, one can surmise that the Republican movement achieved formidable success in generating support for its campaign. Moreover, political posters—such as those examined herein—most likely played a cultural role in boosting morale and solidarity, especially within Republican strongholds, where the struggle was most intense. And, in doing so, those posters have contributed to a dissonance of heritage, collective memory, and ethno-political identity.

CONCLUSION

Among the ironies of censorship and propaganda, as technologies of power, is that they tend to produce various forms of resistance. As mentioned at the onset, in pre-Revolutionary Paris, banned books actually thrived on the black market. Well-known French authors evaded royal censors by having their books printed outside the country. Even more clandestinely, some books were printed in France but had Amsterdam, Geneva, or Kehl inscribed on the frontispiece. Voltaire's works, in fact, were published in that manner, giving his writings a boost for public consumption. Moreover, his arrest and imprisonment in the Bastille added to the martyrdom of authors and intellectuals persecuted by the *ancien régime*. In 1717, at the age of 22, Voltaire was jailed for writing a scurrilous Latin verse about the Regent having incest with his daughter. For eleven months, he was stuck in windowless cell wrapped by walls 10 feet thick. In 1726, he was returned to the Bastille for a 12-day stint following a quarrel with the aristocrat de Rohan-Chabot (Godechot, 1970). Facing indefinite confinement without a trial, Voltaire agreed to be exiled to London, where for two-and-a-half years he immersed himself in its literary circles (BnF, 2010; Gay, 1988). For his legacy of defiance, Voltaire would be inducted into the "cult of patriot-heroes" by having his remains interned in the Pantheon—the "Westminster for the French." In what was staged as a grand spectacle, Voltaire's "body had been transported from Romilly-sur-Seine in a simple wagon . . . escorted by National Guardsmen to the ruins of the Bastille, where the philosopher's smile might contemplate his victory over the fortress in which he had been twice incarcerated" (Schama, 1990: 564).

The elaborate procession to the Pantheon featured a monumental chariot two stories in height with engravings of Voltaire's words. One of the stone models of the Bastille carved by Polloy joined a chorus of men in Roman costumes bearing Voltaire's books. Even in the rain, 100,000 Parisians attended the highly decorated memorial ceremony. Visitors today are invited into the Pantheon, where a statue of Voltaire—"defender of tolerance"—stands in the vestibule. The tribute to Voltaire highlights other exhibits at the Pantheon. Of particular interest is the display titled "Courage and Resistance" that honors "those who helped the Jews to hide during World War II . . . the Resistance fighters . . the spirit of resistance against the Nazi occupier . . . and Rene Cassin, principal author of the Universal Declaration of Human Rights, adopted by the United Nations in 1948" (Pantheon, n.d.). Much like other modes of persuasion, these enlightened words—and noble acts of courage—are a reminder of their potential to transform the mind in a positive direction.

In closing, we should note that the Pantheon represents a significant extension of the Bastille Effect. Quite often in post-conflict societies, memory of repression is activated not only at the actual sites of atrocities but also at other places that undergo cultural transformation. Again, the Irish Republican History Museum in Belfast transitioned from a mundane industrial yard into a space for learning about the Troubles. Along the way, much of its collection of objects and artifacts has been converted into expressions of the ultimate freedom for Irish Republicans—a united Ireland. Republican murals, likewise, reinforce those messages. As examples of a contested heritage, however, Loyalist street art amplifies the commitment to the United Kingdom. In the next chapter, torture is examined in Northern Ireland as well as in the southern cone of Latin America, where transformation of the body serves as another technology of power of the state.

9

Torture and Torment

Transform the Body

Among the often-cited passages in Foucault's *Discipline and Punish* (1979) is his vivid description of the execution of Robert-François Damiens, who was drawn and quartered in 1757 for attempting to assassinate the King of France, Louis XV. As the ordeal begins, Damiens is taken to the main door of the Church of Paris wearing nothing but a shirt and holding a torch of burning wax. He is carted off to the scaffold erected at the Place de Grève, where flesh is ripped from his body with red-hot pincers and sulfur is poured into the open wounds. To complete the brutal task, four horses are harnessed to dismember the body, leaving his torso to be consumed by fire and reduced to ash. What Foucault omits from his account of Damiens is the interrogation that took place prior to his execution. On display at the Conciergerie, in Paris, is an exhibit titled "Un Lieu de Memoire" (A Place of Memory), which attends to the diverse symbols of politics, including the fate of Damiens. An engraving shows the body of Damiens securely fastened to a torture platform, enduring an excruciating inquisition.

Curators at the Conciergerie—as well as Foucault—also do not mention another important extension of the punishment of Damiens. His relatives were deprived of their surname and banished from France. To eliminate all traces of their existence, the family house was razed to the ground (McManners, 1981). Damiens had an accomplice, Auguste-Claude Tavernier. He was spared from death but confined to the Bastille. In a remarkable twist of events, Tavernier was freed upon the storming of the Bastille and ceremoniously joined the six other prisoners as they paraded through the streets of Paris. Five days after being liberated from the Bastille, Tavernier was declared mad and transferred to the insane asylum at Charenton (Godechot, 1970).

The execution of Damiens is analyzed by Foucault (1979) to illustrate how torture –"the art of inflicting pain"—disappeared from the public spectacle, giving way to a redistribution of an entire economy of punishment. The prison, of course, emerged as the hub of that new configuration of penality. Still, the body remains a principle focus of state intervention even as confinement serves to conceal that part of the penal process. In this chapter, political imprisonment is explored by way of torture and torment aimed at re-forming the body. With critical attention to the sites and symbols of bodily—and psychological—cruelty, discussion relies primarily on examples from the dictatorships in the southern cone of Latin America as well as the Troubles in Northern Ireland. In the process, further conceptualizations of power and their cultural representations are brought to light. The first segment situates power, technology, and the body within the strategies of social control. Attending to those lessons, the analysis benefits from a reworking of Foucault's paradigm. Most notably, Beth Lord (2006) demonstrates that museums—and memorial spaces—are capable of shedding their previous status and becoming institutions for progressive commentary. Also rethinking Foucault, C. Fred Alford (2000) proposes that power should be understood as moving along underground axes rather than in purely panoptic forms.

POWER, TECHNOLOGY, AND THE BODY

"The human body," from the standpoint of Foucault, "is the ultimate material which is seized and shaped by all political, economic, and penal institutions" (Garland, 1990: 137). Accordingly, transformations of the body are contoured by external as well as internal forces. In the first instance, forced labor takes aim at the body from the outside. In the second, a "self-controlled" body is subjugated through the influence of what Foucault calls "the soul"—or what is better recognized as "the psyche, the self, subjectivity, consciousness, or the personality" (Garland, 1990: 137). Hence, the psyche becomes the target of disciplinary technology that renders it the "prison of the body" (Foucault, 1979: 30). Those strategies of power constitute a "discernable pattern of institutional practices or political actions which operate across a number of sites" (Garland, 1990: 137). To be clear, power is not an entity possessed by any individual or group; rather, it is a capacity of domination exercised across multiple fields. Foucault chronicles power as it becomes increasingly modernized, departing from the classical age and the penal excesses of the *ancien regime* (see Spierenburg, 1995, 1984). Toward that end, technology—the application of science—stems from knowledge, thereby providing the "know-how" to re-form the body. The more that is known about the body (and psyche), the more controllable it becomes, giving rise to what Foucault (1979, 1980) calls "power-knowledge." The transition from the gothic scaffold to the modern penitentiary is grounded in "power-knowledge" as well as the "sciences of man" that inform techniques aimed at the body (Foucault, 1979: 305; see also Burchell, Gordon, and Miller 1991; Garland, 1990: 137–39).

As trajectories of power transfer the body from the spectacle to the prison, it becomes embedded into the body politic, where that force creates a political technology controlling the general population, or the entire social body. In his conclusion, Foucault (1979: 297) meditates on "the carceral," in which modern society is marked by a series of institutions beyond the frontiers of criminal law, constituting a carceral archipelago. That immense punitive continuum is reduced to a subtle, graduated carceral net in which there are compact sites as well as separate and diffused methods of control. Garland is indeed correct to point out that *Discipline and Punish* should not be treated primarily as a historical text (1990: 162). Rather, it provides a source for theoretical and cultural critique, initiating new ways to think about social institutions. Garland also insists that Foucault's account of penal history is "perspectival"—that is, it views phenomena through the lens of power-knowledge and the body (152; see also Spierenburg, 1984):

> Foucault's description of Western liberal democracy as a society of surveillance, disciplined from end to end, is deliberately reminiscent of totalitarianism which is usually ascribed to others. And in case anyone should miss this implied reference to the Gulag and its confinements, he coins the phrase "carceral archipelago" to describe the chain of institutions which stretches from the prison. (Garland, 1990: 151),

As we segue to the southern cone in Latin America, it is important to note that each of the dictatorships studied here relied on a vast network of clandestine detention and torture centers. In Argentina, for example, the military junta established as many as 500 such sites nationwide, including at least 50 in Buenos Aires (Welch, 2020b). That "carceral archipelago" reached beyond the individual bodies of prisoners to control the larger social body. Whereas Foucault's analysis seems to suggest a smooth refinement of power, case studies elsewhere offer evidence of multiple manifestations of dominance being exercised simultaneously. Across the southern cone, military regimes developed an array of technologies, including the spectacle, surveillance, imprisonment, torture, and disappearance. Those techniques were used to re-form the body at the individual as well as the societal level. In Buenos Aires during the "dirty war," corpses occasionally dotted the urban landscape, hanging from bridges or tied to the landmark obelisk in the Plaza de la Republica (Pitt, 2010; D. Taylor, 1997). Those grotesque spectacles of state terror symbolized the power within a wider campaign to eliminate what the junta referred to as "subversives" (Bilbija and Payne, 2011). "The practice of torture," according to Foucault, was not so much "an economy of example" but rather "a policy of terror to make everyone aware, through the body of the criminal, of an unrestrained presence of the sovereign" (1979: 49). By way of a different technology, the "fishbowl" (*pecera*) hidden deep inside ESMA served as a key site for forced labor, or a "recovery process" intended to "reconvert" the political ideology—or psyche—of certain detainees (Gras, 2010).

FOUCAULT'S MUSEUM: PERFORMING CRITIQUE

The task of rethinking and reanalyzing Foucault's work is part and parcel of a broader intellectual field known as Foucault studies. Just as Garland (1990) and many others have so eloquently revisited Foucault, so too has Beth Lord (2006) with her insightful essay on the museum. In "Of Other Spaces," Foucault (1986) explores the museum as a space of difference and space of representation (see Welch, 2015: 55–60). Lord points out that "Foucault's work has been used to promote a negative view of the museum as an Enlightenment institution that embodies state power and strives to order that world according to universal rules and the concept of total history" (2006: 1). In a direct challenge to that characterization of "Foucault's Museum," Lord contends that such institutions are positive, drawing on the Enlightenment values of critique and freedom. Toward that end, museums are genealogical and have the potential to perform their own critique through an interpretation that conceptually explicates items in its collection.

In the realm of prison museums, many institutions navigate visitors down a progressive *walk through time* that explains how penal practices became increasingly humane (Welch and Macuare, 2011). Among the subsets of prison museums are sites devoted to the display of torture instruments. In London, the Clink Prison Museum is housed in a former dungeon for debtors as well as religious and political dissenters. With its horrific past put safely to rest, the Clink is currently a place for learning, not without some amusement. Storyboards depict the Clink as a "hands-on torture chamber," thereby allowing visitors to participate. The space consists of a series of subterranean galleries featuring a vast collection of torture devices: stocks, pillories, cat-o'-nine tails, and the rack. In support of Lord's (2006) thesis that museums can offer positive and progressive lessons for humanity, curators at the Clink engage tourists by asking them to consider the pain and suffering of those subjected to torture (Welch, 2015, 2013). Similarly, the Torture Museum in Amsterdam focuses on medieval practices of inflicting bodily harm. The assortment of instruments range from whips to the heretic fork consisting of sharp points pressed under the chin as a painful reminder of the consequences of blasphemy. Even more so than the Clink, the Amsterdam Torture Museum delivers a didactic commentary on contemporary human rights:

> Anyone reading the newspapers will know that torture has never been banished. In their persecution of political dissidents, the Security Services of authoritarian regimes have little to learn from the Spanish Inquisition of olden times. Yet even in the centre of Western democracy, executioners have remained in employment. In the United States of America, the very country where the Constitution first guaranteed inviolability of human life, death sentences are still executed. (See Torture Museum, n.d.)

In her critique of "Foucault's Museum," Lord explains how museums perform genealogy and in doing so foster the expansion of capabilities and "contribute to the work of liberation . . . helping societies to heal" (2006: 11). As a case in point, she cites Constitution Hill in Johannesburg, where a museum stands within the former prison complex. The site narrates the campaign against apartheid and the epic turn in history toward democracy in South Africa (see Welch, 2015). Similarly, in Buenos Aires, debate over how to transform ESMA from a former clandestine detention, torture, and extermination center into a memorial space considered many points of view. Most prominently, in planning a space for critique, the performative option advocated wresting the site from its executioners by handing it over to artists and human rights activists, thereby enhancing its signifying-value for greater effect. And, as noted previously, that transformation has allowed a formerly profane place to enter the sphere of the sacred.

GOTHIC TO MODERN TORTURE: THE PARADOX OF PROGRESS

"Torture is a technique . . . [an] art of maintaining life in pain" that is quantitative and calculative by "subdividing [life] into a 'thousand deaths'" (Foucault, 1979: 33–34; see also Scarry, 1985). While Foucault associates torture with the classical age, he concedes that it has persisted well into the modern era, creating a paradox of progress. A critique of torture and other atrocities carried out by military operatives is among the unifying themes at memorial spaces in the southern cone. Curators reveal how the refinement of torture techniques adapted modern advances in technology and science—such as electric shock—to complement otherwise Gothic forms of barbarity (see Welch, 2017b). In Asunción, the Museo de las Memorias, a former detention site, reflects on the Stroessner dictatorship (1954–89) and the vulnerable detainees subjected to torture. The manner in which torture instruments are displayed conveys a paradox of progress, from the archaic to the modern. A spike ball symbolizes a retention of the medieval: the weapon is swung by a chain to strike the body of the prisoner, leaving indelible marks. From a cultural standpoint, the device is enclosed in a locked display case, suggesting that its inherent danger needs to be contained.

At the other end of the spectrum, portable shock generators exemplify modern technology. During the dictatorship, torturers would apply electrical current to sensitive parts of the male and female anatomy, inflicting humiliation as well as irreparable physical and psychological damage. Unlike the visual scars produced by the spiked ball, electrocution leaves no marks on the body, thus concealing evidence of torture (see Welch, 2011c, 2009b). The collection also includes syringes used to inject "the drug of truth" into the bodies of those detained. Interrogators presumed (falsely) that in this way they could obtain valuable confessions while also inflicting intense mental anguish. Curators refer to those instruments as "techniques of State Terror." With respect to a diffusion of knowledge, captions apprise visitors that those techniques were taught to Paraguayan agents by Robert

K. Thierry, a US military adviser. When the "Archives of Terror" were discovered in 1992, documents were found in it that confirmed that Colonel Thierry had "helped draw up the apparatus of the police state as he trained police officers for the Technical Section soon after General Stroessner seized power here in 1954" (Schemo, 1999: A-10). Correspondingly, the exhibit confirms that Stroessner dispatched Antonio Campos Alum, director of the main clandestine detention center, to the US in 1955 to learn a variety of torture techniques (ABC Paraguay, 2012; see also McSherry, 2005).

In line with Lord's (2006) notion of "Foucault's Museum," the Museo de las Memorias boasts large storyboards from the Commission of Truth and Justice (2004–2008), a testament to Paraguay's genuine progress toward a post-dictatorship society. Medical information outlines the physical and psychological effects of torture, including trauma as well as cardiovascular and neurological disorders. References to Amnesty International and the United Nations International Day in Support of the Victims of Torture mark a global commitment to human rights. Those messages are coupled with sculptures capturing the "body in pain" (see Neier, 1995; Scarry, 1985). In its entirety, the Museo de las Memorias is more than a place for learning. With evidence of a Bastille Effect, its transformation from a profane place of state violence into to a sacred site serves as a dynamic metaphor for human rights.

In Santiago, at 120 Santa Lucia, the Director of National Intelligence, Manuel Contreras, operated a torture center from 1977 to 1980. Its code name "Clinica" signifies the extent to which medical practices were integrated into the torture protocol. After Pinochet's regime, the unassuming townhouse was transformed into an office for the Chilean Commission of Human Rights, which, among other things, hosts meetings and related events. The otherwise plain interior is contrasted by posters and drawings illustrating the abuse inflicted on detainees, creating a somber and surreal aura. One sketch in particular highlights the joint cooperation of paramedical staff and military personnel; it shows a detainee restrained to a metal bed frame supervised by two nurses and an armed soldier. At "Clinica," interrogation and torture were administered under close medical attention to expand the limits of pain without imposing death. Empty bed frames were commonly used by torturers in the southern cone as a means to conduct electric shocks through the bodies of prisoners (see Feitlowitz, 1998). In their afterlives, those objects have abandoned their past violence so as to project messages about the value of humanity. Parallel expressions of justice are delivered inside a conference room at "Clinica," where a painting features an ex-prisoner appearing before a judge at a trial. His shirt is partially removed to reveal torture scars inflicted on his body.

Elsewhere in Santiago, the former detention and torture center known as "Villa Grimaldi" has been transformed into a "park for peace." The tranquil surroundings, however, are challenged by reminders of state terror and other strands of Operation Condor. Makeshift prison cells once used by the dictatorship were

FIGURE 19. "The Basement." At ESMA (Buenos Aires), the basement, known as "Sector 4," served as a torture chamber. © retrowelch 2022.

demolished by the military. Those sites of confinement have been reconstructed so that visitors can witness a history of violence. As a memorial, curators rely on a series of drawings by survivor Miguel Montecinos to condemn the torture chambers equipped with metal bed frames and electrical equipment for shocking restrained prisoners. Similarly, the National Stadium, a former detention and torture site, also serves as a memorial to its victims. Tours remind visitors of the horrors that occurred in the stadium during the early phase of military coup. Clearly aware of the power of images, tour guides wear blue T-shirts bearing the logo of the organization for ex-political prisoners. The stark design contains an illustration of a prisoner strapped to a torture chair.

In Buenos Aires, a profane history of prisoner abuse, torture, and electrocution resonates in the collective consciousness. The memorial space at ESMA provides a space where survivors offer detailed testimonies of inhumanity. Lengthy storyboards inform visitors of the role of the basement, a torture site known as "Sector 4" by the repressors (see figure 19). There, detainees were first initiated into a complex ritual of brutality. It was also the last place they were held before they were "transferred"—a euphemism for extermination. In what might be described as a modern dungeon, the otherwise "dim space was constantly lighted by fluorescent tubes. The air circulation was limited since there were only small skylights facing the parking lot" (Strazzeri, 2010). In the words of Angel Strazzeri, who survived his ordeal at ESMA:

> They take me out of the car and made me sit on a chair and then they hit me in the stomach. Then I go few steps down the staircase, they took me to a room that looks like a white infirmary. There were three or four people in there, I had a hood on. Suddenly someone lifts up my hood and tells me 'here you have to tell the entire story, you have to collaborate, if not I'll shoot you and you'll die'. As I deny collaborating with them, they take my clothes off, tie my feet and hands, they make me lie on a metal stretcher and start torturing me with an electric prod. (Strazzeri, 2010; see Testa, 2010)

"Sector 4" was rife with cruelty fueled by sarcasm. Along a row of numbered torture cells, a sign read "Avenue of Happiness." During the interrogation—and torture—sessions, a phonograph played the same Rolling Stones song, again and again (Coquet, 2010; see also Vieyra, 2010). Filthy conditions of confinement, beatings, rape, sexual abuse, and "submarino" (waterboarding) combined for a larger constellation of torture (Milia, Marti, and de Osatinksky, 1980). At the infirmary within "Sector 4," doctors monitored vital signs of detainees to keep them alive during the sessions. In some instances, doctors injected detainees with sedatives (see Basterra, 2010; Girondo, 2010; Lewin, 1985). As Foucault observed, the modernization of punishment was streamlined through the individual inspection and classification of prisoners. At ESMA a similar procedure was followed—with appalling consequences. In what has been described as "Terror Planning" and the "Clandestine Bureaucracy," military documents were stored in filing cabinets with folders alphabetized by name, followed by the designation: D (detention), L (liberation), T (transfer—extermination) (CONADEP, 1986).

Inside one of the many galleries devoted to cultural representations of human rights at ESMA, a collection of political posters are arranged across a long table. Themes of torture are prevalent. An insignia sponsored by an association of former detainees shows a hooded prisoner whose body is contorted into a grotesque position. The upper- and middle-income sections of Buenos Aires appear scrubbed of any graffiti condemning the last dictatorship (e.g., Recoleta, Barrio Norte). In contrast, working-class neighborhoods, such as San Telmo, contain political graffiti to remind the community of the profane past of the last dictatorship. One such stencil parodies the "James Bond" of torture, who is shown equipped with a pistol and electric prod along with the caption "a license to shock." As post-conflict cultures, the cities in the southern cone rely on former detention centers to condemn the military dictatorships. In their afterlives, those sites activate memory so as to remember the victims of tyranny. As we segue to Northern Ireland, similar controversies over torture are critiqued in ways that advance an understanding of state violence in an otherwise democratic society.

FIVE TECHNIQUES OF DEEP-INTERROGATION

In *Formations of Violence*, Allen Feldman offers a narrative on the body alongside the political terror in Northern Ireland during the Troubles. His extensive analysis spans from urban guerrilla warfare to state rituals of torture practiced in interrogation centers and maximum security prisons. Toward that end, Feldman uses Foucauldian concepts to advance a performative theory of social life—and conflict. *Formations of Violence* is a study of surfaces, representing "sites, stages, and templates upon which history is constructed as a cultural object" (1991: 2). Much like Lotman (2000), who recognized the dynamic significance of the boundary, Feldman finds that surfaces and sites of hostility are "frequently located at the edge of social order" (1991: 2). Still, those surface expressions of political violence are symptomatic of *deeper* socio-economic and ideological conditions.

In Belfast during the Troubles, the noise of British military vehicles patrolling Catholic enclaves was unmistakable, an ominous signal of impending house raids. Predawn arrests were "spectacles . . . a display of colonizing power and the command of territory. . . . [They functioned] as a disciplinary incision onto populations and topographies" (Feldman, 1991: 89). Arrest is indeed a performative projection of power, and Feldman is keen to recall Foucault's example of public execution as a "policy of terror to make everyone aware through the body of the criminal, of the unrestrained presence of the sovereign. The public execution did not reestablish justice; it reactivated power" (1979: 49). Arrest, according to Feldman, is "the political art of individualizing disorder" (1991: 109). The body of the subject becomes the "walking panoptic presence of that state in a community that wishes to evade full panopticism" (1991: 109). Feldman draws parallels with Argentina's death squads and disappearances, which injected fear into the social body so as to background violence as the assumed basis for an entire domain of social interaction (1991: 109–10; see also Timerman, 1982: 52).

During the Troubles, powers of arrest and interrogation were means of collecting information on individuals and communities perceived as a threat to social order; those targets were then systematically monitored and surveilled (Hillyard, 1983). The interrogation became one of many rituals of state power, which Feldman (1991) refers to as ceremonies of verification. In the early 1970s, officers in the Special Branch in Northern Ireland received elite training from the British army and intelligence services. The techniques they learned had been in used in other societies under British colonial occupation (e.g., Kenya, Cyprus, Malaya) (Taylor, 2001). Their aim was to "soften" the subject during interrogation in ways that would unfasten personality and impede resistance (see Welch, 2017b, 2016c). In Northern Ireland, those techniques were modeled on methods refined by the KGB. By contrast to Soviet procedures, Ulster methods were "more severe versions of the isolation technique. . . . The components of the process [included] isolation, sleep deprivation, non-specific threat, depersonalization, inadequate diet and in many occasions physical brutality" (Shallice, 1973: 390; see also Adams, 1997; Campbell, McKeown, and O'Hagan, 1998).

As a ceremony of verification, that protocol would come to be known as the Five Techniques—or Deep-Interrogation—administered during a series of mass arrests and imprisonments without trial. The campaign was launched by Operation Demetrius, between August 9 and 10 (1971), over the course of which the government detained about 350 men, mostly Catholics. To reiterate, arrests are displays of colonizing power and the command of territory (Feldman, 1991: 89). On August 9, Jim Auld was strolling home in his Nationalist neighborhood in West Belfast after a night of drinking pints and dancing to rock tunes. When he reached his parents' house at 3:30 a.m. the lights were still on and the door was open—and inside awaited a man with a rifle. Soldiers ambushed Auld and transported him to a secret interrogation facility (Eldemire, 2018).

Auld and 13 other Irish Catholic men were selected for special treatment authorized by top British intelligence officers, becoming guinea pigs for the Five Techniques (i.e., hooding, stress positions, white noise, sleep deprivation, and deprivation of food and water) (Eldemire, 2018; McGuffin, 1974). The ceremony of verification rested on the presumption that Auld—and the other detainees— knew the identity of IRA volunteers. As an initiation ritual to interrogation, Auld was hooded by his captors and loaded onto a helicopter. Once airborne, a soldier kicked him out and seconds later he hit the ground. The aircraft was hovering just six feet off the ground. Once inside the interrogation center, a doctor examined Auld and determined him fit for interrogation. "To this day, Auld is still in disbelief. 'A human being looked at me and approved me to be tortured'" (Eldemire, 2018). In addition to the other techniques, Auld was subjected to wall standing, a form of stress position in which detainees were forced to lean against a wall with their fingers spread. If they moved or fell, they were beaten and placed back into position. After a while, Auld said that he didn't mind the beatings, as they "were allowing your blood to circulate and giving you a relief from the heavy numbness . . . this went on for at least seven days and nights" (Eldemire, 2018).

Auld had a hood placed over his head throughout much of his captivity. Along with the others subjected to "Deep-Interrogation," he became known as one of the "Hooded Men." Auld recalls having the hood removed only once and that a bright light was shined into his eyes. A voice repeated the same question: "Who do you know in the IRA? . . . It was something out of a movie" (Eldemire, 2018). During his confinement, Auld lost consciousness and hallucinated. He did not have access to a toilet, was fed only once, and was not given water for three days. Compounding his ordeal, industrial noise swirled in the background. Auld attempted suicide by bashing his head against a heating pipe. When he awoke, he realized he could not escape the nightmare. "He was still alive" (Eldemire, 2018). Auld was later transferred to another facility for nine months then to a mental hospital to treat his frequent blackouts, symptomatic of post-traumatic syndrome. With more than

350 men rounded up, it is not clear why Auld, from West Belfast, was targeted. However, there is some speculation that geography was considered. McGuffin (1974) reports that initially men from different provinces were selected for "Deep-Interrogation." Hence, the motives behind the roundup are a reminder that colonizing power operates to command territory (Feldman, 1991; Taylor, 1980).

The Five Techniques have been duplicated elsewhere. Citing the 1978 decision *Ireland v. United Kingdom*, 1978, which stated that the methods did not constitute torture, the US defended its "enhanced interrogation" program for the global war on terror. The policy subjected detainees to an American version of the Five Techniques in Afghanistan, Iraq, Guantanamo Bay, and other black sites (Welch, 2009b, 2016c, 2017b). Also in Iraq, British troops reinvigorated the Five Techniques against civilians, resulting in fatal injuries (Corrigan, 2014). More than 20 years after undergoing the Five Techniques, Jim Auld was disheartened to learn that other detainees had been similarly victimized. When he learned about the fate of Moazzam Begg, a former Guantanamo detainee, he reached out to him. Auld and Begg exchanged their inner thoughts and experiences in captivity. This was a rare opportunity, since Auld had been reluctant to discuss his past with anyone else: "It's not great dinner conversation" (Eldemire, 2018). Begg, a British national, has lectured extensively about his years being detained—without charge—by the US military in Afghanistan and Guantanamo Bay (2007; see also Slahi, 2007). His London-based group, Cage, campaigns against abuses of counterterrorism powers. Auld still regrets the original decision by the European Court of Human Rights: "It could have set a precedent, establishing that any use of the Five Techniques after 1978 amounted to torture" (Eldemire, 2018). In Belfast, Auld facilitates conflict resolution, persuading dissident Republicans from resorting to the rituals of reprisal. In one such instance, Auld traveled to Derry to "dissuade someone from delivering a 'kneecapping,' the trademark paramilitary punishment of shooting someone in the knee" (Eldemire, 2018).

Memory of the "Hooded Men" resonates in human rights activism and also threads through other cultural representations, such as the visual arts. In 2016, Musées royaux des Beaux-Arts de Belgique (Brussels) hosted a major retrospective titled "Uncensored Photographs" by Andres Serrano, whose work critiques inhumanity by scanning the imagery of intolerance and barbarism (Musées royaux dex Beaux-Arts de Belgique, 2016). When the Abu Ghraib prison scandal erupted in 2005, Serrano thought about reenacting scenes of medieval torture that would illustrate the persistence of cruelty into the modern age. Juxtaposed with staged photographs of Iraqi detainees is a series of portraits of the "Hooded Men," whom Serrano invited to participate by having them photographed while hooded. "I brought a black hood with me, like the ones placed over their heads during the entire time of their detainment," says Serrano. "They were shocked, because it was reliving something they never wanted to go through again. We talked for a while and then they said, 'Let's do it.' I was very grateful to them—that was very difficult" (Terziyska, 2019).

In Belfast the legacy of the "Hooded Men," the Five Techniques, and internment (detention without trial) resides in the collective memory. At the Irish Republican History Museum, a reminder of the ceremony of verification is expressed through a copy of a local newspaper resting inside a glass display case. Under the banner headline "Torture Resumes at Castlereagh," the article explains that the RUC interrogation center had reopened after a seven-month period during which the government ceased the Interim Custody Orders for internment. Security forces had now resumed the "screening" process:

> "Screening" is a euphemism for the arrest and interrogation of persons from Catholic areas for intelligence-gathering. Despite their innocence, their release is made to depend on their giving information about their neighbours. This blackmail is often carried further by threats that unless they feed information regularly to the security forces, they will be interned or charged or "dumped" in hostile areas or handed over to the paramilitary organizations in their own areas with the label "informer" attached to them. (*Republican News*, 1975: 1; see also Taylor, 1980)

Also in the Irish Republican History Museum, a mock prison cell replicates the Armagh prison that held women political prisoners during the Troubles. On a T-shirt unfurled on a prison cot is the message "Stop Strip Searches," with a sketch of a naked female prisoner being kneed by a guard. The museum's collection also holds a widely circulated poster with a photograph of then Prime Minister Margaret Thatcher captioned "Wanted for murder and torture of Irish prisoners." Another poster announces that "Over 100 Republican Prisoners in Belfast" are being held in the Crumlin Road Jail, 70 of them confined to the "A" wing of that "Bastille" serving sentences of penal servitude ranging up to 15 years. These images and messages constitute a cultural space for collective memory that condemns political oppression of the Irish people in Northern Ireland. As Feldman (1991) observes, resistance to colonial power and its command of territory inflicts a disciplinary incision on populations and topographies.

POWER UNDERGROUND

As another example of rethinking and reworking Foucault, Alford (2000) asks this bold question: What would it matter if everything Foucault said about prison were wrong? Alford begins by noting that Foucault called *Discipline and Punish* his first book, not because it was actually his first but because it best embodied his theory (see Macey, 1993). In particular, *Discipline and Punish* provided a platform for Foucault's notion of capillary power, which reaches so deep into individuals that it shapes who they become (see Foucault, 1980). Capillary power also implies that control migrates from the margins to the center of society. That perspective departs from the classical Weberian concept of power, which argues for a top-to-bottom trajectory. Alford intervenes, proposing that with respect to the prison, false dichotomies have derailed both prevailing theses: capillary versus centralized power, Foucault versus Weber. Moreover, the distinction between margin and center is also faulty. "Margin to center, or center to margin, each assumes that center and margin are places from which one moves, one way or another. What if they are not? What if center and margin are the axes along which power constantly travels?" (Alford, 2000: 126).

Testing that phenomenon, Alford outlines his fieldwork, which he conducted inside a maximum security prison consisting of a series of tunnels (Patuxent Institution, Maryland). There, he observed: "All life is underground. So is power. . . . The real power is exerted underground, in and through the tunnels that connect buildings, making it unnecessary for guard or prisoner to set foot on the surface of the earth" (2000: 130). Alford theorizes that prisons represent not power originating at the margins, but "power that has been moved to the margins from the center, while losing none of its centrality" (2000:139). For instance, relocating a public execution to the prison basement is not a refinement of power; rather, it is a veiling of it. And it is the veil that best exemplifies modern power. The veil not only intensifies reality but also conceals it. Alford does not refute Foucault together. Instead, he simply explains that capillary power moves in both directions and that, consistent with the curve of civilization, brutality and tyranny are displaced to the margins of society, where their inhumanity is less visible (see also Elias, 2005):

> Power has not therefore become more subtle. Power has just gone underground, like the tunnels at Patuxent prison. The ruler still rules, he rules underground. This means that he is able to emerge anywhere in an instant, but generally does not have to, precisely because we know he is there. This is not the same thing as internalizing the gaze, but more like swallowing the sword. (Alford, 2000: 140)

Even Foucault recognized the tyranny of incarceration, embarking on an inquiry to expose the horrific conditions inside French prisons, where men were literally chained in their cells. Foucault and his colleagues were less intent on challenging the tyranny of the panopticon and more committed to uncovering the tyranny of the dungeon (Groupe d'Information sur les Prisons, 1971; see also Welch 2011b, 2010b). Alford reiterates that it is important to realize that power is on the move and that its pathway is the axis connecting the center and margin. For him the tunnel is a better metaphor than the gaze. Alford emphasizes that disciplinary power is very real and very significant, especially since it is attached to political power— "the power to rule. This too is what the tunnels represent" (Alford, 2000: 142).

Throughout the southern cone of Latin America during its dictatorships, kidnappings in broad daylight served as brazen spectacles to inject fear into the civilian population. Still, most human rights atrocities occurred out of public view: victims vanished into clandestine detention, torture, and extermination centers. Notions of underground power are particularly relevant. Recall that the basement at ESMA was reserved for torture sessions in tiny rooms arranged down a corridor that perpetrators named the "Avenue of Happiness." In *The Condor Years*, Dinges describes "El Sepulcro de los Vivas"—the "tomb of the living"—in Asunción just a few blocks from the Paraguayan Parliament. That prison was *ruled* by Pastor Coronel, who took great pride in administering ruthless—medieval—torture techniques:

> The fifteen or so prison cells were to the rear, in what once had been a separate building crudely joined to the headquarters building by narrow doors carved out of walls and ramps bridging the differences in floor elevations. The prison space had a bizarre, disorienting effect. Walls stopped short of the ceiling, columns left over from some previous construction supported nothing. Stairways dead-ended in brick wall. There were no windows to the outside. Cell doors were covered with sheets of iron with a small slit as the only opening. There was only one bathroom, on the ground floor, but prisoners were not allowed to use it. Instead each cell had a large tin can. (Dinges, 2004: 96)

Dinges (2004) reaffirms previously noted aspects of torture in Paraguay under the Stroessner regime, calling them routine but hardly scientific. Coronel fashioned a crude whip—a *tejuruguái*—consisting of heavy cable wrapped in leather. Cast-iron shackles, leg irons, and various other devices immobilized prisoners. While those methods "had changed little since the dungeons of the Dark Ages in Europe," interrogators also modernized their sessions with electric shock (Dinges, 2004: 96–97).

Also in Buenos Aires, the former detention center that served as a transit hub for those abducted in Operation Condor, Automotores Orletti, is identified by a large sign at the entrance: "Here Crimes against Humanity were committed during State Terrorism." Its profane past is palpable. The "dungeon"—or "central cave"—is located upstairs, accessed through a series of winding staircases ("Automotores Orletti," n.d.). Upon entering the torture chambers, the tour guide instructs visitors not to photograph certain rooms, including a shadowy space fitted with a metal hook once used to hoist victims for physical abuse. In one such incident, a detainee "was hung from a hook over a tub of filthy water and repeatedly lowered into it. He appeared to have lost his mind from torture, raving in delirious manner" (McSherry, 2005: 115). Victims reported being injected with drugs and subjected to rape and sexual sadism (see Dinges, 2004; Feitlowitz, 1998). As a place of memory, the curators rely on storyboards to narrate the testimony of survivors. The exhibit recognizes the duality of injustice vis-à-vis justice by also posting mugshots of perpetrators who were tried and sentenced to prison.

In Santiago, 38 Londres remains a riveting place. The elegant townhouse situated in a now posh *barrio* keeps its large double doors open during the day, catching the eye of passersby as they stroll down the pedestrianized street. Upon reading the large posters at the entrance, many visitors somewhat reluctantly step into the former detention and torture center. Inside, curious visitors are navigated by diagrams showing the floor plan and how the space was used by intelligence

FIGURE 20. "This Brit." At the Irish Republican History Museum (Belfast), a poster from the period of the Troubles is a reminder of how much suspicion pervaded certain communities. © retrowelch 2022.

agents. One such drawing identifies the bathroom that interrogators repurposed for torture. In the evening when 38 Londres closes, so too do its double doors. Spray painted on the door panel is this grim message: "Aqui Torturaron A Mi Hijo" ("Here They Tortured My Son").

CONCLUSION

Adding some weight to Alford's (2000) theory that power has the capacity to move along underground axes, Palloy's plans to demolish the Bastille "were expedited by the anxiety among the electors that royal troops might retake the citadel through underground passages that were rumored to extend all the way from the Château de Vincennes" (Schama, 1990: 411). That subterranean unease was felt by residents living near the Bastille, who often imagined hearing groans and voices emanating from deep below ground. Ex-prisoner Mirabeau returned to the Bastille to inspect the dungeons and underground vaults for signs of a labyrinthine connection with Vincennes. He found no such tunnel (Schama, 1990; see also Funk-Brentano, 1899; BnF, 2010). In Northern Ireland during the Troubles, suspicion of underground power was pervasive in cities like Belfast, where residents (correctly) believed that British agents operated undercover (see Feldman, 1990; see also Taylor, 1997, 1999, 2001). A well-circulated poster served as a cautionary tale. It shows a man divided between an army soldier with a weapon and a civilian holding a pint of beer. According to the caption, "This Brit could be standing beside you. Loose talk costs lives!" (see figure 20).

Much of this chapter has meditated on the ways in which the economy of punishment had become redistributed, particularly in the realm of techniques aimed at transforming the body. Discussion of state violence offers sobering evidence of the persistence of inhumanity. However, through Lord (2006) there is reason to appreciate "Foucault's Museum" as an institution that performs critique. In their afterlives, many former torture centers emanate a Bastille Effect by advocating human rights campaigns to hold perpetrators accountable. Past crimes, to be sure, are still being investigated. In 2019, international lawyers finally succeeded in having Mario Sandoval—who had been a professor at the Sorbonne in Paris—extradited to Buenos Aires to face prosecution for torture and crimes against humanity during the last dictatorship. "In the dungeons of the regime, Sandoval was allegedly known as 'Churrasco'—a play on words referring not only to his good looks ('churro' is Argentinian slang for handsome) but also to his alleged skill with an electric cattle prod (a 'churrasco' is a barbecued steak). Political prisoners were routinely strapped to a metal bed frame and electrocuted in the basement of infamous navy mechanics school (ESMA)" (Goñi, 2019). Under his command, many of those victims were subject to being "transferred," a cold euphemism for execution. In the next chapter, similar technologies of power are further examined, especially in light of the dictatorships that resorted to extermination in an effort to reengineer and transform society according to their vision.

10

———

Exterminate and Denial

Transform Society

Informed by cultural studies, scholars explore the meaning of the French Revolution, during which the newly minted patriots extracted from the *ancien régime* its arbitrary power while celebrating the values of the Age of Reason (Hunt, 1984; Sewell, 1996). With messianic zeal, those revolutionaries observed cult-like rituals aimed at purifying "a system of repression that had at its core the polluted symbol of the Bastille and the caprice of the king's *lettre de cachet*, which could condemn citizens to prison without due process" (Smith 2008: 121). At its disposal was the guillotine, a device that had long been used around Europe and now quickly reemerged with forceful significance in France. In the rational and egalitarian climate of the Enlightenment, the guillotine was recognized for its technological efficiency; as Foucault writes, it was a "machine for the production of rapid and discrete deaths" (1979: 15). The Reign of Terror contagiously infiltrated French society, targeting anyone suspected of being an enemy of the state. In 1793 and 1794, more than 2,700 people perished under the "blade of justice" (Conciergerie, n.d.; Schama, 1990).

The guillotine shares many properties with genocide—the deliberate extermination of a distinct class of people. The first of these is the killing of huge numbers of humans; the guillotine was known to have processed as many as 20 victims per hour. Second, both the guillotine and genocide represent a "technological solution to a cultural problem . . . a literal and metaphorical surgical intervention that could cut disease from the body politic" (Smith, 2008: 123, 126). As noted, Foucault (1979) posited that the human body is the subject of every political, economic, and penal agenda. In the thrust of the French Revolution, the body became a signifier for meditating on the profound questions facing a new society (Hunt, 1991; Outram, 1989). The bodies decapitated by the guillotine provided symbolic remnants that would prompt critical debates over notions of justice, science, and progress (Smith, 2008).

Discussed in this chapter are the ways in which genocide was implemented in the southern cone as a technology of power to clean the slate for a new vision of society. As Daniel Feierstein (2014) describes in *Genocide as Social Practice: Reorganizing Society under the Nazis and Argentina's Military Juntas*, extermination annihilates certain people as well as their culture. This destruction also reorganizes social relations, using terror as an instrument. It is important to emphasize that such atrocities are often shrouded in denial, which itself is a mechanism of power in pursuit of a transformed society (Cohen, 2001, 1995; Welch, 2003). To set the stage for critique, this chapter begins with a section on genocide aimed at the indigenous people in Argentina, or what been described as "state racism" directed at "subjects who do not belong to the new nation" (Trinchero, 2006: 122, 132). Attention then turns to matters of state terror and extermination in Chile and Paraguay.

GENOCIDE IN ARGENTINA, AND BEYOND

Narratives on genocide in Argentina run long and wide. At the Museo Etnográfico in the San Telmo section of Buenos Aires, curators assembled an exhibit titled "Challenging the Silence: Indigenous People and the Dictatorship." Visitors were reminded that 2016 marked 40 years since the last coup. A series of texts situated that dramatic shift in history in a broader context of progressive thought, emulating "Foucault's Museum" as explored in the previous chapter (see Lord, 2006). "Remembering the coup requires thinking about state violence, resistance, absences, and the demands of justice." The coup of 1976 was not the only time democracy was consumed by dictatorship; similar overthrows occurred in 1930, 1943, 1962, and 1966. However, it was the "National Reorganization Process" of 1976 that has left an indelible mark on Argentine society due to the use of genocide and state terrorism to impose sweeping political, economic, and cultural changes. Among the more than 30,000 victims were students, educators, and workers as well as union representatives who rallied against the prohibition of political parties.

The expressed goal of the exhibit "Challenging Silence" is to present the plight of the indigenous people who suffered tremendously under state terror. Enhancing that theme, commentary confronts "Two Centuries, Two Genocides." In 1979, the centennial anniversary of the "Desert Campaign"—led by Julio Argentino Roca—was celebrated by the military government with tributes and commemorative medals, stamps, and coins. The principal event was staged in the city of Neuquén, where *de facto* President Jose Videla was joined by Economy Minister José A. Martínez de Hoz and a host of ecclesiastical authorities. "In the official act the process of dispossession and indigenous killing of 1879 was presented as a 'glorious and transcendent making of all the Argentines.'" That "happy integration of a numerous mass of indigenous peoples to the national life" as characterized in similar tributes in 1979 was contested by some clergy. Monsignor Jaime de Nevares issued a statement declaring solidarity with the grief and humiliation inflicted on the Mapuches. The duality of purity and danger makes an important reappearance in the controversies surrounding the Catholic hierarchy and native people.

Museo Etnográfico, as a place of learning about Argentina's profane past, also dwells on forced disappearance. Applying a technology of power, the military targeted migrant workers for the purpose of securing economic gain for the elites. Less than two years after the 1976 coup, more than 100 indigenous laborers were kidnapped; 30 of them are still missing. Managers circulated local legends to explain those disappearances, in this way issuing cautionary tales so as to intimidate indigenous workers. "El Familiar," as one story goes, was a big black dog born from a pact between the sugar mill boss and the Devil. "It feeds from the sweat and blood of the harvesters and ensures the good harvest and profits for the employers." As resistance, indigenous people organized and lobbied for new laws to uphold their rights in the face of state repression. Many of those social movements persist today, drawing support from other progressive strands of Argentine society. At the time, however, military operatives took aim at key activists. Consider, for instance, Marina Vilte, who had trained as a teacher. As Secretary of the Provincial Teachers Association, she worked to improve the working conditions of educators. In 1975 she joined the Revolutionary Front 17 October and was arrested and detained for a month. Upon release, she resumed her activism. She was kidnapped again and remains disappeared. Such atrocities can be traced back to "the Indigenous concentration camps of the late nineteenth century aimed to discipline and 'prepare' those who were supposed to become part of 'civilization,'" as well as to send an effective "message of totalitarian discipline to society as a whole" (Delrio et al., 2010: 143).

"Challenging Silence" is very much a memory project, which raises the question: "Why should we remember them?" One reason, according to curators, is that resistance against repressors continues to fuel indigenous politics. Images of activists are found in neighborhood murals and in photographs carried in demonstrations. Moreover, testimonies in the trials—in which nearly 2,000 military officers have been charged—commemorate their contributions to progressive causes. The exhibit concludes by citing this passage: "Memory does not indicate a break but rather continuity. It does not remember the missing ones who will not return, but turns a worried gaze on those who remain and who cannot go missing again" (*Revista Puentes Editorial*, Provincial Commission for Memory, November 2015). That particular campaign for memory serves as a counterweight to what scholars recognize as invisibility and the hegemonic denial of aboriginal extinction, both of which have played a key role in the statecraft of Argentina. "Therefore, we cannot conceive of the Argentine state without the Indigenous genocide, and vice versa" (Delrio et al., 2010: 149).

The broader technologies of genocide include the separation of families, the redistribution of children, forced labor, material expropriation, and deportation.

Those atrocities are remembered at the Museo Etnográfico and are also revisited elsewhere in Buenos Aires. Museo del Holocausto spans the horrors of the Second World War while keeping an eye on Argentine culture during the same period. A tall banner sets a stark tone with a photograph of a huge Nazi rally. With swastikas in clear sight, the caption declares, "Mientras tanto . . . en Buenos Aires. Año 1937" (Meanwhile . . . in Buenos Aires, Year 1937). Original photographs of a Nazi rally are secured under protective glass. At first glance, the photographs appear to have been taken in Munich or some other German city. A subtitle indicates differently, informing visitors that particular Nazi celebration took place in Buenos Aires on May 8, 1937, at Estadio Luna Park. Curators furnish more details by pointing out that in the mid-1930s, members of the Nazi Party in Germany supported an office in Buenos Aires to maintain contact with German people in Latin America while seeking to raise funds for the fascist movement. They channeled their influence through various social and civic institutions in Buenos Aires, including German-language schools, sports clubs, and youth organizations. Through diplomatic mail, the German embassy in Buenos Aires distributed Nazi propaganda and anti-Semitic materials.

Argentina remained neutral during the Second World War. However, according to one of the many storyboards, there was strong Nazi backing within the political ranks in Buenos Aires that eventually led to the 1943 coup. Subsequently, an escape route for Nazis into Buenos Aires, organized in Rome, was directed by Bishop Alois Hudal. That "ruta de las ratas" ("rat line") was already operating when Juan Domingo Perón took power in 1946. Argentina under Perón continued to authorize their entry so as to attract qualified scientists and engineers—not unlike the US, which also hoped to benefit from their technical expertise. Between 1947 and 1952, many of those fleeing Germany for Argentina were war criminals wanted by the Nuremburg tribunals. Upon arrival they were shielded by the Peronist government and the hierarchy of the Catholic Church and were gradually incorporated into the state. They settled in certain areas that had large German immigrant populations, such as San Carlos de Bariloche, La Cumbrecita, Villa General Belgrano, and the north of Buenos Aires (see Goñi, 2003; Sands, 2021).

The Museo del Holocausto acknowledges the inherent tension in postwar Argentina by juxtaposing the desperation of refugees—most notably Jewish people as well as survivors of the Holocaust—alongside the many war criminals who were allowed to live and move freely in Buenos Aires and the rest of Argentina. Among the former members of the Hitler regime who came to Argentina and who are included in the exhibit are the Nazi doctor Joseph Mengele, "the Angel of Death," and Eduard Roschman, "the Butcher of Riga," who entered Argentina in 1949 and 1948 respectively. The focus then shifts to Adolf Eichmann, who arrived in Buenos Aires in 1950. Eichmann is described as having been in charge of "Jewish Affairs" for the Nazi state and as responsible for the mass deportation of Jews to "the concentration and extermination camps." In 1960, Eichmann was captured in his home; the following year, at a historic trial in Jerusalem, he was convicted of crimes against humanity (see Arendt, [1963]1994).

The exhibit does not spare visitors jarring images of genocide, or "the Final Solution." The curators document a range of profane acts, including mass graves, corpses being pushed into industrial ovens, and gruesome medical experiments carried out on starved prisoners, including children. Altogether, these photographs capture a repulsive panorama of extermination. Still, the emotive messaging is coupled with more didactic lessons. One panel simply states, "Don't forget so that it is not repeated." The irony here is that in fact, extermination did once again occur, this time in Argentina (see Crenzel, 2019; Feierstein, 2006). In the following sections, other memorial sites such as ESMA offer further condemnation of genocide as well as state terror in tandem with state denial.

PUTTING DEATH INTO MOTION

Touring ESMA's memorial space, visitors are provided details that contextualize the last dictatorship, its genocidal tendencies, and the sweeping campaign to transform Argentine society. Themes of danger and purity, as cultural binaries, are profoundly evident. "As from the 1930s, authoritarian, catholic and nationalist ideas had a great impact on Argentine military training, together with Nazi and Fascist ideologies and a growing feeling of anti-Semitism and anti-Communism. The military considered themselves the moral reservoir of the Nation." That self-assigned sense of duty prompted the junta to defend its "free" and "Christian" world against the threat of "subversive" elements (see Der Ghougassian and Brumat, 2018; Robben, 2012).

ESMA provided the leaders of the last dictatorship with a clandestine space where they could carry out genocide in secrecy. Those secret tasks were planned in an area within the Casino called El Dorado. Hidden in the *back stage* of the "dirty war," that ceremonial room served as an intelligence hub. Today, El Dorado occupies a *front stage* and is one of the many performative spaces at ESMA that rely on a sense of temporality to bring the record of past atrocities into the present. In that place, curators provide more excerpts from survivors' testimonies to narrate the now-exposed "theatre of operation" (see D. Taylor, 1997). The Tasks Group was established to impose "its own war doctrine in which the main idea was to exterminate popular activists. . . . Its efficiency in operating is clearly shown in the results obtained; within a year 2,000 Argentine citizens were captured (from March 1976 to March 1977). The number increased to 4,750 by the month March 1978" (Milia, Marti, and Osatinsky, 1979, 1980; see CONADEP, 1986).

As the inner sanctum of the "dirty war," El Dorado set in motion dark, strategic, and inside secrets. In that very room, intelligence officers decided who was to be abducted, and upon their capture, they were brought to basement of the Casino. There detainees were tortured by interrogators, who demanded the names of other civilians. Once those targets were located, military "gangs" carried out more kidnappings, in this way fueling the repressive cycle. While the detainees were being held in the upper floors of the Casino, their fate was being decided by military leaders operating downstairs in El Dorado. To maintain its dark secrets—and later as a mechanism of denial—the military would destroy much of the evidence with a paper shredder known as the "crocodile." Since former officers refuse to divulge information, prosecutors rely heavily on the testimony of detainees who worked in ESMA. Survivor Lidia Cristina Vieyra (2010) testified that officers in El Dorado determined "who was going to live or die. . . . Every Wednesday there were transfers." Such God-like power was pervasive during the last dictatorship (see Actis et al., 2006; CONADEP, 1986).

As noted earlier, the basement of ESMA was given the seemingly mundane name "Sector 4." Yet it was very much a place of profane and calculated violence. A poster explains that "the main method of extermination consisted in throwing prisoners to the ocean, or La Plata river, alive and anesthetized. That technique was later known as the *flights of death.*" Putting death into motion, prisoners were subjected to the following ritual:

> At about 5pm, in "Capucha" (The Hood), the sub officers started to call the detained people by their numbers. They were made to stand in a straight line, held one another at their shoulders, in hoods and shackles at their feet. In those conditions, from the third floor they went down through the stairs in the whole building. In the Basement, a nurse gave them an injection of Pentothal, a drug that the repressors called 'pentonaval' [as an inside joke about the navy]. The sedative made them unconscious but it did not kill them. Under those conditions they were taken through a lateral door, taken into a truck waiting outside in the parking lot and drove to the Airport or military airports.

The military blatantly denied that it used death flights. In one remarkable disclosure in 1995, however, ex-Captain Adolfo Scilingo publicly confessed to participating in two death flights. In one mission, he pushed thirty naked, drugged victims out of an airplane into the Atlantic Ocean. Scilingo was sentenced to more than 1,000 years in prison (Verbitsky, 1996; see also Feitlowitz, 1998).

The "transfers" and death flights were premeditated murder; they were also a means to conceal extermination. The death flights were finally exposed when corpses began washing ashore on the beaches of neighboring Uruguay. Survivor Susana Burgos (1984) recalls a conversation she had with Lieutenant Aztiz (the "Blond Angel of Death"). Sharing a strategic secret, Aztiz told her, "The sea helps us. You may know the river has given the bodies back, so we thought about the Argentine Sea. We throw them from planes, the sea is blessed, from that height the sea is not soft it turns into a steel plate, that is why they break their necks, but in case they do not die, the whales do their job. We throw them asleep, of course" (Graziano, 1992). Argentine writer Rodolfo Walsh (1977) openly condemned the dictatorship's efforts to eradicate a segment of the population and "carpet the River

Plate with dead bodies" as having the "systematic character of extermination." Walsh added that the "mutilated bodies afloat in the Uruguay shores" included a 15-year-old boy, Floreal Avellaneda, whose autopsy revealed "injuries in the anal area and visible broken bones."

CHILDREN BORN IN CAPTIVITY

In 1976, in the wake of the military coup, ESMA transitioned from primarily a training academy to a "clandestine detention center of torture and extermination." The military now transformed the entire compound in order to conceal its activities. The garage, for example, was used to disguise cars that the junta had stolen from detainees by repainting them and changing their license plates. The printing house produced forged documents, such as falsified deeds for homes seized from the abducted. Even more horrific was the abduction of children born into captivity at ESMA. On the infirmary staff were doctors who would deliver the babies of tortured detainees; those infants were given to military families and their mothers were exterminated.

Recall Nora's (2002) remarks on the "upsurge of memory" that challenges the "official" stories of history, pursues the recovery of aspects of the past that have been confiscated, and stresses the importance of heritage, which individuals seek as they learn more about their own identity. Those concerns are evident in the fate of pregnant detainees and their children. That controversy has produced many roles in the resistance against the last dictatorship, but one group stands out, namely the Grandmothers of Plaza de Mayo (Asociación Civil Abuelas de Plaza de Mayo). The Grandmothers remain committed to identifying the "stolen" babies whose mothers were disappeared by the junta. It is estimated that more than 500 babies were born in detention and then "adopted" by military families (see Park, 2014). In memory of the pregnant women—and their infants—detained at ESMA, a series of exhibits inform visitors of that tragic chapter in Argentine history. In the attic of the Casino, a dimly lit message is written on the floor of an empty room: "Como era possible que en este lugar nacieran chicos?" (How is it possible for children to be born in this place?). Visitors tend to stare motionless into the void, and some of them openly weep.

Curators reveal the details of these systematic abductions—*confiscationes*—of children while keeping the emphasis on memory. Lila Pastoriza (abducted from June 15, 1977, to October 25, 1978) testified at the ESMA Trial in 2010: "I asked [Officer] D'Imperio how it was possible that children were born in that place, in that place where people were tortured and he said: 'Look the children are innocent, they are not to blame for having terrorist parents, that is why we give them to families that are going to educate them differently out of the terrorist world'" (ESMA Trial Testimony Case, 1270, July 8, 2010). Being pregnant did not prevent detainees from being tortured, abused, and subjected to inhuman conditions of confinement at ESMA. A few days after giving birth, the mothers were murdered. However, before her death, the mother would be told that her baby would be given to her own family, and she would be instructed to prepare a letter with the child's information. The text of one such letter has been posted in the area where an estimated 30 children were born:

> Dear Mum. Today you have news from me after such a long time. I'm so sorry for not having written before but I wasn't able to do so as I was abroad working. This is my baby boy. His name is Sebastian. He was born in a clinic in Buenos Aires. . . . I am in perfect shape, the person carrying the baby is a friend of mine, and he is doing me a favor as I can't do it myself at the moment. I want you to be calm as I'm all right and I will contact you again soon. . . . Paty.

In most instances, the letter was destroyed and the infant was given to an unrelated family. Through the tireless efforts of the Grandmothers of Plaza de Mayo, more than 100 of those children, as adults, have been identified and reunited with their biological families. The former dictator General Jorge Videla was convicted and sentenced to a 50-year prison term for his involvement in the unlawful adoptions. So that visitors will not forget those merciless acts, ESMA displays a list of doctors who participated in the birth scheme. The military and the medical staff referred to the child abduction process as "a well-oiled machine" (Feitlowitz, 1998; see *The Official Story*, 1985).

Since visitors actually enter the very space where these atrocities occurred, sitedness—the power of place—is established to promote its memory project. At several points, signs are posted to remind visitors that "here, a crime against humanity was perpetrated." The legacy of the "dirty war" pervades Argentine culture as well as thinking about the past. However, rather than positioning the sacred against the profane, the narrative situates one profane against another. Here enters Teoria de los Dos Demonios (Two Demons Theory), which sets out to explain—and excuse—political violence during the last dictatorship. In brief, it suggests that the junta was responding to guerrilla factions that had taken aim at the government. The military and the armed resistance fought a war that engulfed the rest of civil society (Familiares, 2006). Some of the political prisoners were also members of revolutionary groups; thus, they were labeled as terrorists. The military justified its violent methods by claiming to be the "lesser evil."

As a deeply entrenched form of denial, Two Demons Theory supposedly safeguarded the "civil society's endorsement of the genocide" (Trinchero, 2006: 123; see Perelli, 1994):

> To clarify, the Two Demons Theory did acknowledge that victims existed but only a certain type of victim. According to this theory, the main group of victims was the general public—the citizens who were caught between the military and guerrilla violence and were silent either by fear or by choice. Those who disappeared were reimagined as innocent youths, and they were also considered victims. (Park, 2014: 26)

In many of the trials of former military officers, prosecutors focused on victims who had no political affiliation. The Two Demons Theory continues to be evoked in proposals for amnesty and eligibility for early release. Outside ESMA's gates, banners condemn those forms of impunity. Most recognizable is the catchphrase "No Al 2 × 1" ("No To The 2 for 1"), which challenges proposals that convicted officers be able to earn two years of "good time" for every year served in prison. That particular controversy continues to resonate in Argentine culture as an ongoing push and pull between justice and injustice.

MIENTRAS TANTO . . . EN SANTIAGO, AÑO 1973

Meanwhile in Santiago, the events surrounding September 11, 1973, inflicted enduring anguish on the country and its people. The bloodshed directed by General Pinochet was so rampant that the CIA's own sources struggled to keep track of the casualties. By the end of Pinochet's 17-year reign, more than 3,000 Chilean citizens had been eliminated through state-sponsored terror (Rettig Commission Report, 1993). Under the dictatorship, all threats to its authority were swiftly eradicated. Thousands of civilians were subjected to the brutal technologies of power, including mass detention, torture, and assassination. Civil society was immediately transformed: the junta suspended political parties, shut down Congress, took over universities, and imposed tight control over the media. On October 12, 1973, a diplomatic cable from US Ambassador Nathaniel Davis discussed his private meeting with Pinochet, who was soliciting economic and military assistance. When Davis expressed concerns about human rights atrocities, Pinochet replied that he would do his "best to prevent violations and loss of life" (Kornbluh, 2013: 163).

Apparently, the dictator was merely posturing. Three days later, Pinochet launched the Caravana de la Muerte (Caravan of Death). General Sergio Arellano Stark, a coup leader, was dispatched to exact revenge on political prisoners. For four days, Stark and his death squad of elite officers traveled by Puma helicopter to key provincial regions. At each stop along the way, Stark would enter a detention center, identify prisoners—most of whom had surrendered upon an official arrest warrant—then summarily torture, bayonet, and execute them. In an interview years later, General Joaquin Lagos Osorio said that Arellano had shown him paperwork in 1973 documenting his authority as Pinochet's official delegate and his order to "review and accelerate" the judicial process. Lagos offered a graphic account of their actions:

> They cut eyes out with daggers. They broke their jaws and legs, Lagos said, adding that firing squads were used to inflict maximum pain instead of instant death. They shot them to pieces, first the legs, then the sexual organs, then the heart, all with machine guns. . . . They were no longer human bodies. I wanted to at least put the bodies back together again, to leave them more decent, but you couldn't. (Bernstein, 2016; see Ewel, 2018)

The Caravan of Death would leave a trail of 68 victims. US intelligence officers were aware of the massacres but reported them in vague terms, even characterizing the victims as extreme leftists. In fact, most of those killed were upstanding civil leaders and well-respected members of their communities, among them municipal leaders, lawyers, professors, and prominent union representatives (Spooner, 1999; Verdugo, 2001).

In 1998, 25 years after the coup, Pinochet was arrested in London, where he would remain in detention for 504 days while legal proceedings weighed the crimes of his dictatorship, including the Caravan of Death. The case against Pinochet had implications for the entire world as well as in Chile, where citizens underwent an "irruption of memory" (Wilde, 1999: 473). In 2000, Pinochet returned to face more than 70 judicial cases. Just 72 hours after Pinochet's plane landed in Santiago, Judge Juan Guzmán filed a motion to have Pinochet's immunity lifted so that he could prosecuted for his role in the Caravan of Death. On December 1 (2000), Guzmán indicted Pinochet as "the intellectual author of the Caravan of Death" (Kornbluh, 2013: 477). Pinochet was placed under house arrest and interrogated by investigators. On December 10, 2006, Pinochet died before any trials could take place. While Pinochet had his share of mourners, crowds of detractors celebrated in the streets of Santiago. Observers noted that—ironically—he had died on International Human Rights Day. "The criminal has departed without ever being sentenced for all the acts he was responsible for during his dictatorship," said Hugo Gutierrez, a lawyer who had represented many victims (*Guelph Mercury*, 2006). President Michelle Bachelet, herself a victim of Pinochet, refused to provide a state funeral: "It would embarrass Chile's conscience to honor somebody who was involved not only in human rights issues but even in misappropriation of public funds" (Agence France-Press, December 11, 2006).

With strange fanfare, however, the Chilean Military School sponsored Pinochet's funeral, becoming a "national spectacle. . . . The ceremony attracted thousands of supporters, several of whom were caught on camera giving the Nazi salute to the deceased ex-dictator" (Kornbluh, 2013: 496). The event was another exercise in collective denial: Pinochet's grandson, Augusto III, delivered a eulogy lauding his grandfather as a hero who had defeated Marxism. Augusto III also chastised the judges for prosecuting the cases against Pinochet. For breaching the government-imposed protocol for the funeral, Augusto III was dismissed from the military (Agence France-Press, December 13, 2006; Associated Press, 2006). As evidence of an emerging "Pinochet Effect" by which perpetrators would ultimately face justice, other military leaders with links to the Caravan of Death were tried and convicted (Roht-Arriaza, 2005). For their roles, General Manuel Contreras received a seven-year prison sentence and Colonel Pedro Espinoza, six years. The Chilean Supreme Court ruled that General Arellano should serve six years in prison, but the sentence was suspended due to his rapidly deteriorating mental health (Bernstein, 2016).

In Santiago, memories of state terror continue to resonate at various sites. Recall Casa de José Domingo Cañas, a memorial on the demolished property of a former detention/torture center, where many narratives are delivered on human rights violations committed by the Pinochet regime (Arenas Uriarte, 2016). The most conspicuous atrocity is the pre-Condor—cross-border—mission called Operation Colombo, which today is signaled throughout the city with the foreboding number 119. In 1975, DINA disappeared at least 119 Chileans who had been labeled "subversives." The operation was followed by a classic example of "black propaganda" as publications (funded by the CIA) released stories reporting that the 119 Chileans had been killed in the course of guerrilla activities in Argentina or during fighting between leftist factions. Photographs showed dead bodies recovered in Argentina, many of which had been mutilated to conceal their identity. As Dinges explains in *The Condor Years:* "The ID cards with the bodies were Chilean, but the bodies were not. They belonged to Argentine victims of the AAA death squads" (2004: 235–36). At Casa de José Domingo Cañas, a well-known reminder speaks to those murders in the form of a newspaper headline "Exterminados Como Ratones" ("Exterminated Like Mice"). Alongside a black and red banner with the number 119, pictures of the Chilean victims are memorialized on small pedestals surrounded by objects re-collected from the ruins of the Casa. The commemorative space is supported by a collective that animates memory through political—at times combative—activism, a move that is in sharp contrast to the "museological" approach at Villa Grimaldi (Collins and Hite, 2013).

The Caravan of Death, Operation Colombo, and other crimes of the Chilean dictatorship reactivate a profound consciousness each September 11, the date of the coup. In 2017, on "Once de Septiembre"—as the day is known locally—groups of demonstrators make their way through downtown Santiago to remember the loss of life in 1973. In front of La Moneda, the presidential palace where President Salvatore Allende committed suicide amid air raids, several young adults gather. There they protest in silence, wearing large white paper hats to make them appear as mice. To underscore the meaning of their performance, they conspicuously hold up newspapers bearing the infamous headline "Exterminados Como Ratones" ("Exterminated Like Mice") (see figure 21).

FROM "PARAISO" TO VALPARAISO

At other sites in Santiago, crimes of the dictatorship have entered the collective consciousness. Most notable is Villa Grimaldi, which in its previous incarnation was a popular restaurant known as "Paraíso" ("Paradise"). In a sharp turn for the worse, from 1974 to 1978, it served as a secret "Center of Abduction, Torture and Extermination." Operating under the code name "Cuartel Terranova," DINA agents tortured more than 4,500 political prisoners. As many as 229 of them were executed on the premises, which were was later demolished to conceal criminal evidence. As noted earlier, the villa was transformed into a solemn peace park

FIGURE 21. "Exterminated Like Mice." In Santiago, on September 11, 2017, protesters gathered in front La Moneda, where they dressed as mice and held newspapers with the headline "Exterminados Como Ratones" ("Exterminated Like Mice") in reference to Operation Colombo. © retrowelch 2022.

in 2004. Narratives about its cruel past, however, remain. The use of conceptual art adds elements of mystique. On the edge of the property is a large cube tilted in a manner that seems to defy gravity. It is a monument to the victims of Operation Puerto Montt (1974–78). Information posted next to the cube explains that prisoners were taken from secret torture centers, such as Villa Grimaldi, José Domingo Cañas, and 38 Londres, then transferred to other locations where they were injected with substances that numbed (or killed) them. Their limp bodies were secured to pieces of metal railing so as to add weight. They were then loaded onto a Puma helicopter that flew along the coast until all of the victims had been pushed out into the sea. Eventually some bodies began to float and wash up on the beach. Investigators discovered pieces of rusty metal that had been used during the operation. The installation was conceived as a "silent witness of horror," with the cube representing a container that had lost "historical stability." A short footbridge invites visitors to enter the cube and view remnants of the rails recovered from the ocean floor.

The various spaces within Villa Grimaldi consist of reconstructed prison cells, memorial gardens, and scholarly poster boards. Altogether, they point to a Bastille Effect by a stating its mission: "For a culture of human rights: Fighting against oblivion in Villa Grimaldi." In its afterlife, that place of memory insists that "Nadie esta olvidado" ("Nobody is forgotten"). A timeline chronicles the transformation of the site into a memorial space. The last entry is for October 14, 2006. On that date President Michelle Bachelet visited Villa Grimaldi, "and she is the only President of Democratic Chile to do so." When Pinochet seized power, Bachelet's father Alberto—who headed the Food Distribution Office under Allende—was detained for treason. After months of torture, he died in custody in 1974. The following year, Michelle and her mother were confined to Villa Grimaldi, where they too were subjected to abuse and torture. In 2013, Bachelet disclosed that while she was held at Grimaldi, she was personally interrogated by Manuel Contreras, the head of DINA. Bachelet went on to serve two terms as President of Chile (2006–10, 2014–18). In 2018, she was named the UN High Commissioner for Human Rights (Cea, 2013; see also Collins, Hite, and Joignant, 2013).

Elsewhere in Chile, political imprisonment under the dictatorship is cast into memory. Consider, for instance, the city of Valparaíso ("Vale of Paradise"), birthplace of both Allende and Pinochet. There, the former prison Cerro Carcel contains historical fragments of state repression. Tucked into a hillside, surrounded by rugged working-class neighborhoods, Cerro Carcel is decidedly part of the community. Officially named Parque Cultural de Valparaíso, the memorial space functions as an elaborate visual and performing arts center offering a busy schedule of theatre, dance, exhibitions, and lectures. On one of the interior walls of the ex-prison, former political prisoners are commemorated in large high-resolution portraits. Down the hill, in the city center, a modern monument remembers the disappeared by listing the local victims by name and the dates they went missing or were executed by the military.

FIGURE 22. "The Selk'nam." On a street in Valparaiso, an artist tells the story of the Selk'nam people who were subjected to genocide by European settlers in the 19th century. © retrowelch 2022.

Valparaíso—or just Valpo—is synonymous with public art: murals and political
graffiti saturate the urban landscape, attracting tourists from all over the world.
Some of the messages deliver historical and cultural lessons about the territory
and its people. One series of brightly colored paintings tells the story of the "The
Selk'nam (or Ona)" people, who

were a nomadic tribe, indigenous to the Tierra del Fuego region of southern Chile and Argentina. They believed that in the time of the ancestors all things walked as people: the Sun, Moon Mountains, everything. With the arrival of the Europeans in the late 19th century, the Selk'nam were hunted and murdered to rid them from the land, which the Chilean government was parceling out to Europeans. Chile paid a bounty for each carcass, as given proof of delivering an ear. After 10,000 years in Patagonia, their genocide took less than thirty. They are now considered extinct—Hailey Gaiser [artist], 2017. (See figure 22)

On the other side of the city, in 2017, the Museo de Bellas Artes (Museum of Fine Arts) sponsored an exhibit on the Selk'nam. Of particular interest, the gallery displayed photographs by Martin Gusinde (2015), who conducted anthropological research with the indigenous people of Tierra del Fuego in southern Chile. In the early 20th century, Gusinde, an ordained minister from Austria, immersed himself in the tribe for 22 months and was allowed to participate in initiation rites. He also recorded songs and chants, which have been archived at the Martin Gusinde Anthropological Museum in Puerto Williams, on Navarino Island south of Tierra del Fuego (see Chapman, 1982). Other artistic and scholarly critique on colonial power as it intersects indigenous people is displayed in other cities in the southern cone of Latin America, including Asunción (Paraguay).

LEGACY OF COLONIAL POWER IN PARAGUAY

In the foyer of the Archives of Terror in Asunción, an elaborate display on the rise of colonial power in Paraguay throws critical light onto an apparatus of abuse inflicted on the indigenous people. The first in a series of panels containing images and text informs visitors that initially the Spanish were friendly with the Indians. However, those relations eroded as the Indians—in particular the Guaraní—were treated as "vassal servants," which drove a wedge between the two cultural groups. That tension had already been instilled by a feudal system of economic exploitation. Over time, customary tribal sanctions intended to maintain community cohesion were replaced by more monarchical-based penalties. Illustrations of corporal punishments and medieval executions demonstrate a turn toward European punishments, such as breaking on the wheel, stocks and pillories, and a primitive guillotine. Guaraní society was also injected with elements of the Inquisition. Colonizers tortured Indians for "crimes against faith," thus blurring the lines between the sacred and the profane as well as danger and purity. Even in the face of a reformed "Justicia Colonial," provisions to protect the indigenous people often went unfulfilled.

As a place of learning, the exhibit leaps ahead to the Stroessner dictatorship (1954–89). The regime launched a fierce anti-communist campaign and imposed repression on vast sectors of Paraguayans. Photographs of police beating members of a small crowd in broad daylight confirm a collective fear. Mass detentions, torture, and disappearances were directed at workers, farmhands, and students. More images of the detention cells, currently open to the public at the Memorial Museum, remind visitors of the brutalization of civilians through the use of electric shock and *la pileta* (the filthy bathtub used for mock drowning). "Campos de Concentración" have an appalling history in Paraguay; compounding matters, Stroessner also displaced people to remote areas of the country. The text of the exhibit is punctuated with padlocks, creating a visceral effect of a country under lockdown. In the early 1990s, the transition to democracy embraced the rule of law, especially the rights of women, children, and indigenous people. The final installment of the display turns special attention to the lifting of impunity for crimes against humanity and genocide. Much like the critique of "Foucault's Museum," which promotes a progressive commentary on human rights, the presentation concludes with an optimistic tone by depicting justice as a force that prevails over injustice.

With respect to contemporary attacks on the indigenous communities, however, the exhibit provides few details. Filling that void, international activists have exposed compelling evidence of extermination. In 1973, Mark Munzel released findings in a document titled *The Ache Indians: Genocide in Paraguay*. The report concludes that the UN Charter of Human Rights had been denied to the Ache Indians, "not through indifference or neglect, but by a deliberate Government policy of genocide disguised as benevolence" (1973: 5). The study goes on to contextualize the war against the Ache as an extension of colonial rule that served to conquer new territories and capture indigenous people for cheap as well as slave labor. Massacres, manhunts, and other forms of calculated violence contributed to what J. A. Borgognon, a member of the armed forces and at the time Vice Director of the Native Affairs Department in the Ministry of Defense, described as a tribe "close to extinction" (1968: 360). The methodical extermination involved the hunting and selling of Indian children, often to sex traffickers (Cadogan, 1967). The separation of families has been justified by the dubious claim that the children would be better cared for by non-Indian parents. That convenience of denial is "a remarkable example of the colonial mentality still rampant among some Paraguayans, who always suppose that Ache parents are unable to give their children a decent education" (Munzel, 1973: 15; see also Barros, Campos, and Griffin, 2018; Costa, 2019b).

Activist clergy, however, resisted the regime and its abuse of the Ache people. Father Bartomeu Meliá, an anthropologist and linguist, devoted his work to the indigenous people and in 1976 was deported from Paraguay by Stroessner. Meliá, who died in 2019, recalled being in his bathroom when police entered his home; at gunpoint, he was ordered to leave the country immediately. Meliá was targeted for his condemnation of the dictatorship's systematic massacres of the Ache carried out by soldiers and mercenaries, who also kidnapped children and enslaved them as servants. His criticism gained international recognition, prompting US President Jimmy Carter to demand that the Paraguayan government investigate incidents of genocide. "The military regime's response was to deny everything and expel the complainants" (Carneri, 2019; see also Harder Horst, 2007). Formal charges of genocide have been lodged, but judicial bodies have deflected them by insisting that proof requiring "specific intent" is lacking. Nevertheless, the Inter-American Human Rights Commission has issued concerns that grave abuses against the indigenous people were committed by the Stroessner government (Cooper, 2008; Quigley, 2006).

Collective memory—and denial—in Paraguay is further complicated by Stroessner's eagerness to harbor Nazis fleeing Germany to avoid being prosecuted for genocide and crimes against humanity. Without characterizing the entire German immigrant community as supporting fascism, it should be noted the first Nazi party outside of Germany was established in Paraguay in the 1930s. During the Second World War, Paraguay maintained political distance from Germany; in 1945, it declared war on Germany, albeit just three months before its defeat. When Stroessner, of German descent, assumed power, he implemented an authoritarian style reminiscent of the Nazis. Much like Perón in Argentina, Stroessner opened the "rat lines" for Nazi fugitives, so that his country became known as the "poor man's Nazi regime" (Cooper, 2008: 167; Sands, 2021). Among those welcomed to Paraguay were Joseph Mengele (who naturalized as a Paraguayan citizen), Marko Colak, Erwin Fleiss, Ante Pavelić, and Edward Roschmann (Goñi, 2003, Steinacher, 2012). In reference to Nazi collaborators living with impunity during the Cold War, Dasa Drndic writes: "Wars are an orgy of forgetting" (2019: 22).

CONCLUSION

Returning to the cultural meaning of the guillotine, it is important to note just how deeply mythologized that form of execution really was. Smith (2008) captures that significance by theorizing about the symbolism of death as it relates to complex imaginaries of the body, pollution, and salvation (see Bataille, 1991; Hertz, [1960]2009). At the time, advocates of the guillotine insisted that the instrument would accommodate the 1791 penal code requiring executions to be carried out without pain inflicted on the body. Dr. Guillotine, whose name is synonymous with the device, famously declared to the National Assembly, "With my machine I'll cut off your head in the blink of the eye, and you will feel nothing but a slight coolness on the back of the neck" (1790: 278). Such pronouncements added to a broader legitimacy of the machine; they also channeled currents of meaning and utopian narratives, thus paving the way for an emergent ideology of a new political order (see Alexander, 2005). Correspondingly, the guillotine provided a ritual extervention on the body that carried magical properties and inspired awe (Turner, 1977; Smith, 2008). Still, opposition to Dr. Guillotine's argument mounted as counterclaims proposed that the device did not deliver instantaneous death; rather, it caused moments of intense pain. The procedure, therefore, breeched revolutionary penal policy and the humanistic values of the Enlightenment. In the end, the mutilated body signified pollution that impeded civilization and progress, casting a gothic shadow over modernity (Hurley, 1996).

Smith suggests that the guillotine stands as strategic research site for exploring the cultural ramifications of penal technologies; in the same vein, a critique of extermination provides opportunities for careful circumspection of the duality between purity and danger. Recall the pretentious claims of the Argentine generals who hailed the death flights as a divinely ordained ritual. Those pronouncements went well beyond blatant denial. From the standpoint of the junta, such euphemisms spoke to a presumably higher purpose of extermination – that it was an attempt to purify a Western and Christian civilization by eradicating "subversive" elements. To the contrary, the "dirty wars" in Argentina and elsewhere in the southern cone have inflicted sustained harm on society, leaving its people—and indigenous communities—in a state of grief. As Trinchero observes: "Native peoples have internalized the memory of war in their consciousness as a state policy against them" (2006: 133). Of course, confronting denial remains a key strategy of human rights activism. "We must," in the words of Stan Cohen, "make it difficult for people to say that they 'don't know'" (2001: 11). The National Institute against Discrimination condemns expressions of denial or minimization of the Holocaust, the Armenian genocide, and the genocide by Argentina's last dictatorship. Conspicuously absent from that proclamation is any mention of the indigenous people of the southern cone (Delrio et al. 2010; see also Sozzo, 2016; Zysman, 2017).

PART FIVE

Performing Memory

11

Consecrate and Desecrate

In a secluded chamber deep within the Conciergerie, in Paris, away from the heavy traffic of tourists, is a serene space called the Girondins' Chapel. Its vaulted ceilings are contoured by shafts of light entering through elevated portals. The chapel is located on the very site of the king's medieval oratory—a "place of prayer" (Conciergerie, n.d.). Its sacred ambience is maintained by honoring the 21 Girondins who feasted there prior to their execution on October 30, 1793. A large portrait of the Girondins performs memory and activates a sense of tragedy in the face of the Reign of Terror then sweeping France. The Girondins, a radical group that supported the overthrow of the monarchy but denounced the spiraling violence, were not spared that carnage. A stark painting by Julien-Leopold Boilly, titled "Banquet of the Girondins" (1847), adds historical context to the chapel. Interestingly, the event captured on canvas is remembered through the many moods of the Girondins. At the center is a small dining table at which a few Girondins are sharing a final intellectual soirée; in the background, others appear a bit more boisterous. Even with all that activity, the viewer fixes on a corpse covered in a white sheet, where only a single mourner is conveying grief. The content of the painting is explained in a caption labeled "Memory of the Girondins." It informs viewers that a few hours earlier the Revolutionary Tribunal had condemned the Girondins, including Brissot, Vergniaud, and Gensonne. "According to tradition, they gathered together on their last night for a fraternal banquet, probably in the prison chapel, while one of them, Dufriche-Valaze, lay dead after committing suicide by plunging a stiletto in his heart."

In the performance of memory, the sacred occupies a unique stage where acts of consecration ritualistically unfold, producing affirmative gestures that bond certain people together. Communal identities are thus maintained in ways that reinforce ethnic, religious, and even political heritage. The sacred, especially from a Durkheimian perspective, is a potent force that not only evokes awe but also triggers countervailing impulses that defile and pollute. Those forms of desecration are as subjective as consecration itself, contributing to cultures that are often contested (Welch, 2000). In this chapter, those polarities of remembrance are explored so as to detect symbolic harmony as well as dissonance. In an examination of collective memory in Ireland—North and South—during the Troubles, critical attention is turned to the many expressions of consecration vis-à-vis desecration. The sanctity of death and that of sacrifice are among the socio-religious concepts to be inspected, largely because they are grounded in the transformed sites of political imprisonment. Along the way, the phenomena surrounding hunger strikes are surveyed due to their cultural production of martyrdom. More abstractly, bodily sacrifice serves to mobilize the hunger striker as a mediator between the worlds of the sacred and the profane (Hubert and Mauss, [1898]1981; Smith, 2008).

Discussion of consecration and desecration extends to the southern cone of Latin America, where similar socio-religious symbolism is manifest at memorial sites in Buenos Aires, Santiago, Montevideo, and Asunción. There, technological forces are considered as they interact with the sacred and the profane. The death flights carried out by the Argentine military, for instance, demonstrate the use of technological procedures aimed at sanitizing crimes against humanity. As described in previous chapters, before being murdered, victims were ritualistically sedated so as to cleanse their unholy death and manage the pollution caused by genocide. Other insignias represent the gross desecration of victims, such as mass graves simply marked "N.N."—no names. In Santiago, certain sites and symbols remind visitors of enduring tensions in a post-dictatorship society, typically by honoring the memory of Allende while ridiculing the legacy of Pinochet. Similar performances have unfolded in Montevideo and Asunción, with special reverence for the "student martyrs" killed by police and soldiers during political protests. As noted in previous chapters, many former detention, torture, and extermination centers in the southern cone underwent purification ceremonies so that in their afterlives they could properly function as memorial sites and metaphors for human rights.

SANCTITY OF DEATH AND IRISH REPUBLICANISM

As noted earlier, memory of political imprisonment is deeply embedded in Irish history, especially during both periods of conflict known as the Troubles. Adding to the cultural landscape, narratives of those events often evoke socio-religious meaning by defining Irish Republicanism in terms of sacrifice and martyrdom. From a Durkheimian perspective, those emotive impulses activate what can be described as the sanctity of death, thus buttressing demands for proper memorialization following the tragic loss of life (Welch, 2016a). Robert Hertz, an early Durkheimian scholar, delved into that phenomenon, declaring that "death has a specific meaning for the social consciousness; it is the object of a collective representation" ([1960]2009: 28). Burial rites, to be sure, figure prominently in

Irish culture, and those rituals are powerful expressions of shared values among certain people.

Before embarking on an interpretation of the sites and symbols that project the sanctity of death, some conceptual overtures are in order. An important starting point is Emile Durkheim ([1915]2008) and the Année sociologique, an intellectual group that included the young pioneering theorists Marcel Mauss and Robert Hertz (Guyer, 2014). Together, those luminaries of the early French sociological school set out to "discover the origin of social solidarity in a modern and secular way by departing from traditional, theological explanations" (Kwon, 2014: 123; see Durkheim and Mauss, [1903]1963; Riley, 1999). Despite their shared perspectives on various socio-religious phenomena, they diverged in important ways. For instance, Durkheim focused on the creation and maintenance of social solidarity (see Smith and Alexander, 2005). By contrast, Hertz assumed "the task of studying the responses of society to breaches in that solidarity" (Hertz, [1988]1994: 18). In deciphering a Troubled Ireland, it is important to bear in mind that violations of the sanctity of death not only create resistance but also, in doing so, perpetuate conflict driven by unresolved injustices.

A promising scholar—and pupil of Durkheim—Hertz was among the casualties of the First World War. At the age of 33, he was killed leading his military unit in an attack on Marcheville. Hertz's scholarly legacy survives through the translation of *Death and the Right Hand* (1960]2009). That volume consists of two separate works. For our purposes, focus remains on the first essay, "A Contribution to the Study of the Collective Representation of Death" (1907). Hertz begins by reminding us that "we all believe we know what death is because it is a familiar event and one that arouses intense emotion" (2009: 27). Perhaps hinting at the sanctity of death, he goes on to observe that "the body of the deceased is not regarded like the carcass of some animal: specific care must be given to it and a correct burial; not merely for reasons of hygiene but out of moral obligation" (2009: 27). Toward that end, Hertz concludes that the final ceremony serves several social—and spiritual—functions. It provides a proper burial to the remains of the deceased so as to grant peace to the soul. The final ritual liberates the living from their obligations of mourning and allows them to rejoin "communion with society" (2009: 62).

Returning to the realm of a troubled Ireland, we remain mindful of the meaning of the sanctity of death along with community efforts to restore its violations. The Collins Barracks Museum in Dublin serves as a place of learning about different aspects of the Irish struggle, including hunger strikes. Curators are quick to point to a tradition of hunger striking by commemorating Thomas Ashe, who died on a hunger strike in 1917. Despite some concessions, the protests continued. In 1920, 60 Irish prisoners went on a hunger strike. That year, Terence MacSwiney died at the Brixton jail (England) after 74 days on a hunger strike, an event that attracted international attention to the plight of Irish prisoners of war. A vintage photograph documents an act of solidarity with the hunger strikers at Mountjoy prison in 1921. Among the four women protesting outside the prison gates was Charlotte Despard, a socialist, Republican activist, and suffragist. It should be noted that the Suffragettes, who themselves used hunger strikes to protest their imprisonment, inspired the Irish Republican movement to maximize that form of resistance (Grant, 2019; Murphy, 2014).

Various forms of prisoner resistance at the Maze (e.g., blanket protest, dirty protest) culminated into the 1981 hunger strike, which thrust Bobby Sands into the center of a wider narrative on martyrdom. The Irish Republican History Museum goes to great lengths to honor that sacrifice by quoting Sands: "Greater love hath no man that this, that he lay down his life for his friends" (see Sands, 1998; Beresford, 1987). A higher order of nationalism surrounds the memory of the hunger strikers. Political posters are decorated with renderings of the Irish flag alongside the list of five demands:

1) No prison uniform
2) No prison work
3) Free association
4) Visits, letters, parcels, and recreational facilities
5) Full remission

That posting pleads "Don't Let Them Die!" and features an illustration of a woman prisoner with her fist raised in defiance. Martyrdom is conveyed not only in written language but also in visual terms. Sands is often presented as a Christ-like figure: as a prisoner dying on a crucifix. Many posters blend the fine details of Catholic and paramilitary protocol. One poster depicts a funeral procession in which the casket, covered in the Irish tricolor flag, is carried through the streets by men in civilian clothes. Escorting them is an IRA volunteer dressed in a black turtleneck sweater, black gloves, beret, and shades. The caption draws historical lines between the recent Troubles and an earlier era by quoting 1916 rebel leader, P. H. Pearse: "They shall be spoken of among their people and generations shall call them blessed." To commemorate the fallen, portraits of hunger strikers identified by name arranged around the border of the artwork. The paramilitary tradition known as the "firing party" appears in several photographs. During that ceremony, which is often performed at public funerals, three soldiers in unison each fire three shots aimed over the casket. The ritual can be traced back to the European dynastic wars, when battles were suspended to bury the dead. That "three volley salute" marks the continuation of fighting and struggle (see Moloney, 2007).

Perhaps the most honored "firing party" was the one performed at the funeral of Bobby Sands. A poster brings the viewer into close range as three IRA commanders position their rifles. A photograph of Sands contains his words: "I refuse to change to suit the people who oppress, torture, and imprison me, who wish to dehumanise me. . . . I have the spirit of freedom which cannot be quenched by even the most horrendous treatment. Of course, I can be murdered, but I remain what I am—a political prisoner of war" (see Sands, 1998). His death was mourned worldwide. More than 100,000 attendees lined the funeral route to the cemetery, his final resting place. Many illustrations in the archive display other symbols of Irish Catholicism, including the Celtic Cross and the even more politically charged the Easter Lily. Members of the Official IRA have been nicknamed the "Stickies" because their supporters are known to "stick Easter lilies on their lapels" to commemorate the Easter Rising of 1916 (P. Taylor, 1997: 369). Altogether those sacred rituals and venerated objects reflect the sanctity of death in ways that enhance solidarity.

In *An Archaeology of the Troubles: The Dark Heritage of Long Kesh/Maze Prison*, Laura McAtackney offers a rare study of the remains of the H Blocks that were eventually demolished, including documents (e.g., secret prisoner communications), artifacts (e.g., a plastic cup holding a small incendiary device), and landscapes (e.g., murals). Having been transformed from their use-value to their signifying-value, those objects serve to narrate the Irish heritage of political imprisonment. Her description of this "highly mythologized site" provides an avenue for theorizing about culture, identity, and power. McAtackney shares her material and conceptual observations of the "death bed" of Bobby Sands that is on display at McCorley's Club in Belfast. Surrounded by emblems of martyrdom, the bed draws a degree of respect that is "palpable," revealing "how the emotive quality of place can transcend its physical structures" (2014: 270). McAtackney concedes that in all probability, that particular bed is not the actual one in which Sands died. But that doesn't really matter since its immense symbolism—it is a touchstone of Irish Republican culture—has already been established for those who wish to revere it (Graham and McDowell, 2007; Welch, 2016b).

Martyrdom by way of a hunger strike carries enormous sociological significance. Returning to lessons from Durkheimian thought, there is much to learn from a sharper interpretation of sacrifice. From that perspective, Henri Hubert and Marcel Mauss extract the underlying meaning of sacrifice, which "consists in establishing a means of communication between the sacred and profane worlds through the mediation of the victim, that is, of a thing that in the course of ceremony is destroyed" ([1898]1981: 97; see also Welch, 2006). The sacrifice imparts to the victim a power that is exercised through a ritual. In the case of a hunger strike, the victim is a conduit for passing on a sacred element of the religious world to the profane world, or vice versa. The direction of that current is indifferent to the victim because the victim is merely an intermediary. A hunger strike is a rite that puts into motion an entire complex of sacred entities; the sacrifice is part of a wider system of consecration.

Ostensibly, both sacrifice and hunger strikes involve destruction. Hubert and Mauss theorize: "If the religious forces are the very principle of the forces of life, they are themselves of such a nature that contact with them is a fearful thing for the ordinary man. Above all, when they reach a certain level of intensity, they cannot be concentrated in a profane object without destroying it" ([1898]1981: 98; see also Smith, 2008: 165–66). Situated between those powers is the intermediary, and as the chosen victim, it "penetrates into a perilous domain of sacrifice, it dies there, and indeed it is there in order to die" ([1898]1981: 98). In the case of a hunger strike, the ritual is not simply symbolic of a partisan struggle. It is a conduit that unites the sacred and profane, and in doing so, it bonds the prisoner's immediate plight to a mythological space involving an imagined political identity. And that is why death by hunger has so much meaning for believers in the Irish Republican cause. That powerful rite—transmitted through a martyr—connects the historical markers between the past and the present as well as the future.

THE SACRED AND PROFANE IN THE SOUTHERN CONE

Elaborating further on a sociology of culture, Smith (2008) sorts out the nuances of technology, particularly as they make contact with the sacred and the profane. Technology is used to cleanse certain forms of death—such as executions—in ways that "remove semantic irregularities and indignities" (142). By doing so, it produces a message about purification, civilization, and the sacred dignity of the person, even as the body is destroyed. Technology also "transforms into a totem and signifier in a complex semiotic universe of sacred and profane iconography" (142). The death flights that were carried out by the Argentine dictatorship have profound Durkheimian import. Prior to their execution, victims were subjected to a technological ritual in which they were injected with a sedative. That protocol conforms to Smith's observations that "judicial death, like all sacrifice, seems to require special cultural preparations" so as to manage pollution (2008: 153). It is crucial to note that the secret procedure occurred in the basement of ESMA, a restricted area separated from other sectors of the compound. Smith similarly notes that executions take place in a designated "death house" because "the sacred is dangerous and so needs to be segregated from the profane or everyday" (153; see also Johnson, 1990).

The modern technology of execution is designed to avoid indicators of chaos, such as an unruly body. For instance, in the US, lethal injection was introduced to replace the grisly product of the electric chair. Lethal injection, with all its medical pretense, is understood to be a "defensive reaction to the semiotic excess of the electric chair, working not so much to remove cruelty as to limit production of signs and disorder and degradation" (Smith, 2008: 166). Far from being a purely sanitized form of extermination, death flights breached the hallowed principle of violating the body since it retained sacred powers. Recall the words that Lieutenant Aztiz—the "Blond Angel of Death"—used to describe the death flights in which victims were thrown from aircraft into an ocean that was hard as a "steel plate," thereby breaking their necks (Graziano, 1992). Many of those mutilated bodies washed ashore, revealing more warnings of disorder and pollution that, as Smith contends, are not easily regulated and contained (see Douglas, 1966).

FIGURE 23. "Sculpture of Pablo." At the Memorial Park in Buenos Aires, Claudia Fontes installed her work "Reconstruction of the Portrait of Pablo Miguez" just off the waterfront. © retrowelch 2022.

In Buenos Aires, El Parque de la Memoria serves as a monument to the victims of state terrorism. The site, along the Rio de la Plata, was selected so that visitors could make visual contact with the channel of water where many of the disappeared met their fate. The river was used by the dictatorship to harshly dispose of its victims, yet it maintains qualities that are potentially tranquil and purifying. Thus, the location is remarkably suitable for memorialization, serving as it does as an open-air gallery to commemorate human rights. The park's vast landscape is contoured with imposing art installations. Among them is a piece by Claudia Fontes, who was commissioned to deliver a "Reconstruction of the Portrait of Pablo Miguez." The sculpture is placed in the river but close enough to be viewed from the waterfront. Its shape "articulates the concepts of appearance/disappearance and is based on the portrait of an adolescent who was disappeared when he was only 14 years old. The work was inspired by the case of Pablo Miguez, who, if he were still alive today, would be the same age as the artist" (Monumento a las Victimas del Terrorismo de Estado: Parque de la Memoria, n.d.; figure 23).

Nearby another artist has posted a sign with simple message—"N.N."—referring to the mass graves of victims who were buried with "no names." The caption of that piece contemplates the inhumanity and indignity of what has been discussed previously as breaching the sanctity of death. That desecration, however, is often countered by performances of consecration. Consider the site at Iglesia Santa Cruz. The courtyard of that church hosts a memorial to those who "struggled to find their loved during the state terror (1976–1983)." Twelve victims are remembered with headstones bearing their names; they include Leonie Duquet and Alice Domon, the French nuns murdered by death flights. Another recognizable name, Azucena Villaflor, appears as it does at so many memorials around the city. Villaflor was a founder of the Madres de la Plaza de Mayo, the activist group that confronted the military dictatorship over the disappearances of their children. Villaflor was also the victim of a death flight, but in her case, her bodily remains were recovered. Her ashes were deposited in the Pyramid of the Plaza de Mayo, and a street in Buenos Aires has been named in her honor (Bosco, 2006).

Another former detention center, known as Club Atletico, is dedicated to the "Project for the Recovery of Memory." Recovery here refers not only to emotional and psychological healing but also to the physical unearthing of the site. The Atletico offers both a memorial space and a collection of objects, but principally it is an excavation site where investigators continue to search for evidence of political violence. In its previous life, the Atletico served as an administrative unit for the federal police in the San Telmo neighborhood of Buenos Aires. From February to December 1977, the basement was used for detention. The building was then demolished for the construction of a major motorway. Through the rubble, the original floor could be seen from the street. Based on this, survivors testified that they were certain they had been held at the Atletico because even though they had been blindfolded while confined there, they could see the checkerboard floor below them. Human rights organizations descended on the property to protect it from further destruction. Once it was realized that the Atletico held valuable clues about its role as a detention center, it was transformed into an active archaeological recovery site.

The Atletico is more than an excavation site where its life as a clandestine center is being uncovered; as one poster explains, it is also a symbol of the pursuit of truth. The site reaches deep below the surface beyond view, but it is accompanied by an enormous silhouette of a victim that is illuminated throughout the night. That artwork joins a billboard displaying photographs of those who were detained—and were disappeared—at the Atletico (see Longoni and Bruzzone, 2008). Those cultural representations of the victims make the Atletico "a spontaneous call to memory at a symbolically 'loaded' location . . . assuming a life of its own, becoming a space for informal memorials," such as graffiti, poems, and drawings (Gates-Madsen, 2011). Adding even greater primordial sacred importance to the site, a totem has been installed on one of the columns. Artists have shaped sculptures of twisted—unruly—bodies of blindfolded and handcuffed detainees, thereby projecting a tense aura where the sacred and profane collide.

Themes of consecration and desecration also abound today in Santiago. The most formal expression of commemoration is Cementario General, where Chile's most revered historical figures are buried, most notably Salvador Allende. His tomb, a painful reminder of the nation's tumultuous past, is joined by a memorial to those civilians who were detained, disappeared, and executed by Pinochet's forces. Other public sites possess emotive power because of the victims who were actually murdered on the premises. At the National Stadium, candles burn in memory of Americans Charles Horman and Frank Teruggi as well as countless others. In the stadium's concourse, images of desecration are displayed, such as a photograph of a soldier burning books amid the coup. A closer look reveals "Cuba" in the title, perhaps a sign of danger and disorder from the standpoint of Pinochet, who was preoccupied with the threat of Marxist ideology. With much less subtlety, pictures show a smoldering La Moneda after it was repeatedly bombed by fighter jets on September 11, 1973. The desecration of the seat of executive government is more than emblematic of the destruction of Allende's presidency; it also portends the coming dictatorship. Those dramatic events are chronicled at Museo Histórico Nacional. The collection contains Allende's broken glasses, which have been transformed from use-value to signifying-value. Nearby, a series of international newspapers are posted to amplify the global significance of the coup. London's *Observer* printed the headline "Champagne and death in Santiago." Revealingly, that article is not the most prominent story on its front page. It is overshadowed by a more ominous danger: "'Beware,' IRA warns Heath" (a reference to the British prime minister at the time). Companion articles echo that danger: "UDA fears for chief" (a reference to the Loyalist paramilitary, the Ulster Defence Association, targeted by the IRA in Northern Ireland) and "Police warn of new blasts" (in reference to an expanding IRA bombing campaign).

In Santiago, and in other Chilean cities, the Pinochet regime is regularly scorned in popular culture. At Bar Radicales, patrons are immersed in a cultural milieu of dense ridicule as the image and memory of Pinochet is desecrated with dark humor. Next to a bustling dining and drinking area stands a mock museum boasting the dubious achievements of Pinochet. Electric candles illuminate a parlor featuring a "wanted poster" of Pinochet. The exhibit's curators joke about an imaginary tour of Cementario General, as it is common knowledge that then-President Bachelet denied Pinochet a state funeral (see Joignant, 2013). In another salon of the sprawling Bar Radicales, a portrait engages in satirical veneration by depicting Bachelet as "Santa Gladys: Ruega por Nosotros" ("Saint Gladys: Pray for Us"; see Collins, Hite, and Joignant, 2013).

Elsewhere in Santiago, parodies of Pinochet abound at another drinking establishment known simply as The Clinic. The lively night spot first opened under the name The London Clinic, alluding to the site where Pinochet was arrested while undergoing medical treatment. Compared to Bar Radicales, The Clinic seems edgier. A life-size wooden panel is painted showing Pinochet dressed in his signature Prussian cape—often mocked as "Darth Vader" (Oquendo-Villar, 2011: 274). A thick noose is wrapped around his neck, and various crimes are listed under his feet: theft, kidnapping, assassination, and genocide. In contrast to modern forms of execution, such as lethal injection, which are aimed at concealing and managing bodily mutilation, the mock hanging of Pinochet resembles the crass execution of common criminals deprived of dignity and the sanctity of death. As a bookend to that narrative, a framed photograph of lawyer Baltasar Garzón is posted across the barroom—perhaps as an expression of gratitude, for it was he who filed Pinochet's arrest warrant (see Roht-Arriaza, 2005).

Museo de la Memoria, in Montevideo, exhibits distressing images and narratives of desecration during the dictatorship. Photographs show the interior of a ransacked church. Shattered pews and broken stained glass are evidence of the violent disorder inflicted on a venerated space of worship by the military, which viewed religious groups as dangerously subversive. Similarly, universities—spaces for enlightenment—were searched and placed under intense surveillance. Students organized and resisted the military's encroachment on their campus. In 1968, police stormed a protest and injured student Liber Arce, who died two days later at the age of 28. "On the 14th of August a big crowd accompanied the funeral procession walking to the Buceo Cemetery. The crowd was expressing indignation and disgust over this assassination. From the following year and until today the anniversary of Liber Arce's death constitutes a symbolic date in memory of the 'student martyrs.'"

Desecration of a different sort seems to confirms Foucault's (1979) theory that the body is the ultimate material on which political agendas are inscribed (see Garland, 1990). A large news clipping from Montevideo shows a jarring photograph of Nazi swastikas carved into the legs of a young woman. The article explains that in 1962, Soledad Barrett Viedma was kidnapped by four men who threatened to kill her. They demanded that she shout "Viva Hitler" and "Death to Fidel [Castro]." Her attack compounded the plight of her family, who had fled to Uruguay to escape persecution by the Stroessner regime in Paraguay. Soledad's mutilated body is a physical *and* symbolic reminder of the disorder within ideological spheres that rely on repression to establish a certain form of order that—ironically—manifests itself as violence (see figure 24).

The city of Asunción, in 1537, was named by the Spanish conquistador Juan de Ayolas in honor of Our Lady Saint Mary of the Assumption. The Feast of the Assumption commemorates Mary as her body ascends to heaven, departing from her earthly life. At Museo de las Memorias, an artwork titled "The Tree of Life" is accompanied by a photograph of Pope John Paul II, who performed a purifying ceremony for the Paraguayan people in 1988. The following year, the brutal dictatorship came to an end. Stroessner is remembered, according to a separate placard, for his persecution of Catholic priests, who had been maligned as "subversives and communists" (see Mora, 1998). Strangely situated next to the Presidential Palace is Plaza de los Desaparecidos, where twisted sculptures capture the body in pain (see Scarry, 1995). The site's close proximity to the palace creates cultural tension between perpetrators and victims, hinting at binary themes of danger and purity.

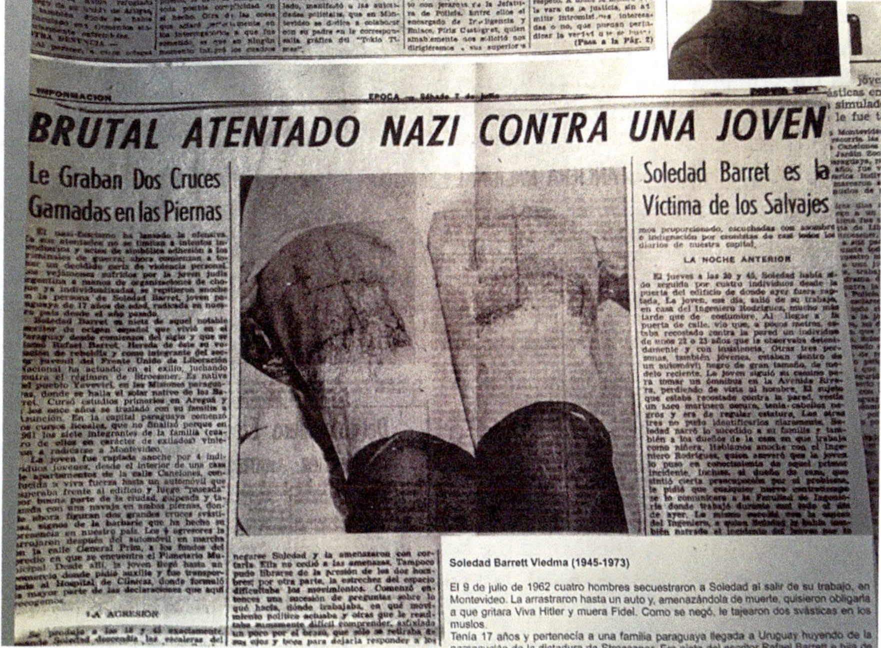

FIGURE 24. "Soledad and Swastikas." On display at the Museo de la Memoria in Montevideo is a photograph appearing in a newspaper article on the attack of Soledad Barrett Viedma, whose legs were disfigured with swastikas. © retrowelch 2022.

Down the avenue, another memorial site narrates the difficult transition toward democracy in the 1990s. The Monument to the Marzo Paraguayo stands amid a checkerboard of black-and-white tiles at the foot of Congress. Just before Easter, in 1999, students and pro-democracy protesters clashed with the "Oviedistas," who riddled the crowd with powerful fireworks and sniper fire. To defend themselves, the demonstrators pulled up the tiles, hurling them at their attackers. The violence escalated until eight were killed and more than 700 wounded, 90 by bullets. A makeshift memorial is devoted to the victims, who "gave their lives to make us free . . . Justice! Liberty! Democracy!"

Those events, known as the Marzo Paraguayo (Paraguayan March), can be understood as a youth movement aimed at ridding society of the persistent residue of the dictatorship. At the center of the controversy is General Lino Oviedo, who was convicted of planning a coup in 1996 and sentenced to 10 years in prison. That same year, a fanatic named Tomas Velazquez staged a hunger strike to draw attention to what he described as the political persecution of Oviedo. The public spectacle, in front of the Supreme Court, culminated in Velazquez being bound and then hoisted onto a large wooden cross. He allowed his fellow protesters to drive nails through his palms in an act of crucifixion (BBC, 1996). The cultural significance of crucifixion ought not be overlooked. James Q. Whitman points out the symbolic value of the cross has carried throughout Christianity because "crucifixion was the most degrading low-status punishment inflicted by the Romans, and the crucifixion of Christ, like the wearing of the cross by individual Christians, was long remembered as a fundamental symbol of a Christian uneasiness about status. It drew its power precisely from the revulsion created by low-status punishment. Embracing low-status punishment was a shocking act" (2003: 29). Other supporters, the "Oviedistas," intensified their violence during the riots of the Marzo Paraguayo, and on March 23, 1999, Luis Maria Argana, the country's vice president and a political rival of Oviedo, was assassinated. Soon after, Pablo Vera Esteche was arrested for the murder of Argana. In his defense he testified that he and two other gunmen had been paid US$300,000, authorized by Ovieda. The court sentenced Vera Esteche to a 20-year prison term (*Miami Herald*, 1999).

Returning to Buenos Aires, stark symbolism endures along lines of consecration and desecration. In what remains as an unresolved mystery, the hands of controversial President Juan Perón were sawed off his corpse as it lay in the family tomb. In 1987, burglars broke into the crypt—a sacred space—and mutilated the body. Adding further allegory to the act of desecration, Perón's military cap, ceremonial sword, and a poem by his last wife, Isabel, were also stolen. An anonymous ransom letter was sent to the Peronist Justicialist Party demanding $8 million. The ransom was rebuffed, and several suspects were arrested but released after a judge determined they had no involvement in the crime (Christian, 1987). In *Death, Dismemberment, and Memory: Body Politics in Latin America*, anthropologist Rosana Guber contends that in Argentine society, Perón's missing hands not only are symbolic of his political power but also arouse anxiety over a post-dictatorship culture (Johnson, 2004: 251–53). Indeed, central to the haunting aura of a dismembered cadaver is the power of the sacred as it intersects with danger and disorder (Welch, 2016a; Verdery, 1999).

CONCLUSION

In the opening passage of this chapter, the cultural significance of the Girondins' Chapel was carefully considered. As a place of worship, its sacredness is enhanced by being spatially partitioned from the main flow of tourist circulation at the Conciergerie. Beyond the visual narrative contained in Julien-Leopold Boilly's painting "Banquet of the Girondins" (1847), the ultimate fate of the Girondins is remembered through forms of consecration as well as desecration. On October 31, 1793, the day after the banquet, the Girondins were summarily executed. "On the scaffold, Sanson took just thirty-six minutes to cut twenty-two heads, and was remarkably pleased at this further evidence of the efficiency of the *rasior national*" (Schama, 1990: 804–5). Adding a surreal touch to the spectacle, the prosecutor, Fouquier-Tinville, apparently miffed that Dufriche-Valaze had taken his own life, demanded that his cadaver also be guillotined—thus, defiled. Schama observes that "though there was something like an epidemic of suicides among fallen revolutionaries, the Girondins seem to have been especially susceptible to the poetry of self-destruction" (1990: 804). In 1795, the memory of the Girondins was honored in a special *fete* for the "martyrs of liberty" (Sarmiento, 2005: 274). It is worth noting that inside the Girondins' Chapel, those themes of martyrdom echo through a parallel painting of Christ's crucifixion. French culture retains the memory of the Girondins as victims of the Terror in the form of a monument unveiled in Bordeaux in 1902.

The sacred and the profane, and the sanctity of death and sacrifice, figure prominently in the sites and symbols of political imprisonment. In the southern cone of Latin America, memorials sanctify the very places where atrocities occurred. Before those afterlives could be established, however, purifying ceremonies had to cleanse the space of its pollution. Turning the pages of history in those nations ravaged by dictatorships is not a smooth process. Resistance continues to manifest itself in many public demonstrations during which the names of the disappeared are slowly recited. In a call-and-response ritual, the audience chants in unison "Presente!"—a vocal affirmation that the victim is still with the community, at least metaphorically or spiritually. The performance of memory in Northern Ireland takes a different cultural tone. As noted, there are no state-sponsored memorials to civilians who died in the course of the Troubles in Belfast, and beyond. That cultural void demonstrates the extent to which the government deliberately avoids the legacy of the past and its thousands of fatalities (Graham and Whelan, 2007). To compensate for that official denial of memory, commemoration is expressed throughout special gardens, private exhibits, and personal collections.

Beyond the lack of state recognition of victimhood amid the Troubles, sites and symbols of political imprisonment continue to resonate in political exchanges between the Irish and the British. In 2014, a momentous occasion took place at the Crumlin Road Gaol (Belfast), where Queen Elizabeth toured the former prison, which has since been transformed into a history museum. Her Majesty was accompanied by then–First Minister Peter Robinson and then–Deputy First Minister Martin McGuinness. Both of those members of the power-sharing regime in Northern Ireland had served time at the Crum. McGuinness was confined there for more than a month in 1976 on a charge of IRA membership; a court later dismissed the case. Robinson was held at the Crum on several occasions during the 1980s for his involvement in protests against the Anglo-Irish Agreement. "In a landmark visit marking Northern Ireland's steady transition from a violent past to a peaceful future, the symbolic visit to the once forbidding Crumlin Gaol," the Queen announced: "Belfast should be an example to the world of people overcoming differences." Her concluding remarks at the photo-op served as a reminder of the ways in which the sacred is expressed in communal prose: "always remember that the thoughts and prayers of millions, including my own, are with you" (Carty and Young, 2014: 2–3; O'Connor, 2014).

12

Places of Resistance

As noted at the beginning of this book, the place de la Bastille would have many afterlives. Eventually, that once momentous site would be eclipsed by two other emblems of the nation, the Arc de Triomphe and the Eiffel Tower. That cultural competition pushed the Bastille, and its symbolic purchase, to the margins of the Parisian landscape. A poster promoting the 1889 centennial features the Eiffel Tower in the foreground with the Bastille in the background (BnF, 2010: 183). For the bicentennial, in 1989, the Bastille was conspicuously overshadowed by official events at other locations, such as the Trocadero, the Louvre, and the Grande Arche de la Defense. It seems odd that the holiday known as Bastille Day favors state-sponsored celebrations at other sites, thus displacing the place de la Bastille. Filling the void, however, activists of the political left have seized on the place de la Bastille to protest the establishment. In 1989, as a counterweight to the official festivities, demonstrators rallied there to condemn French President François Mitterand's sponsorship of the G7 summit, lingering colonialism, and Third World debt. Other imperial campaigns were again challenged in 1991, when more than 40,000 activists gathered at the venue for an anti–Gulf War rally. Despite occasional gatherings at the place de la Bastille, the site has slipped into the mundane: the Colonne de Juillet "stands isolated, unvisited, unapproachable and almost unnoticed in a multi-lane whirlpool of traffic whose roads run over the unmarked locations of the old fortress walls" (Smith, 1999: 35).

In this final chapter, critical thought is directed again at how a sociology of place informs places of resistance. Recall that Pierre Nora (1989) observed that history bonds with events whereas memory tends to take refuge in places. To untangle the complex threads of resistance, discussion returns to place identity and how sites are transformed according to the dynamics of history and culture. Forceful expressions of resistance are examined in the southern cone of Latin America. For example, in Buenos Aires, community activists transform mundane places into profane places through rituals called *escraches*. Those noisy gatherings target retired military officers accused of crimes under the last dictatorship, subjecting them to public shaming. As we shall see, places of shame can be transformed into places of resistance while serving as metaphors for human rights.

In Belfast—a place of resistance as well as a place full of places of resistance—the city contends with the complicated symbolism embedded in its post-conflict heritage. There, peace walls figure prominently in the streetscape, forging material and symbolic wedges that contour place identity. Narratives of how political prisoners engaged in collective resistance are among the many messages conveyed about the Troubles, allowing certain profane places to emerge as signs of struggle. Legendary accounts of prison escapes further enhance themes of ascent so as to define and elevate ethnic and political identity. At the end of this chapter, I offer some final thoughts about the afterlives of sites of political imprisonment.

ESCRACHE AS PERFORMING OF RESISTANCE

The notion of place carries tension in post-dictatorship cultures in which repressors are able to live openly and with impunity alongside victims and their relatives (Feierstein, 2014). Such "normalization" of denial generates "an unhealthy tolerance for criminality" that provides torturers and assassins "a place" on the streets and in restaurants, as well as on television screens and at official ceremonies (Kaiser, 2002: 502). Many perpetrators of human rights abuses have been allowed to "recycle" themselves as trusted politicians and business leaders. In Buenos Aires, human rights activists organize events to resist such complacency. Their creative and confrontational tactics transform mundane places into places of the profane. These acts of resistance, known locally as *escraches*, are a unique form of social performance initiated by the grown children of the disappeared. *Escrache*—Argentine slang for "uncover"—crystalizes as "campaigns of public condemnation through demonstrations that aim to expose the identities of hundreds of torturers and assassins benefitting from amnesty laws" (Kaiser, 2002: 499). Large numbers of marchers target neighborhoods where repressors live. There, they hoist banners and chant slogans, such as "Alert! Alert! Alert all neighbors, there's an assassin living next door to you!" and "Just like the Nazis it will happen to you, wherever you go we'll go after you" (Kaiser, 2002: 499). These activists are engaging in consciousness-raising, shaming, and stigmatization in ways that collide with the prevailing amnesia.

A sociology of place is in order here. *Escrache* organizers alter the equilibrium of mundane places such as an apartment house by inflicting profane messages on them. Flyers are distributed about the *escrachado* that include his name, his photograph, his address and current occupation, and his complicity in the dictatorship. Once positioned in front of his home, the marchers share a brief ceremony accompanied by speeches, street theatre, and music—all honoring the spirits of the disappeared. Then the profanity begins: the building and sidewalk are painted with slogans of condemnation. Red paint is commonly used to signify the bloodshed inflicted by the military, a form of pollution reminiscent of the stigma imposed on lepers in medieval times. *Escracheros* use place to agitate the present by bringing back the past, in this way publicly defying impunity and political silence. Protests also have a future trajectory, in that they demand that repressors be stripped of their immunity and prosecuted for crimes against humanity (see D. Taylor, 1997).

At ESMA, a place of memory, posters promoting *escraches* are extensively displayed. Graphics infuse the confrontational tactics surrounding the public spectacle. In advertising one such protest, graphic designers superimposed the images of Cardenal Aramburu and Roberto Alemann, shaming them as "ministers of genocide." The sponsors, HIJOS, add more detail to the biographies of their *escrachados*, referring to Aramburu as the ex–Archbishop of Buenos Aires and Alemann as the former Minister of the Economy during the dictatorship. Both were allowed to retire "with privilege" (see Morello, 2019). Opposition to the controversial "2 × 1" plan to reduce the prison sentences of repressors is crudely styled with a skull and bones, underscoring the evil of mass murder. Posters announcing *escraches* include precise information about the event: day, date, time, and location all pivot on the notion of place as a venue for action.

Post-dictatorship societies like Argentina retain elements of authoritarianism and even respect for military officers who fought "subversion." Unsurprisingly, their supporters often use the media to portray the *escrachados* as the *real* victims (i.e., of the political left), drawing on a sympathetic television audience (Ranalletti, 2010). *Escrachados* depict themselves not only as nationalists but also as "good parents" of the children they "adopted" during the "dirty war." In doing so, they are attempting to turn the profane into the sacred. Enter into the fray HIJOS, the Daughters and Sons For Identity and Justice against Forgetting and Silence, a group organized by the grown children of the disappeared. Alongside other activists, members of HIJOS (the Spanish word for "children") remind the public that many of the repressors who claim to have been "good parents" were actually raising kidnapped children after their biological parents were murdered by the state. In doing so, they are challenging the status quo and striving to rewrite the political narrative of a benevolent junta (see *The Official Story*, 1985).

Much as in other post-Condor nations, human rights activism in Argentina has for its ally international law, under which torturers and assassins are now more likely to face justice. The arrest of Chilean dictator Pinochet in London in 1998 was an ominous warning to those have committed atrocities that they are taking chances if they travel abroad (Rhot-Arriaza, 2005). So repressors remain at home, confined to a place has been described as an "aguantadero" (mafia hideout) (Kaiser, 2002: 502). Performers of *escraches* practice place to restrict the societal space that repressors have gained from impunity; this allows the gradual "metaphorical repossession of the streets by freeing them from these criminals' presence . . . a move to tear off the protective shield of anonymity behind which hundreds of torturers hid" (Kaiser, 2002: 504; 2020). Through *escraches*, activists use mundane place to perform profane rituals so as to eradicate pollution; the events thereby provide emotional catharsis for members of HIJOS and other protesters.

RESISTING BELFAST

Once derided as the "Pariah City"—due to the Troubles—Belfast has resisted its reputation as a place to avoid (see Neill, Fitzsimmons, and Murtagh, 1995; Shirlow and Murtagh, 2006). Tourists have discovered a vibrant city that is still managing its difficult past. From the standpoint of a sociology of place, profane themes of descent are rivaled by sacred themes of ascent, thereby establishing cultural binaries that invite a deeper look at Belfast (see Smith, 1999). Even before visitors can absorb the complicated emblems of various neighborhoods, the imposing peace walls give them pause. Although they seem like things of the past, there remain at least 88 partitions designed to separate antagonistic communities (Community Relations Council, 2009). As a diversion from the lingering tensions of the Troubles, the *Titanic* museum, murals, and memorials offer tourists a place to reflect on the greatness of shipbuilding (ascent) in Belfast alongside that vessel's tragic sinking (descent) in 1912. Its "centenary was viewed by the city council as both a potential tourist attraction and as a nonsectarian symbol for the still materially segregated area . . . with evolving processes of post-conflict place making" (McAtackney, 2020: 78).

Beyond the places devoted to the *Titanic*, the city is defined by its peace walls. In both Unionist/Loyalist and Nationalist/Republican neighborhoods, peace walls provide a canvas for murals and graffiti to communicate ethnic and political identity as well as an identity of place, altogether boasting themes of heroic ascent (see Nisbett and Rapson, 2020; Rolston, 1992, 1998). Murals can also be read as places of resistance where paramilitaries are vividly remembered for their commitment to the struggle. Other places of resistance, such as the Irish Republican History Museum, deliver heavily sectarian narratives on ethno-politics. Images and objects resonate with sacred themes of ascent, including nationalism, sacrifice, and the defense of the eternal good (Smith, 1999; see Katz, 1988). To establish such noble ascent, repressive state power is depicted as a profane force. The cultural binary is thus set for justice to prevail over injustice. For hundreds of years, the Irish response to British colonization has been grounded in strict defiance. One poster, bluntly titled "resistance," features an intimidating picture of a masked paramilitary volunteer aiming a rifle. The strident words of Bobby Sands reinforce its message.

> There can never be peace in Ireland until the foreign, oppressive British presence is removed, leaving all the Irish people as a unit to control their own affairs and determine their own destinies as a sovereign people, free in mind and body, separate and distinct physically, culturally, and economically.

For the Republican movement in the 1980s, the struggle against the British in Northern Ireland gradually incorporated parallel political tactics known as "Armalite and Ballot Box" (McAllister, 2004). Shipments of Armalites (AR-15, AR-18 semi-automatic rifles) were smuggled in from the US to equip the IRA, becoming an emotive symbol of the Republican resistance (Bell, 2000; P. Taylor, 1997). In fact, many of the images of assault weapons in the posters resemble Armalites—nicknamed "the Widowmaker." The electoral/militant strategy is best exemplified in the campaign conducted by Sands, who was elected to the British parliament while on a hunger strike, a protest that fused resistance with sacrifice. The "Armalite and Ballot Box" slogan is traced back to Danny Morrison, who spoke at the 1981 Sinn Fein conference: "Who here really believes we can win the war through the ballot box? But will anyone here object if, with a paper ballot in this hand and an Armalite in the other, we can take power in Ireland" (English, 2005: 224–25; see also Moloney, 2007; P. Taylor, 1997).

To illustrate the "fight/peace" duality as it thrived in the Republican movement, a series of posters insert another visual device used by graphic artists. The figure makes a decidedly gestalt impression in that it blends a fist with a dove (Humphrey, 1924). At a glance, the fist/dove symbol can be interpreted as either a message of conflict or one of harmony, or both. That parallel political agenda becomes clearer when we remember that Sinn Fein's POW Committee printed the fist/dove emblem on many of its posters. Especially in West Belfast, Sinn Fein messages endorsing national unity inundate the streetscapes. Since that particular Republican neighborhood borders on a Loyalist one, there is a noticeable symbolic intensity (see Graham and McDowell, 2007; Lindström, Kull, and Palang, 2011).

As noted earlier, visual narrations of the Troubles tend to be highly skewed toward masculinity (Dowler, 1998; Graham and Whelan, 2007). Even the strong role women played in the Republican struggle is often compromised by the presence of dominant male figures (McAtackney, 2018; Scarlata, 2014). One poster, showing two armed women posing with an armed male comrade, is labeled "Oglaigh na hEireann." (Warriors of Ireland). The three subjects together form a trinity or geometry of force. However, the man is standing while the two women are kneeling, thus projecting a male hierarchy even though the women are presented as brave (and skilled) "warriors" (Welch, 2019). Perhaps the most iconic expression of the female warrior is found in a poster that borrows from a French masterpiece, Eugene Delacroix's "Liberty Leading the People" (1830). Delacroix romanticizes the July Revolution of 1830 by showing a bare-breasted woman dramatically raising the French tricolor in one hand and holding a bayoneted musket in the other. The scene is depicted with controlled chaos; she towers over fallen bodies and defies the armed men who are charging her. At her feet, a young boy adores her

FIGURE 25. "Liberty Leading the People." An Irish political poster borrows from a classical French masterpiece by Eugene Delacroix titled "Liberty Leading the People" that romanticizes the July Revolution of 1830. © retrowelch 2022.

majestic courage; another youngster holds up a pistol in choreographed solidarity. The painting's symbolism is direct. Liberty—also known as Marianne—represents an allegorical goddess guiding France into a new era of Republican Enlightenment (see Boime, 2008). In the Irish version of the warrior, Liberty holds the Republican (tricolor) flag of Ireland. This scene, captioned "the struggle continues . . . 1989

Ireland," employs a unique visual technique in an effort to lend the image a veneer of authenticity. Rather than appearing as a crass rip-off, the poster renders the original canvas in a manner that reinforces the historical continuity between the Irish struggle and that of the oppressed French (figure 25).

Broader themes of ascent of the Irish Republican struggles are also remembered in the form of institutions. Former prisons, even those (mostly) demolished and off-limits to the public, such as the Maze, remain potent places of resistance. Themes of profane descent as well as sacred ascent are rarely separated. As discussed in chapter 6, the British government under Margaret Thatcher moved to "criminalize" paramilitaries in Northern Ireland by holding them in the Maze prison, which had been built to replace "the Cages" (Long Kesh internment camp). Once confined, political prisoners would be denied Special Category Status. As stigma of their lower status as "ordinary criminals," prisoners would be compelled to wear state-issued uniforms. That requirement (and loss of special status) was met with fierce opposition, sparking a "blanket protest" that would persist for five years. The first "blanket man" was Kieran Nugent, who became a recognizable figure in the Republican struggle. Refusing to accept the prison uniform, he insisted on wearing only a blanket, which emerged as a symbol of non-compliance. Nugent famously declared: "If they want me to wear a uniform they'll have to nail it to my back" (Bishop and Mallie, 1987: 349–50). Hundreds of prisoners from the Republican (and Socialist) movement would join the "blanket men" as a shared expression of sacrifice (Campbell, McKeown, and O'Hagan, 1994; O'Rawe, 2005). Several posters in the archive pay tribute to the "blanket men," including one that shows a photograph of a large public demonstration with marchers holding a banner "Victory to the Blanket Men."

In 1978, prisoners converted the Maze into a profane place of resistance. Their collective actions escalated into a "dirty [no wash] protest" whereby they refused to empty their chamber pots (the cells lacked toilets and sinks). Upwards of 300 prisoners then smeared their excrement on the walls. By March 1981, that rebuke of confinement had reached primordial levels of pollution and disgust (see Adams's foreword to Sands, 1998; Douglas, 1966). While visiting the prisoners, Archbishop Cardinal Tomás Ó Fiaich curiously compared the stench and filth to "the sewer pipes in the slums of Calcutta. . . . I was unable to speak for fear of vomiting" (P. Taylor, 1997: 221–22). Ó Fiaich, nevertheless, was struck by their high morale. It seemed that prisoners were keeping their sanity by studying Irish. Some even wrote Irish words into the excrement covering the walls of their cells, a ritual that could be understood as a primitive rite of resistance (Bishop and Mallie, 1987; see Katz, 1988). In solidarity, the "dirty protest" spread to other prisons, including Maghaberry. A poster commemorates the struggle: "Support 1981–2011: The Maghaberry Dirty Protest." A photograph of a prisoner scrawling on a cell wall coated in excrement is conspicuously positioned within the graphic, thus documenting the profane defiance.

At the Armagh Women's Prison, Mairead Farrell and 30 other Republican prisoners joined the "dirty protest" in 1980. Since they retained their right to wear their own clothes there was no "blanket" protest; still, they smeared their menstrual blood across the cell walls (Coogan, 2002). A poster commemorates the "blanketmen/armagh women historic reunion" (2011). A slogan speaks to the enduring spirit of resistance and solidarity: "Some bonds can never be broken. . . . And they are still loved, by all who knew them well; In a romantic chamber of the heart and in a nostalgic country of the mind where it will always be—1981." The same photograph of the prisoner shown in the "Maghaberry Dirty Protest" is coupled with an illustration of a woman prisoner captioned "STOP strip-searches." An aerial shot of the H-blocks of the Maze prison adds authority to the poster's design; indeed, the H symbol endures simultaneously as an emblem of state oppression and of prisoner resistance. As the Irish prisoners entered the hunger phase of their strike, they made the collective decision to purify themselves by showering, shaving, and allowing their cells to be cleaned by high-powered hoses. As places of resistance, those prisons would transit through various elements of the profane and ultimately be remembered as sacred sites in which the deaths of the hunger strikers would shape a collective consciousness (see Olley, 2007; Purbrick, 2004; Wylie, 2004).

GREAT ESCAPES

Themes of descent coupled with those of ascent inject the Bastille with legendary tales of its famous prisoners. Jean-Henri Chevalier de Latude, in his *Memoirs of Vengeance*, does not disappoint his readers. Latude was no stranger to the Bastille. Over the course of his 28 years in confinement, he had been in and out of the Bastille several times. In 1750, his poorly executed plot to scam the Royal Court landed him in the Bastille, setting the stage for his first escape. Rather than hunkering down and receding into the background, Latude breached his liberty by contacting the monarchy with the wild expectation of receiving a pardon. The plan failed, and he found himself back in the Bastille. Over the next six months, he and his cellmate Alegre threaded together a 300-foot rope ladder. "This extraordinary piece of work required considerable sacrifice since the rungs had to be made from the firewood given to the prisoners during the winter" (Schama, 1990: 395). Becoming personally attached to the ladder, Latude gave his instrument of freedom the names *Jacob* and *Dove* before securing his second escape from the Bastille (Barriere, 1886). He hid out in Amsterdam for nearly three months while agents of the king eventually tracked him down. Upon returning to the Bastille, Latude was placed in the appalling subterranean *cachots*, which ended his winning streak of escapes. In 1777, he was released, but the publication of his memoir caused such a stir that the authorities imprisoned him in the Petit Châtelet and later the Bicetre. Finally, in 1784, he was exiled from Paris, albeit with a royal pension of 400 livres a year. For all his trials and tribulations, Latude was able to survive by his wits, even becoming a celebrity. The Académie Française showered him with praise, and Thomas Jefferson, then US Ambassador to France, sought his company (Godechot, 1970; Schama, 1990).

The relationship between the Bastille and Latude was renewed when he was invited to survey the site on the July 16, 1789. At that legendary reunion, Latude was presented with the original rope and ladder used for his escape; those charismatic artifacts had been faithfully hidden by the guards for 33 years. "They were ceremoniously offered to the famous escapee as "'property acquired by just title.' . . . In the Salon that autumn they were exhibited alongside a splendid portrait of Latude by Antoine Vestier in which the hero points to his escape route and shows the ladder as the attribute of his revolutionary sainthood" (Schama, 1990: 408; BnF, 2010: 61, 145). The afterlife of the Bastille further preserves the adventures of Latude. As part of a collection of souvenirs crafted by Patriot Palloy, a model of the Bastille was fitted with working doors and drawbridges. The clock was set at 5:30: the very moment of surrender. Adding a final touch to the replica, a miniature of Latude's ladder is hooked to the appropriate turret (Godechot, 1970).

In Montevideo, the City without Memory, some places of resistance are remembered to this day. As noted in previous chapters, the former prison Punta Carretas was transformed—physically and culturally—into a massive shopping mall. In its current incarnation, that commercial compound is decorated with pop art in the form of tall, multicolored shoes and oversized lawn chairs. The details of the fortress-style façade have been refurbished in a style that is non-threatening, defying its past as a place of danger. The edifice now projects a theme-park motif that abandons its original neo-Gothic design. References to its days as a prison are limited to two remnants. First, a photograph of the penitentiary (c. 1985) has been placed inconspicuously near a footpath. Second, a theatre (Teatro de la Candela) on the edge of the property advertises a dramatic production titled "El Abuso: La Fuga de Punta Carretas." As a departure from commerce and shopping, the story's main audience is one that has not forgotten the political significance of an ingenious prison escape. In 1971, more than 100 political prisoners (members of an urban guerrilla group, the Tupamaros) carried out an escape code-named "El Abuso" (The Abuse)—the largest jailbreak in world history (see Fernandez, 1998). The artwork on the advertisement contains the letter "T" inside a star— the logo of the Tupamaros. That leftist organization gained notoriety in the 1960s and 1970s for its spectacular kidnappings and assassinations. Among its targets was Dan Mitrione, an FBI agent who was rumoured to have taught torture techniques to the police by practicing his sadistic tactics on the homeless (see Dinges, 2004; McSherry, 2005). The larger story is the subject of the film *States of Siege* (by Costa-Gavras, who also directed *Missing*). Notwithstanding those references to resistance, the dominant narrative at Punta Carretas is still consumerism, which has erased the memory of political repression (see Draper, 2012).

In Belfast, accounts of famous prison escapes are frequently remembered and retold. Stories of Republican jailbreaks are punctuated with ideological expressions that project the perils of descent as well as the triumph of ascent. In Irish culture, prison escapes are an important element of heritage and ritual dating back to 1591, when the Irish clan leaders Hugh Ruadh O'Donnell and Art O'Neil broke away from their English jailers (Foster, 1988). Irish prisoners of war in the modern era have seen it as their duty to escape (P. Taylor, 1997). Defiance is among the chief motives of prison escapes: in an act of solidarity, they join their "fellows in making life as difficult as possible for the authorities" (Cohen and Taylor, 1972: 48). In doing so, they relieve their own boredom, frustrate their captors, share a collective adventure, and contribute to the war effort. According to an IRA commander, "escapes demonstrate to the British that they cannot imprison our struggle, that it continues behind the prison walls and that despite the might of the war machine, their supposedly escape proof prisons, with determination, skill and patience, our Volunteers can defeat them" (McEvoy, 2001: 49). IRA prison escapes are a propaganda coup as well as a valuable source of material and symbolic resistance that mocks the myth of the omnipotent British state. Such victories bolster Irish Republican morale and are celebrated in songs, poetry, and legends that represent Ireland's long struggle for freedom (O'Donoghue, 1971).

Borrowing the visual dynamics of an action movie, a political poster at the Irish Republican History Museum commemorates the 1981 "Great Escape" from the Crumlin Road Prison in which eight IRA volunteers broke out by brandishing three pistols and wearing the uniforms of the officers taken hostage. Illustrations show IRA prisoners bursting out the front gate of the heavily secured jail. Blurry brush strokes accentuate the intensity and velocity of the dramatic escape, with the prisoners firing handguns and knocking down officers. A poem honors those who escaped by referring to them as the "M60 Gang," a four-man active service unit known for their use of heavy machine-guns in targeting British military patrols. The gang included Joe Doherty, who fled to New York City. There, he became a *cause célèbre* as he fought extradition. "For the next nine years, a series of legal battles waged, and Doherty's case became a constellation of highly charged issues, including immigration, Thatcherism, the definition of a political prisoner, Irish American ethnic identity, and ethno-nationalist conflict in Northern Ireland" (Searcy, 2015). Frank Durkan, an Irish American human rights attorney, contacted then– New York City mayor David Dinkins in 1990 just before Nelson Mandela's historic visit to the city, writing: "A short distance from your office, another political prisoner is about to begin his eighth year of incarceration although never having been convicted of—or even charged with—a crime in the United States" (Searcy, 2015). Doherty's protracted legal battle ended with his deportation to Northern Ireland, where he was reincarcerated. His political legacy endures in lower Manhattan, where the street intersection near the federal jail has been named "Joseph

Doherty Corner," becoming a cultural monument to the Irish Republican struggle as honored by the Irish diaspora (see Dillon, 1992; Greg, 2013).

Back in Belfast, memories of the Maze as a place of resistance are cherished in the most daring prison escape in IRA history. The plan was launched in 1983 inside the H-Blocks, considered the most secure prison in Europe. The fortified institution was tucked behind 15-foot fences and an 18-foot concrete containment wall wrapped in barbed wire. Solid steel gates were electronically controlled by a state-of-the-art communication system. The escape benefited from lengthy deliberations among the IRA leadership. As in previous breakouts, the plot involved smuggling in weapons, taking guards hostage, and confiscating their uniforms. In all, 38 prisoners broke out, prompting an extensive manhunt into Europe and the US that would last for years. An upbeat image—and dramatic theme of ascent—reminds us that anniversaries are important cultural moments in Irish Republican history: "the great escape: 25th Anniversary, 25 Years to the Exact Day." A photographic collage commemorates each of the escapees. Assembled into a group shot, the image speaks to their collective defiance and shared solidarity. A picture of an H-Block guard tower makes a brooding appearance, symbolizing the role of imprisonment in the British occupation of Ireland. In the form of a montage, the imagery captures the intersection and interaction of themes of descent with themes of ascent, casting a sociology of place onto a wider topography.

AFTERLIVES AND AFTERTHOUGHTS

As conceptualized throughout this book, the Bastille Effect represents the unique ways former prisons and detention centers are transformed both physically and culturally. In their afterlives, those sites deliver critiques on justice as it prevails over injustice. However, for that narrative to emerge, the sites must be purified of their profane past, giving them a new place identity. By relinquishing their use-value attached to incarceration and embracing their signifying-value, many of these sites have been reconfigured into a places of enlightenment that offer inspiring allegories on human rights and the struggle against state repression.

To summarize briefly how the Bastille Effect served as organizing principle for this project, four main parts were established so as to frame particular chapters. In Part One, "The Sacred and the Profane," the notion of cultural afterlives allowed us to decipher the dynamic interchange between forces purity and danger. Those binaries very much inform a sociology of place. In many of the examples scattered throughout the book, we discovered that in the course of transforming a former site of political imprisonment into a memorial, the space is animated by being *personed*. Consider an imaginary Nelson Mandela in his cell at Robben Island. While discussing the States of Confinement, we learned that certain political prisoners are transformed from low to high status. Through that conversion, the foundation of human rights is also elevated. Part Two, "In Search of Signs," introduced us to the Sites of Trouble in Northern Ireland. In that context, the heritage of political prisoners is emotionally contested. Depending on one's ethnic point of view, the low status of a "common criminal" is inverted into the high status of a "freedom fighter," or vice versa. The presence of boundaries in the form of partitions and peace walls heightens those distinctions. Shifting focus to the southern cone of Latin America, Operation Condor and its parallel "dirty wars" unfolded in response to the anxieties of danger and "subversion"—only to be resolved in justice campaigns as those nations transitioned to democracy. Indeed, places such as ESMA in Buenos Aries project a resounding Bastille Effect as a metaphor for humanity. Other transformed sites, most notably the shopping mall at Punta Carretas, demonstrate the failure of memorialization, a reminder that a Bastille Effect is not inevitable.

Part Three, "The Diagrams of Control," delved into economics, religion, and architecture. Among the valuable lessons from Montreal during the rebellions of 1837 and 1838 was that the struggle over commerce and agriculture is also influenced by contested heritage. As with the failed uprising against the British in Dublin in 1916, the Patriotes' insurgence and their subsequent executions transformed local and regional culture. La Prison-des-Patriots, like the "Bastille of Ireland," has been injected with memories of courage and nationalism. The nuances of Catholicism, the next topic explored, throw crucial light onto the sacred and profane in that religious workers in Argentina were scapegoated as "subversive" and confined to clandestine detention centers. Within those polluted places, political prisoners were tortured and later exterminated. Their memories, however, persevere in ways that acknowledge moral purity. As another diagram of control, the use of panoptics to penetrate an entire social body speaks to the power of architecture. Resorting to violent spectacles, dictatorships in the southern cone created the allusion of an omniscient deity in which citizens absorbed the gaze of a God-like tyrant.

The chapters in Part Four scan the "Technologies of Power" as they transform the mind (through censorship and propaganda), the body (through torture), and society (through extermination). Those breaches of human rights are carefully documented in former prisons and detention centers, allowing those sites to be repurposed from places of pain to places of learning. The book concludes with a pair of writings on the performance of memory. To reiterate, the duality of danger and purity is unleashed in complex forms of consecration and desecration. Even in instances where a former prison is physically demolished, such as the Maze, the spirits of martyred political prisoners reside elsewhere, in heritage museums and memorial gardens. To be sure, the Bastille Effect is not restricted to particular places. Rather it is culturally fluid, migrating with transcendence—and with themes of ascent, those forces spill into a collective consciousness.

REFERENCES

ABC Paraguay. 2012. "Falleció Antonio Campos Alum, director de centro detención clandestina stronista," February 14. www.abc.com.py/nacionales/fallecio-antonio-campos-alum-director-de-centro-detencion-clandestina-stronista-366219.html.

Achugar, H. 2000. "Territorios y memorias versus lógica del mercado. (A propósito de cartografías y shopping malls)," *Arte Latina* (November). http://acd.ufrj.br/pacc/artelatina/hugo.html.

Actis, M., C. Aldini, L. Gardella, M. Lewin, and E. Tokar. 2006. *That Inferno*. Translated by G. Siebentritt. Nashville: Vanderbilt University Press.

Adams, G. 1997. *Cage Eleven*. Boulder: Roberts Rinehart.

Adams, J. 2000. "Movement Socialization in Art Workshops: A Case from Pinochet's Chile." *Sociological Quarterly* 41(4): 615–38.

Agence France-Press. 2006. "Pinochet to be Buried without State Funeral Mourning." December 11.

———. 2006. "Bachelet Calls Army to Punish Pinochet Grandson for Remarks." December 13.

Agnew, J. A., and J. S. Duncan. 1989. *The Power of Place*. Boston: Unwin Hyman.

Alexander, J. 2005. "The Inner Development of Durkheim's Sociological Theory." In *The Cambridge Companion to Durkheim*, edited by J. Alexander and P. Smith. New York: Cambridge University Press.

Alford, C. F. 2000. "What Would it Matter If Everything Foucault Said about Prisons was Wrong?" *Theory and Society* 29: 125–46.

Almada, M. 1993. *Paraguay: La Carcel Olvidada, El Pais Exiliado*. Asuncion: Imprenta Salesiana.

———. 2005. Foreword to *Predatory States* by J. P. McSherry. New York: Rowman and Littlefield.

Amnesty International. 2011. "Uruguay: Congress Adopts Landmark Law to Tackle Impunity." https://www.amnesty.org/en/latest/news/2011/10/uruguay-congress-adopts-landmark -law-tackle-impunity.

Andermann, J. 2012. "Returning to the Site of Horror." *Theory, Culture, and Society*, 29(1): 76–98.

Andermann, J., and S. Arnold-de Simine. 2012. "Introduction: Memory, Community, and the New Museum." *Theory, Culture, and Society* 29(1): 3–13.

Andersen, M. 1993. *Dossier Secreto*. Boulder: Westview.

Arendt, H. 1994. *Eichmann in Jerusalem* [1963]. New York: Penguin.

Arenas Uriarte, S. 2016. *La Sorda Juticia: El "Hoyo" de Jose Domingo Cañas, Cuartel Ollague de la DINA*. Santiago: Foundacion 1367 Casa Memoria Jose Domingo Cañas.

Associated Press. 2006. "Army Ousts Pinochet's Kin." *New York Times*, December 14, Section A, 27.

"Automotores Orletti." n.d. Espacio Para la Memoria y la Promocion de los Derechos Humanos. Buenos Aires: Archivo Nacional de la Memoria.

Avellaneda, A. 1986. *Censura, Autoritarismo y Cultura: Argentina 1960–1983*. Vol. 2. Buenos Aires: Biblioteca Politica Argentina.

Bailey, C. B. 2016. "Hubert Robert and the Joy of Ruins." *New York Review of Books*, October 13, 5–37.

Bargu, B. 2014. *Starve and Immolate*. New York: Columbia University Press.

Barriere, B. F. 1886. *Memoires de linguet et de latude*. Paris: Librairie de Firmin Didot Freres.

Barrionuevo, A. 2007. "Argentine Priest Testifies about Church's Role in the 'Dirty War.'" *New York Times*, September 17. https://www.nytimes.com/2007/09/17/world/americas /17iht-argentina.1.7531520.html.

Barros, C., A. Campos, and J. Griffin. 2018. "Forced Labour in Paraguay." *The Guardian*, September 18. https://www.theguardian.com/environment/2018/sep/18/forced-labour-in -paraguay-the-darkness-at-the-bottom-of-the-global-supply-chain.

Basterra, V. 2010. Abducted from August 10, 1979, to year 1983. ESMA Trial Testimony, Case 1270, April 30.

Bataille, G. 1991. *The Accursed Share*. New York: Zone Books.

Baudrillard, J. 1994. *Simulacra and Simulation*. Ann Arbor: University of Michigan Press.

BBC News. 1996. "Paraguay Man Crucified in Public." November 30. http://news.bbc.co .uk/2/hi/americas/6158229.stm.

Begg, M. 2007. *Enemy Combatant*. New York: New Press.

Bell, J. B. 2000. *The IRA, 1968–2000: Analysis of a Secret Army*. New York: Taylor and Francis.

Bell, M. M. 1997. "The Ghosts of Place." *Theory and Society* 26: 813–36.

Bello, A. 2010. Abducted from December 6, 1978, to September 1979. ESMA Trial Testimony, Case 1270, July 16.

Bender, J. 1987. *Imagining the Penitentiary*. Chicago: University of Chicago Press.

Bennett, T. 1995. *The Birth of the Museum*. London: Routledge.

Bentham, J. 1995. *The Panopticon Writings* [1787], edited by M. Bozovic. New York: Verso.

Beresford, D. 1987. *Ten Dead Men: The Story of the 1981 Irish Hunger Strike*. New York: Atlantic Monthly Press.

Bernstein, A. 2016. "Sergio Arellano Stark, driver of the 'Caravan of Death' under Pinochet, dies at 94." *Washington Post*, March 10. https://www.washingtonpost.com/world/the_

americas/sergio-arellano-stark-driver-of-the-caravan-of-death-under-pinochet-dies-at
-94/2016/03/10/ad7bdd32-e6d5-11e5-b0fd-073d5930a7b7_story.html.

Bilbija, K., and L. Payne. 2011. *Accounting for Violence: The Memory Market in Latin America*. Durham: Duke University Press.

Bishop, K. 2014. "The Architectural History of Disappearance." *Journal of the Society of Architectural Historians* 73(4): 556–78.

Bishop, P., and E. Mallie. 1987. *The Provisional IRA*. London: Corgi Books.

Blainey, G. 1966. *The Tyranny of Distance: How Distance Shaped Australia's History*. New York: Macmillan.

Bluche, F. 1986. *Septembre 1792: Logiques d'in massacre*. Paris: Editions Robert Laffont.

BnF (Bibliotheque nationale de France). 2010. *La Bastille ou "l'enfer des Vivants."* Paris.

Boal, F. W. 2002. "Belfast: Walls Within." *Political Geography* 21: 687–94.

Bodnar, J. 1992. *Remaking America*. Princeton: Princeton University Press.

Boime, A. 2008. *Art in an Age of Civil Struggle, 1848–1871*. Chicago: University of Chicago Press.

Bongie, L. 2004. *From Rogue to Everyman*. Montreal and Kingston: McGill–Queen's University Press.

Borgognon, J. A. 1968. "Panorama Indigena Paraguayo." *Suplemento Antropologico de la Revista del Ateneo Paraguaye*, III, 1–2 (Octobre). Asuncion.

Bosco, F. J. 2006. "The Madres de Plaza de Mayo and Three Decades of Human Rights' Activism: Embeddedness, Emotions, and Social Movements." *Annals in Association of American Geographers* 96(2): 342–65.

Bowen, D. 1988. "Ultramontanism in Quebec and the Irish Connection." In *The Untold Story: The Irish in Canada*, ed. R. O'Driscoll and L. Reynolds. Toronto: Celtic Arts of Canada.

Branch, T., and E. Propper. 1982. *Labyrinth*. New York: Viking Press.

Brodsky, M. 2005. *Memoria en construccion: el debate sobre la ESMA*. Buenos Aires: La Marca.

Brown, M. 2009. *The Culture of Punishment*. New York: NYU Press.

Burchell, G., C. Gordon, and P. Miller. 1991. *The Foucault Effect*. Chicago: University of Chicago Press.

Burke, K. 1966. *Language as Symbolic Action*. Berkeley: University of California Press.

Burgos, S. 1984. Abducted from January 26, 1977, to January 25, 1979. CONADEP Testimony.

Butler, J. 2004. *Precarious Life*. London: Verso.

Cadogan, L. 1967. "La Tragedia Guarani." *Suplemento Antropologico de la Revista del Ateneo Paraguaye*, II, 2 (Septiembre). Asuncion.

Campbell, B., L. McKeown, and F. O'Hagan. 1998. *Nor Meekly Serve My Time: The H Block Struggle (1976–1981)*. Belfast: Beyond the Pale.

Carneri, S. 2019. "Spanish Jesuit, Linguist Once Expelled by Dictator, Dies in Paraguay," *National Catholic Reporter*, December 10. https://www.ncronline.org/news/people/spanish -jesuit-linguist-once-expelled-dictator-dies-paraguay.

Caron, P. 1935. *Les massacres de septembre*. Paris: Maison du Livre Francais.

Carrabine, E. 2014. "Seeing Things." *Theoretical Criminology* 18(2): 134–58.

Carty, E., and D. Young. 2014. "Martin and Peter Go Back to Crumlin Gaol at Her Majesty's Pleasure." *Irish Independent*, June 25, 2–3.

Casey, V. 2003. "The Museum Effect." *Archives and Museum Informatics, Europe: Cultural Institutions and Digital Technology*. Paris: Ecole du Louvre, September 8–12.

Catala, S. 2013. *Les Hubert Robert de Besançon*. Milan: Silvana Editoriale.

Cea, R. 2013. "Bachelet revela que fue interrogada por el jefe de la Policia Secreta de Pinochet." *El Pais*, October 8. https://elpais.com/internacional/2013/10/08/actualidad/1381202095 _923747.html.

Cerruti, I. 2010. *Olimpo*. Buenos Aires: Instituto Espacio de la Memoria.

Chapman, A. 1982. *Drama and Power in a Hunting Society: The Selk'nam of Tierra del Fuego*. Cambridge: Cambridge University Press.

Christian, S. 1987. "Peron Hands." *New York Times*, September 6, Section 1, 25. https://www .nytimes.co.m/1987/09/06/world/peron-hands-police-find-trail-elusive.html.

Clark, L. B., and L. Payne. 2011. "Trauma Tourism in Latin America." In *Accounting for Violence*, edited by K. Bilbija and L. Payne. Durham: Duke University Press.

Cohen, S. 1995. "State Crimes of Previous Regimes." *Law and Social Inquiry* 20(1): 7–50.

———. 2001. *States of Denial*. Cambridge: Polity Press.

Cohen, S., and L. Taylor. 1972. *Psychological Survival*. Harmondsworth: Penguin.

Collins, C. 2011. "The Moral Economy of Memory: Public and Private Commemorative Space in Post-Pinochet Chile." In *Accounting for Violence*. Edited by K. Bilbija and L. Payne, 235–64. Durham: Duke University Press.

Collins, C., and K. Hite. 2013. "Memorial, Silences, and Reawakenings." In *The Politics of Memory in Chile*, edited by C. Collins, K. Hite, and Alfredo Joignant. Boulder: First Forum Press/Lynne Rienner.

Collins, P. 2017. "Orange Order: Protestants Told Not to Use 'RIP' As It Is Catholic Superstition." *Guardian*, July 29. https://www.theguardian.com/world/2017/jul/29/orange-order -protestants-told-not-to-use-rip-as-it-is-catholic-superstition.

Collins, C., K. Hite, and A. Joignant. 2013. *The Politics of Memory in Chile*. Boulder: First Forum Press/Lynne Rienner.

Community Relations Council. 2009. *Towards Sustainable Security: Interface Barriers and the Legacy of Segregation in Belfast*. Belfast: Community Relations Council.

CONADEP: National Commission on the Disappearance of Persons. 1986. *Nunca Mas* (Never Again). London: Faber and Faber.

Conciergerie. n.d. Conciergerie brochure (English). Paris: Centre des Monuments Nationaux.

Constitution Hill. n.d. Visitor's brochure.

Coogan, T. P. 2002. *The Troubles: Ireland's Ordeal and the Search for Peace*. New York and London: Palgrave Macmillan.

Cooke, P. 2014. *A History of Kilmainham Gaol: 1796–1924*. Dublin: Office of Public Works.

Cooper, A. D. 2008. *The Geography of Genocide*. Latham: University Press of America.

Coquet, R. 2010. Abducted from March 10, 1977, to December 8, 1978. EMSA Trial Testimony, Case 1270, August 5.

Costa, W. 2019a. "Paraguay Investigates Human Remains Found on Ex-Dictator Former Property." *The Guardian*, September 8.

———. 2019b. "Past Weighs Heavy as Paraguay Struggles with Ghosts of Dictatorship." *The Guardian*, December 10. https://www.theguardian.com/world/2019/dec/10/paraguay-dictator -alfredo-stroessner-dictatorship.

Cottle, S. 1997. "Reporting the Troubles in Northern Ireland: Paradigms and Media Propaganda." *Critical Studies in Mass Communication* 14: 282–96.

Creighton, D. 1956. *The Empire of Saint Lawrence.* Toronto: Macmillan.

Crenzel, E. 2019. "Crimes of the Last Dictatorship in Argentina and Its Qualification as Genocide." *Global Society* 33(3): 365–81.

Crooke, E. 2005. "Dealing with the Past." *International Journal of Heritage Studies* 11(2): 131–42.

Curtis, L. 1984. *Ireland: The Propaganda War, the British Media, and the Battle for Hearts and Minds.* London: Pluto Press.

Daleo, G. 2010. Abducted from October 18, 1977, to April 20, 1979. ESMA Trial Testimony, Case 1270, April 29.

Davis, A. 1971. *If They Come in the Morning.* New York: Third Press.

———. 2016a. *Angela Davis.* New York: International.

———. 2016b. "Radical Visions of Justice." JUSTICE IN ACTION public lectures. New Brunswick: Rutgers University, October 5. https://www.youtube.com/watch?v=ilrk5LXUj2Y.

———. 2016c. "The Prison Industrial Complex and Critical Resistance." Seminar moderated by Michael Welch. New Brunswick: Paul Robeson Cultural Center, Rutgers University, October 5.

Davis, M. 1990. *City of Quartz.* New York: Vintage.

Day, J. 2013. *Corrections and Collections.* New York: Routledge.

Debord, G. 1967. *The Society of the Spectacle.* Cambridge, MA: Zone Books.

De Certeau, M. 1984. *The Practice of Everyday Life.* Translated by S. Randall. Berkeley: University of California Press.

Delrio, W., D. Lenton, M. Musante, and M. Nagy. 2010. "Discussing Indigenous Genocide in Argentina." *Genocide Studies and Prevention: An International Journal* 5(2): 138–59.

de Paor, L. 1985. "The Rebel Mind." In *The Irish Mind,* edited by R. Kearny. Dublin: Wolfhound Press.

Der Ghougassian, K., and L. Brumat. 2018. "The Argentine Military and the Antisubversivo Genocide." *Genocide Studies International* 12(1): 48–71.

Dickinson, J., and B. Young. 1993. *A Short History of Quebec.* Toronto: Copp Clark Pitman.

Dillon, M. 1992. *Killer in Clowntown: Joe Doherty, the IRA, and the Special Relationship.* London: Hutchinson.

Dilts, A., and B. E. Harcourt. 2008. "Discipline, Security, and Beyond." *Carceral Notebooks* 4: 1–6.

Di Paolantonio, M. 2008. "A Site of Struggle, a Site of Conflicting Pedagogical Proposals: The Debate over Suitable Commemorative Form and Content for ESMA." *Journal of the Canadian Association for Curriculum Studies* 6(2): 25–42.

Dinges, J. 2004. *The Condor Years.* New York: Free Press.

Dinges, J., and S. Landau. 1980. *Assassination on Embassy Row.* New York: Pantheon Books.

Dooley, B. 1998. *Black and Green: The Fight for Civil Rights in Northern Ireland and Black America.* London: Pluto Press.

Douglas, M. 1966. *Purity and Danger.* London: Routledge and Kegan Paul.

Dowler, L. 1998. "'And They Think I'm Just a Nice Old Lady': Women and War in Belfast, Northern Ireland." *Gender, Place, and Culture* 5: 159–76.

Draper, S. 2011. "The Business of Memory: Reconstructing Torture Centers as Shopping Malls and Tourist Sites." In *Accounting for Violence*, edited by K. Bilbija and L. Payne. Durham: Duke University Press.

———. 2012. *Afterlives of Confinement: Spatial Transitions in Postdictatorship Latin America.* Pittsburgh: University of Pittsburgh Press.

Drndic, D. 2019. *EEG.* Translated by Celia Hawkesworth. New York: New Directions.

Ducharme, M. 2007. "Closing the Last Chapter of the Atlantic Revolution." *Proceedings of the American Antiquarian Society* 116(2): 413–30.

Dunning, T. 2009. "The Canadian Rebellions of 1817 and 1838 as a Borderland War." *Ontario History* 10I(2): 129–41.

Durkheim, E. 2008. *The Elementary Forms of Religious Life* [1915]. Translated by C. Cosman. New York: Oxford University Press.

Durkheim, E., and M. Mauss. 1963. *Primitive Classification* [1903]. Translated by R. Needham. Chicago: University of Chicago Press.

Eldemire, S. 2018. "From Belfast to Guantanamo." *The Intercept*, March 22. https://theintercept.com/2018/03/22/ireland-hooded-men-torture.

Elias, N. 2005. *The Civilizing Process.* Translated by Edmund Jephcott. Oxford: Blackwell.

Ellison, G., and M. O'Rawe. 2010. "Security Governance in Transition: The Compartmentalizing, Crowding Out, and Corralling of Policing and Security in Northern Ireland." *Theoretical Criminology* 14(1): 31–57.

Ellison, G., and C. O'Reilly. 2008. "Ulster's Policing Goes Global." *Crime, Law, Social Change,* 50: 331–51.

Ellison, G., N. Pino, and P. Shirlow. 2013. "Assessing the Determinants of Public Confidence in the Police." *Criminology and Criminal Justice* 13(5): 552–76.

English, R. 1998. *Ernie O'Malley: IRA Intellectual.* Oxford: Oxford University Press.

———. 2005. *Armed Struggle: The History of the IRA.* Oxford: Oxford University Press.

Erikson, K. 1966. *Wayward Puritans.* New York: John Wiley and Sons.

Evans, R. 1982. *The Fabrication of Virtue: English Prison Architecture, 1750–1840.* Cambridge: Cambridge University Press.

Ewel, N. 2018. "45 Years The Caravan of Death." *Chile Today*, September 28. https://chiletoday.cl/site/45-years-the-caravan-of-death-chiles-notorious-death-squad-remains-an-open-wound.

Familiares. 2006. "La teoria de los dos demonios: Una falsa justificacion del terrorismo de Estado" (The Two Demons Theory: A False Justification of State Terrorism), Archival Document, 7. Cordoba: Familiares de Deseparacidos y Detenidos por Razones Politicas de Cordoba.

Feierstein, D. 2014. *Genocide as Social Practice.* New Brunswick, NJ: Rutgers University Press.

Feierstein, L. 2014. "A Quilt of Memory." *European Review* 22: 585–93.

Feitlowitz, M. 1998. *A Lexicon of Terror: Argentina and the Legacies of Torture.* New York: Oxford University Press.

Feldman, A. 1991. *Formations of Violence.* Chicago: University of Chicago Press.

Flander, S., A. Chen, J. Piche, and K. Walby. 2016. "Critical Punishment Memorialization in Canada." *Critical Criminology* 24: 1–18.

Fletcher, L., and E. Stover. 2009. *The Guantanamo Effect.* Berkeley: University of California Press.

Foster, R. F. 1988. *Modern Ireland, 1600–1972*. London: Penguin.

Foucault, M. 1979. *Discipline and Punish*. Translated by A. Sheridan. New York: Vintage.

———. 1980. "Prison Talk." In *Power/Knowledge*, edited by C. Gordon. New York: Pantheon Books.

———. 1986. "Of Other Spaces." *Diacritics* 16(1): 22–27.

———. 1996. "The Eye of Power." In *Foucault Live*, edited by S. Lotringer. New York: Semiotext(e).

Fournel, V. 1892. *La Patriote Palloy et l'exploitation de la Bastille*. Paris: H. Champion.

Friedman, M. 1962. *Capitalism and Freedom*. Chicago: University of Chicago Press.

———. 1982. "Free Markets and the Generals." *Newsweek*, January 25, 59.

Funck-Brentano, F. 1979. *La Bastille et sus secrets* [1898]. Paris: J. Tallandier.

Garland, D. 1990. *Punishment and Modern Society*. Chicago: University of Chicago Press.

Gates-Madsen, N. 2011. "Marketing and Sacred Space: The Parque de la Memoria in Buenos Aires." In *Accounting for Violence*. Edited by K. Bilbija and L. Payne, 151–78. Durham: Duke University Press.

Gay, P. 1988. *Voltaire's Politics*. New Haven: Yale University Press.

Ginzburg, V. 2008. "Los nuevos habitants de la ESMA." *Pagina/12*, Marzo 12.

Girondo, A. 2010. Abducted from May 15, 1977, to end of January 19, 1979. ESMA Trial Testimony, Case 1270, July 1.

Gladstone, R., and P. Robins. 2021. "The Ghosts of Northern Ireland's Troubles Are Back: What's Going On?" *New York Times*, April 12. https://www.nytimes.com/2021/04/12/world/europe/Northern-Ireland-Brexit-Covid-Troubles.html?action=click&module=In%20Other%20News&pgtype=Homepage.

Godechot, J. 1970. *The Taking of the Bastille*. Translated by Jean Stewart. New York: Faber and Faber.

———. 1986. *Les Révolutions (1770–1799)* [1963]. Paris: Presses Universitaires de France.

Goffman, E. 1959. *The Presentation of Self in Everyday Life*. New York: Anchor.

Goñi, U. 2003. *The Real Odessa: How Peron Brought the Nazi War Criminals to Argentina*. London: Granta.

———. 2011. "Argentina's 'Angel of Death' Jailed for Crimes Against Humanity." *The Guardian*, October 27. https://www.theguardian.com/world/2011/oct/27/argentinas-angel-of-death-jailed.

———. 2017. "Argentina 'Death Flight' Pilots Sentenced for Deaths Including Pope's Friend." *The Guardian*, November 29. https://www.theguardian.com/world/2017/nov/29/argentina-death-flight-pilots-sentenced-for-deaths-including-popes-friend.

———. 2018. "Argentina: Two Ex-Ford Executives Convicted in Torture Case." *The Guardian*, December 11. https://www.theguardian.com/world/2018/dec/11/pedro-muller-hedro-sibilla-ford-executives-argentina-torture-case.

———. 2019. "How Did an Accused Torturer End Up Teaching at the Sorbonne?" *The Guardian*, December 22. https://www.theguardian.com/world/2019/dec/22/argentina-sorbonne-accused-torturer-mario-sandoval.

Goodell, C. 1973. *Political Prisoners in America*. New York: Random House.

Graham, B. 1996. "The Contested Interpretation of Heritage Landscapes in Northern Ireland." *International Journal of Heritage Studies* 2 (1–2): 10–22.

Graham, B., and S. McDowell. 2007. "Meaning in the Maze." *Cultural Geographies* 14(3): 343–68.

Graham, B., and Y. Whelan. 2007. "The Legacies of the Dead." *Environment and Planning D: Society and Space* 25: 476–95.

Grant, K. 2019. *Last Weapons: Hunger Strikes and Fasts in the British Empire, 1890–1948.* Berkeley: University of California Press.

Gras, M. 2010. Abducted at ESMA between January 1977 and mid-1978. ESMA Trial Testimony, Case 1270, ESMA Trial Testimony, Case 1270: revised and ratified by the survivor.

Green, M. 1998. *The Prison Experience: A Loyalist Perspective.* Belfast: EPIC.

Greer, A. 1993. *The Patriots and the People.* Toronto: University of Toronto Press.

———. 1995. "1837–38 Rebellion Reconsidered." *Canadian Historical Review* 76(1): 1–18.

Greg, P. 2013. *The Crum.* Belfast: Glen.

Gregory, D. 2004. *The Colonial Present.* Oxford: Blackwell.

Grupo de Estudios Urbanos. 1983. *Una ciudad sin memoria.* Montevideo: Ediciones de la Banda Oriental.

Groupe d'Information sur les Prisons. 1971. *Enquete dan vingt prisons.* Paris: Editions Champ-Libre.

Guelph Mercury. 2006. "Former Chilean Dictator Augusto Pinochet Dies." December 11.

Guillotine, J. 1790. Reported Speech in the Assemblee National Transcript for January 21, in Archives Parlementaires de 1787 a 1860, p. 278.

Gumede, W. M. 2005. *Thabo Mbeki and the Battle for the Soul of the ANC.* Cape Town: Zebra Press.

Gunder Funk, A. 1976. *Economic Genocide in Chile.* Nottingham: Spokesman Books.

Gusinde, M. 2015. *El espiritu de los hombres de Tierra del Fuego.* Paris: Editions Xavier Barral, Beaux Livres.

Guyer J. 2014. "The True Gift: Thoughts on L'Année sociologique of 1925." *Journal of Classical Sociology* 14(1): 11–21.

Guzmán, P. 1993. *Batalla de Chile.* New York: First Run Films.

Harcourt, B. E. 2011. *The Illusion of Free Markets.* Cambridge, MA: Harvard University Press.

Harder Horst, R. D. 2007. *The Stroessner Regime and Indigenous Resistance in Paraguay.* Gainesville: University Press of Florida.

Hearty, K. 2014. "A Shared Narrative? A Case Study of the Contested Legacy of Policing in the North of Ireland." *British Journal of Criminology* 54(6): 1047–66.

Hennessy, T. 2005. *Northern Ireland: The Origins of the Troubles.* Dublin: Gill and Macmillan.

Hertz R. 1994. *Sin and Expiation in Primitive Society* [1988], edited and translated by R. Parkin. Occasional Paper no. 2. Oxford: British Centre for Durkheimian Studies.

———. 2009. *Death and the Right Hand* [1960], edited and translated by R. Needham and C. Needham. Introduction by E. E. Evans-Pritchard. London: Cohen and West.

Hinds, L. S. 2016. "Reflections of a People's Lawyer." JUSTICE IN ACTION public lectures. New Brunswick: Rutgers University, October 5. https://www.youtube.com/watch?v=ilrk5LXUj2Y.

———. 2019. *Illusions of Justice,* 2nd ed. Iowa City: University of Iowa.

Hite, K. 2004. "Chile's National Stadium: As Monument and Memorial." *ReVista: Harvard Review of Latin America* (Spring): 58–61.

Hubert, H., and M. Mauss. 1981. *Sacrifice.* Translated by W. D. Halls. Chicago: University of Chicago Press.

Humphrey, G. 1924. "The Psychology of the Gestalt." *Journal of Educational Psychology* 15(7): 401–12.

Hunt, L. 1984. *Politics, Culture, and Class in the French Revolution.* Berkeley: University of California Press.

Hurley, K. 1996. *The Gothic Body.* Cambridge: Cambridge University Press.

Huyssen, A. 2003. *Present Pasts.* Stanford: Stanford University Press.

Invernizzi, H., and J. Gociol. 2003. *Un golpe a los libros.* Buenos Aires: Eudeba.

Irish Times. 2010. "Human Rights Activist Pat Rice Dies at 64." https://web.archive.org/web/20121021105255/http://www.irishtimes.com/newspaper/ireland/2010/0709/1224274349711.html.

Jacobs, J. 1977. *Stateville.* Chicago: University of Chicago Press.

Jelin, E. 2003. *State Repression and the Labors of Memory.* Translated by J. Rein and M. Godoy-Anativia. Minneapolis: University of Minnesota Press.

Jelin, E., and S. Kaufman. 2000. "Layers of Memories." In *The Politics of War,* edited by T. Ashplant, G. Dawson, and M. Roper. London: Routledge.

Johnson, L. 2004. *Death, Dismemberment, and Memory.* Albuquerque: University of New Mexico Press.

Johnson, R. 1998. *Deathwork.* Belmont: Wadsworth.

Johnston, N. 1978. *The Human Cage.* New York: Walker and Company.

Joignant, A. 2013. "Pinochet's Funeral." In *The Politics of Memory in Chile,* edited by C. Collins, K. Hite, and Alfredo Joignant. Boulder: FirstForumPress/Lynne Rienner.

Kaiser, S. 2002. "Escraches." *Media, Culture, and Society* 24: 499–516.

———. 2011. "Memory Inventory." In *Accounting for Violence,* edited by K Bilbija and L Payne. Durham: Duke University Press.

———. 2020. "Writing and Reading Memories at a Buenos Aires Memorial Site: The Ex-ESMA." *History and Memory* 32 (1): 69–99.

Katz, J. 1988. *Seductions of Crime.* New York: Basic Books.

Kilmainham Gaol. n.d. *Visitors' Guide.* Dublin: Office of Public Works.

Kindynis, T., and B. Garrett. 2015. "Entering the Maze." *Crime Media Culture* 11(1): 5–20.

Kinzer, S. 1983. "Church in Chile Doesn't Just Pray for Reform." *New York Times,* November 20. https://www.nytimes.com/1983/11/20/weekinreview/church-in-chile-doesn-t-just-pray-for-reform.html.

Klein, N. 2007. *The Shock Doctrine.* New York: Picador.

Knight, F. H. 1932. "The Newer Economics and the Control of Economic Activity." *Journal of Political Economy* 40(4): 455–71.

Kornbluh, P. 2013. *The Pinochet File.* New York: Free Press.

Kubiak, A. 1987. "Disappearances as History." *Theatre Journal* 39(1): 78–88.

———. 1989. "Stages of Terror." *Journal of Dramatic Theory and Criticism,* Fall: 3–30.

Kusnetzoff, J. 1986. "Renegacion, desmentida, desaparicion y percepticido como tecnicas psicopaticas de la salvacion de la patria." In *Argentina Psicoanalisis Represion Politica,* edited by O. Abudara. Buenos Aires: Ediciones Kargieman.

Kwon, H. 2014. "Spirits in the Work of Durkheim, Hertz, and Mauss: Reflections on Post-War Vietnam." *Journal of Classical Sociology* 14(1): 122–31.

La Prison-des-Patriotes. n.d. Exhibition Center brochure. Montreal: La Prison-des-Patriotes.

Lemoine, H. 1930. *Le demolisseur de la Bastille.* Paris: Perrin.

Lennon, J., and M. Foley. 2010. *Dark Tourism*. London: Thompson Learning.

Lernoux, P. 1985. "Blood Taints Church in Argentina." *National Catholic Reporter*, December 4.

Letelier, O. 1976. "The 'Chicago Boys' in Chile." *The Nation*, August 28. https://www.thenation.com/article/archive/the-chicago-boys-in-chile-economic-freedoms-awful-toll.

Levitt, P. 2015. *Artifacts and Allegiances*. Berkeley: University California Press.

Lewin, M. 1985. Abducted from March 25, 1978, to January 10, 1979. Juntas Trial Testimony, Case 13, July 18.

Lindström, K., K. Kull, and H. Palang. 2011. "Semiotic Study of Landscapes." *Sign Systems Studies* 39(2–4): 12–36.

Linguet, S. 2015. *Memoirs of the Bastille* [1884]. London: Forgotten Books.

Lira, E., and B. Loveman. 2013. "Torture as Public Policy, 1810–2011." In *The Politics of Memory in Chile*, edited by C. Collins, K. Hite, and Alfredo Joignant. Boulder: FirstForumPress/Lynne Rienner.

Longoni, A., and G. Bruzzone. 2008. *El siluetazo*. Buenos Aires: Adriana Hildago.

Lopez, M. 2013. *A pesar de las sombras: Imagenes del ex Centro Clandestino de Detencion, Tortura, y Exterminio "Olimpo."* Buenos Aires: Instituto Espacio Para la Memoria.

Lord, B. 2006. "Foucault's Museum." *Museum and Society* 4(1): 1–14.

Lotman, J. 2000. *Universe of the Mind*. Translated by A. Shukman. Bloomington: Indiana University Press.

———. 2004. *Culture and Explosion*, edited by Marina Grishakova. Translated by Wilma Clark. New York: Mouton de Gruyter.

———. 2005. "On The Semiosphere." Translated by W. Clark. *Sign Systems Studies* 33(1): 206–29.

Loza, C. 2010. Abducted from December 16, 1976, to January 6, 1977. ESMA Trial Testimony, Case 1270.

Ludmer, J. 1994. "Introduction." In *Las culturas de fin de siglo en América Latina: Coloquio en Yale, 8 y 9 de abril de 1994*, 7–24. Rosario: Beatriz Viterbo.

Lynch, J. 2019. *The Partition of Ireland: 1918–1925*. Cambridge: Cambridge University Press.

Maas, P. 1987. Introduction to *Ten Dead Men* by D. Beresford. New York: Atlantic Monthly Press.

Mac Lochlainn, P. 2006. *Last Words*. Dublin: Department of Arts, Heritage.

Macey, D. 1993. *The Lives of Michel Foucault*. New York: Vintage.

Mandela, N. 1994. *Long Walk to Freedom*. London: Little, Brown.

Marais, H. 2001. *South Africa: Limits to Change: The Political Economy of Transition*. Cape Town: University of Cape Town Press.

Marchak, P. 1999. *God's Assassins*. Montreal and Kingston: McGill–Queens University Press.

Marti, A. M. 2010. Abducted from March 18, 1977, to December 19, 1978. ESMA Trial Testimony, Case 1270, June 26.

Mayerfeld, A., and T. Murray 2001. "The Ghosts of Place." *Theory and Society* 26(6): 813–36.

McAllister, I. 2004. "'The Armalite and the Ballot Box.'" *Electoral Studies* 23: 123–42.

McAtackney, L. 2013. "Dealing With Difficult Pasts." *Prison Service Journal* 210: 17–23.

———. 2014. *An Archaeology of the Troubles*. Oxford: Oxford University Press.

———. 2015. "Memorials and Marching." *Historical Archaeology* 49(3): 110–25.

———. 2018. "Where Are All the Women." In *Heritage after Conflict: Northern Ireland*, edited by C. Crooke and T. Maguire. London: Routledge.

———. 2020. "Segregation Walls and Public Memory in Contemporary Belfast." In *Walling In and Walling Out*, edited by L. McAtackney and R. McGuire. Albuquerque: University of New Mexico Press.

McCaughan, M. 2002. *True Crimes: Rodolfo Walsh*. London: Latin American Bureau.

McConville, S. 1995. "The Victorian Prison." In *The Oxford History of Prisons*, edited by N. Morris and D. Rothman. Oxford: Oxford University Press.

McDonald, H. 2016. "Easter Rising Commemoration Draws Thousands in Dublin." *The Guardian*, March 27. http://www.theguardian.com/world/2016/mar/27/easter-rising-centenary -to-be-marked-in-dublin-gpo-amid-heavy-security.

McDowell, S. 2008. "Selling Conflict Heritage through Tourism in Peacetime." *International Journal of Heritage Studies* 14(5): 405–21.

McEvoy, K. 2001. *Paramilitary Imprisonment in Northern Ireland*. Oxford: Oxford University Press.

McEvoy, K., and H. Conway. 2004. "The Dead, the Law, and the Politics of the Past." *Journal of Law and Society* 31: 359–62.

McEvoy, K., and P. Shirlow. 2009. "Reimagining DDR: Ex-Combatants, Leadership, and Moral Agency in Conflict Transformation." *Theoretical Criminology* 13(1): 31–59.

McGlinchey, M. 2019. *Unfinished Business: The Politics of "Dissident" Irish Republicanism*. Manchester: University of Manchester Press.

McGuffin, J. 1974. *The Guineapigs*. London: Penguin.

McKittrick, D., S. Kelters, B. Feeney, and C. Thornton. 2001. *Lives Lost*, 2nd ed. Belfast: Blackstaff Press.

McManners, J. 1981. *Death and the Enlightenment*. Oxford: Oxford University Press.

McQueen, S. 2008. *Hunger*. Directed by Steve McQueen. Film4 Productions.

McSherry, J. P. 1999. "Operation Condor." *Social Justice* 26(4): 144–74.

———. 2005. *Predatory States: Operation Condor and Covert War in Latin America*. New York: Rowman and Littlefield.

Mendez Carreras, H., and M. Villagran San Millan. 1982. "On Holmberg's Case." *Buenos Aires Herald*, September 18, 22.

Miami Herald. 1999. "Arrested Gunman Implicates Oviedo, Cubas in Argana Assassination." October 29. http://www.latinamericanstudies.org/paraguay/gunman.htm.

Michelet, J. 2008. *History of the French Revolution* [1847]. Translated by C. Cocks. Oxford: Oxford University Press.

Milia, M. A., A. M. Marti, and de S. S. Osatinsky. 1979. Testimony jointly presented on October 1 before the French National Assembly. Published by the Argentine Commission on Human Rights (CADHU), Genocide Testimonies, 1980.

Mirabeau, V. R. 2010. *La theorie de l'impôt* (*Theory of Taxation*) [1760]. Nabu Press (French edition).

Moloney, E. 2007. *A Secret History of the IRA*, 2nd ed. New York: Penguin Books.

———. 1991. "Closing Down the Airwaves." In *The Media and Northern Ireland*, edited by B. Rolston. Houndmills: Macmillan.

Morello, G. 2019. *The Catholic Church and Argentina's Dirty War*. New York: Oxford University Press.

Mumford, L. 1970. *The Culture of Cities* [1938]. New York: Mariner.

Munzel, M. 1972. *The Ache Indians*. Copenhagen: International Work Group for Indigenous Affairs.

Murphy, W. 2014. *Political Imprisonment and the Irish, 1912–1921*. Oxford: Oxford University Press.

Musées royaux des Beaux-Arts de Belgique. 2016. "Andres Serrano: Uncensored Photographs." Brochure. Brussels.

Nation [Chile]. 2007. "DD.HH: Confirman Condena a Coronel (R) Por Muerte de Joan Alsina." March 30. http://www.lanacion.cl/prontus_noticias/site/artic/20070330/pags/20070330175145.html.

Neier, A. 1995. "Confining Dissent." In *The Oxford History of the Prison of Punishment in Western Society*, edited by N. Morris and D. Rothman. New York: Oxford University Press.

Neill, W. 2017. "Representing the Maze/Long Kesh Prison in Northern Ireland." In *The Palgrave Handbook of Prison Tourism*, edited by J. Wilson et al. London: Palgrave Macmillan.

Neill, W., D. Fitzsimmons, and B. Murtagh. 1995. *Reimagining the Pariah City*. Avebury: Aldershot.

Newburn, T., and R. Sparks. 2004. *Criminal Justice and Political Cultures*. Cullompton: Willan.

Nisbett, M., and J. Rapson. 2020. "The Role of Ex-Paramilitaries and Former Prisoners in Political Tourism." *Political Geography* 80: 102–85.

Nora, P. 1989. "Between Memory and History." *Representations* 26: 7–24.

———. 2002. "The Reasons for the Upsurge in Memory." *Transit-Virtuelles Forum* 22. https://www.eurozine.com/reasons-for-the-current-upsurge-in-memory.

Nunca Mas. 1986. The Report of the Argentine National Commission on the Disappeared. New York: Farrar, Straus & Giroux.

O'Carroll, L. 2018. "Brexit Warning from US Senator Who Brokered Northern Ireland Peace George Mitchell Says 'Serious Trouble' Could Lie Ahead If Border Checks Are Reinstated." *The Guardian*, March 4. https://www.theguardian.com/world/2018/mar/03/brexit-warning-us-senator-brokered-northern-ircland-peace-george-mitchell.

O'Connor, N. 2014. "Queen Sets an Example Other Leaders Should Follow." *Irish Independent*, June 25, 3.

O'Donoghue, F. 1971. *Sworn to Be Free: The Complete Book of the IRA Jail-Breaks, 1918–1921*. Tralee: Anvil Books.

O'Dwyer, R. 2010. *The Bastille of Ireland*. Dublin: The History Press Ireland.

O'Gallagher, M. 1988. "The Irish in Quebec." in *The Untold Story: The Irish in Canada*, edited by R. O'Driscoll and L. Reynolds. Toronto: Celtic Arts of Canada.

Olley, J. 2007. *Castles of Ulster*. Belfast: Factotum.

O'Rawe, R. 2005. *Blanketmen*. Dublin: New Island.

Oquendo-Villar, C. 2011. "Dress for Success." In *Accounting for Violence*. Edited by K. Bilbija and L. Payne, 265–90. Durham: Duke University Press.

Outram, D. 1989. *The Body and the French Revolution*. New Haven: Yale University Press.

Pantheon. n.d. *Pantheon*. Brochure: English version.

Park, Rebekah. 2014. *The Reappeared: Argentine Former Political Prisoners*. New Brunswick: Rutgers University Press.

Park, Robert. 1915. "The City." *American Journal of Sociology* 20(5): 577–612.

Perelli, C. 1994. "Memoria de Sangre." In *Remapping Memory*, edited by J. Boyarin. Minneapolis: University of Minnesota Press.

Pitt, K. 2010. *Body, Nation, and Narrative in the Americas.* London: Palgrave Macmillan.

Pittsburgh Post-Gazette. 1988. "British Government Bans Song by Irish Group." November 28, 6.

Purbrick, L. 2004. "The Architecture of Containment." In D. Wylie, *The Maze.* London: Granta.

Quinn, C. 2019. "Fian Gerald McAuley's Mum Speaks on his 50th Anniversary. 15 August. Belfastmedia.com. https://belfastmedia.com/fian-gerald-mcauleys-mum-speaks-on-his -50th-anniversary.

Quigley, J. B. 2006. *The Genocide Convention.* Burlington: Ashgate.

Ramsamy, E. 2016. "The International Community and Transformation in South Africa." In *Social Justice and Transformative Learning*, edited by S. Thomlinson-Clarke and D. Clarke. New York: Routledge.

Ranalletti, M. 2010. "Denial of the Reality of State Terrorism in Argentina as Narrative of the Recent Past." *Genocide Studies and Prevention: An International Journal* 5(2): 160–73.

Remm, T. 2011. "Understanding the City through Its Semiotic Spatialities," *Sign Systems Studies* 39(2–4): 124–44.

Republican News: The Voice of Republican Ulster. 1975. "Torture Resumes at Castlereagh." 5(35), September 13, 1.

Rettig Commission Report. 1993. *Report on the National Commission on Truth and Reconciliation* (English version). Notre Dame: University of Notre Dame Press.

Reuters. 2018. "Victor Jara Murder: Ex-Military Officers Sentenced in Chile for 1973 Death." *The Guardian*, July 3. https://www.theguardian.com/world/2018/jul/03/victor-jara -ex-military-officers-sentenced-in-chile-for-1973-death.

Riley, A. T. 1999. "Whence Durkheim's Nietzschean Grandchildren." *European Journal of Sociology / Archives Européennes de Sociologie* 40: 302–30.

Robben, A. 2005. *Political Violence and Trauma in Argentina.* Philadelphia: University of Pennsylvania Press.

———. 2012. "From Dirty War to Genocide." *Memory Studies* 5(3): 305–15.

Robin, M. M. 2003. "Les escadrons de la mort: L'École Franco-Algérienne." https://www .youtube.com/watch?v=8IaA8rTeQRY.

Robinson, R. 1989. "Subtle Protests You Can Hang on the Wall." *New York Times*, August 24. https://www.nytimes.com/1989/08/24/garden/subtle-protests-you-can-hang-on-the -wall.html.

Roht-Arriaza, N. 2005. *The Pinochet Effect: Transnational Justice in Age of Human Rights.* Philadelphia: University of Pennsylvania Press.

Rolston, B. 1992. *Drawing Support: Murals in the North of Ireland (1).* Dublin: Beyond the Pale.

———. 1998. *Drawing Support: Murals of War and Peace (2).* Dublin: Beyond the Pale.

———. 2003. *Drawing Support: Murals and Transition in the North of Ireland (3).* Dublin: Beyond the Pale.

———. 2013. *Drawing Support: Murals and Conflict Transformation in Northern Ireland (4).* Dublin: Beyond the Pale.

Ruetalo, V. 2008. "From Penal Institution to Shopping Mecca." *Cultural Critique* 68: 38–65.

Sachs, A. 2007. "I Sang in My Cell Because I Wouldn't 'Sing' and Other Tales." In *Sociology and Politics of Denial*, edited by David Downes, Paul Rock, Christine Chinkin, and Conor Gearty. Cullumpton: Willan.

Said, E. 1993. *Culture and Imperialism*. New York: Vintage.

Sands, B. 1998. *Writings from Prison*. Cork City: Mercier Press.

Sands, P. 2021. *The Ratline*. New York: Penguin.

Saoirse. 2013. "Statement From a Member of Republican Sinn Fein." No. 310 (February), Dublin.

Sarmiento, D. F. 2005. *Recollections of Provincial Past*. Oxford: Oxford University Press.

Scarlata, J. 2014. *Rethinking Occupied Ireland*. Syracuse: Syracuse University Press.

Scarry, E. 1985. *The Body in Pain*. Oxford: Oxford University Press.

Schama, S. 1990. *Citizens: A Chronicle of the French Revolution*. New York: Vintage.

Schemo, D. J. 1999. "Files in Paraguay Detail Atrocities of U.S. Allies." *New York Times*, August 11, Section A, 10. https://www.nytimes.com/1999/08/11/world/files-in-paraguay-detail -atrocities-of-us-allies.html.

Schwartz, M. 2018. *Public Pages*. Austin: University of Texas Press.

Searcy, R. A. 2015. "Joe Doherty Corner: The Troubles in America." *The Back Table: Archives and Special Collections at New York University*, March 13. https://wp.nyu.edu/specialcollections /2015/03/13/joe-doherty-corner-the-troubles-in-america.

Segal, L. 2006. *Number Four*. Johannesburg: Penguin.

Sennett, R. 1969. *Classic Essays on the Culture of Cities*. Englewood Cliffs: Prentice-Hall.

Seodaemun Prison History Hall. n.d. English Version Brochure. Seoul.

Seodaemun Prison History Hall. 2010. *A Place of Independence and Democracy*. Seoul.

Sevenko, L. 2004. *The Power of Place*. Minneapolis: Center for Victims of Torture.

Sewell, W. 1996. "Historical Events as Transformations of Structures: Inventing Revolution at the Bastille." *Theory and Society* 25: 841–81.

Shallice, T. 1973. "The Ulster Depth Interrogation Techniques." *Cognition* 1: 385–405.

Shirlow, P., and B. Murtagh. 2006. *Belfast*. London: Pluto.

Simpson, J., and J. Bennett. 1985. *The Disappeared*. London: Robson.

Slahi, M. O. 2015. *Guantanamo Diary*. New York: Little, Brown.

Slattery, M. 1980. "Dr. Edmund Bailey O'Callaghan of New York." *CCHA, Study Sessions* 47: 23–40.

———. 1997. "Irish Radicalism and the Roman Catholic Church in Quebec and Ireland, 1833–1834." *CCHA, Historical Studies* 63: 29–58.

Smith, L. 2006. *Uses of Heritage*. London: Routledge.

———. 2011. "The 'Doing' of Heritage: Heritage as Performance." In *Performing Heritage Research, Practice, and Development in Museum Theatre and Live Interpretation*, edited by A. Jackson and J Kidd. Manchester: Manchester University Press.

Smith, P. 1999. "The Elementary Forms of Place and Their Transformations." *Qualitative Sociology* 22(1): 13–36.

———. 2008. *Punishment and Culture*. Chicago: University of Chicago Press.

Smith, P., and J. Alexander. 2005. "The New Durkheim." In *The Cambridge Companion to Durkheim*, edited by J. Alexander and P. Smith. New York: Cambridge University Press.

Soffiantini, A. M. 2010. Abducted from August 16, 1977, until mid-1978. ESMA Trial Testimony, Case 1270, November 11.

Sokolowski, T. 2019. Introducing *Angela Davis—Seize the Time*. The Jane Voorhees Zimmerli Art Museum, Rutgers University, New Brunswick. Organizing committee correspondence.

Sorbille, M. 2008. "Argentine Military Terrorism." *Cultural Critique* 68: 86–128.

Souvenir Guidebook to Crumlin Road Gaol. n.d. Belfast.

Sozzo, M. 2016. "Democratization, Politics, and Punishment in Argentina." *Punishment and Society* 18(3): 301–24.

Spierenburg, P. 1984. *The Spectacle of Suffering*. Cambridge: Cambridge University Press.

———. 1995. "The Body and the State." In *The Oxford History of the Prison of Punishment in Western Society*, edited by N. Morris and D. Rothman. New York: Oxford University Press.

Spire, J. 1991. "La Detention a Fresnes durant la Guerre d'Algerie." In *Fresnes, la Prison, Les Establissements Penitentiaries de France: 1895–1990*, edited by C. Carlier, J. Spire, and F. Wasserman. Fresnes: Ecomusee.

Spooner, M. H. 1999. *Soldiers in a Narrow Land*. Berkeley: University of California Press.

Spy in the IRA. 2017. Gerry Adams and the Murder of Denis Donaldson. September 21. https://www.youtube.com/watch?v=apBLMtOtI9Q.

Steinacher, G. 2012. *Nazis on the Run: How Hitler's Henchmen Fled Justice*. Oxford: Oxford University Press.

Strazzeri, A. 2010. Abducted from December 22, 1978, to the end of March 1980. ESMA Trial Testimony, Case 1270, November 11.

Suarez-Orozco, M. 1991. "The Heritage of Enduring a 'Dirty War.'" *Journal of Psychohistory* 18(4): 469–505.

Sudjic, D. 2006. "Engineering Conflict." *New York Times Magazine*, May 21, 23–33.

Tackett, T. 2011. "Rumor and Revolution." *French History and Civilization* 4: 54–64.

Taylor, D. 1997. *Disappearing Acts: Spectacles of Gender and Nationalism in Argentina*. Durham: Duke University Press.

Taylor, P. 1986. "The Semantics of Violence." In *Communicating Politics*, edited by P. Golding, G. Murdock, and P. Schlesinger. Leicester: Leicester University Press.

———. 1997. *Provos: The IRA and Sinn Fein*. 1980. *Beating the Terrorists? Interrogation in Omagh, Gough, and Castlereagh*. New York: Penguin.

———. 1999. *Loyalists: War and Peace in Northern Ireland*. New York: TV Books.

———. 2001. *Brits: The War against the IRA*. London: Bloomsbury.

Terziyska, Y. 2019. "A History of Violence." *The Guardian*, February 13. https://www.theguardian.com/artanddesign/2019/feb/13/andres-serrano-interview-torture.

Testa, A. M. I. 2010. Abducted from November 13, 1979, to end of March 1980. ESMA Trial Testimony, Case 1270, May 7.

The Official Story [*La Historia Oficial*]. 1985. Directed by Luis Puenzo, written by Puenzo and Aida Bortnik.

Tilley, C. 1970. "Preface" to *The Taking of the Bastille: July 14, 1789* by J. Godechot. Translated by Jean Stewart. New York: Faber and Faber.

Timerman, J. 1998. *Prisoner Without a Name, Cell Without a Number* [1981]. Translated by T. Talbot. New York: Vintage Books.

Torture Museum. n.d. *Medieval Exhibition*. Brochure. Amsterdam: SignenPrint.nl.

Touhill, B. M. 1981. *William Smith O'Brien and His Revolutionary Companions in Penal Exile*. Columbia: University of Missouri Press.

Trinchero, H. H. 2006. "The Genocide of Indigenous Peoples in the Formation of the Argentine Nation-State." *Journal of Genocide Research* (8)2: 121–35.

Turner, V. 1977. *The Ritual Process*. Ithaca: Cornell University Press.

Valdes, J. G. 1995. *Pinochet's Economists*. Cambridge: Cambridge University Press.

Vasquez, L. A. 2010. Abducted from October 9, 1976, to October 22, 1976. ESMA Trial Testimony Case 1270, December 22.

Verbitsky, H. 1996. *The Flight*. New York: New Press.

Verdery, K. 1999. *The Political Lives of Dead Bodies: Reburial and Post-Socialist Change*. New York: Columbia University Press.

Verdugo, P. 2001. *Chile, Pinochet, and the Caravan of Death*. Miami: North-South Center Press.

Verney, J. 1994. *O'Callaghan*. Ottawa: Carleton University Press.

Vidal, J. M. 2004. "Juan Carlos Aramburu, el cardenal que 'bendijo' la dictadura argentina." *El Mundo*. http://www.elmundo.es/elmundo/2004/11/19/obituarios/1100887302.html.

Vimont, J. C. 1990. "Enfermer les politiques: La mise en place progressive des regimes politiques' d'incarceration (1815–1848)." In P. Vigier et al. *Repression et prisons politiques en France et en Europe au XIXe siècle*. Paris: Creaphis.

———. 1993. *La Prison Politique: Genese d'une mode d'incarceration specifique, XVIIIe–XXe siecle*. Paris: Anthropos: Diffusion, Economica.

Visitors' Guide. n.d. Kilmainham Gaol. Dublin: Office of Public Works.

"Vierry Cevallos." n.d. Brochure. Archivo Nacional de la Memoria. Buenos Aires: Ministerio de Justicia y Derechos Humanos, Presidencia de la Nacion.

Vieyra, L. 2010. Abducted from March 11, 1977, to July 26, 1978. ESMA Trial Testimony, Case 1270, September 15.

Virilio, P. 1994. *The Vision Machine*. Bloomington: University of Indiana Press.

Wallot, J. P. 1973. "Révolution et réformisme dans le Bas-Canada (1773–1815)." *Annales hisitoriques de la Révolution française* 45: 213–35.

Walsh, R. 1977. "Open Letter from a Writer to the Military Junta." March 24. https://www.historyisaweapon.com/defcon1/walshopenletterargjunta.html.

Waterton, E. 2008. "Sights of Sites." *Journal of Heritage Tourism* 4(1): 37–56.

Waxman, O. 2018. "The U.S. Government Had Nelson Mandela on the Terrorist Watch Lists Until 2008. Here's Why." *Time*, July 18. https://time.com/5338569/nelson-mandela-terror-list.

Welch, M. 2000. *Flag Burning: Moral Panic and the Criminalization of Protest*. New York: de Gruyter.

———. 2003. "Trampling of Human Rights in the War on Terror: Implications to the Sociology of Denial." *Critical Criminology: An International Journal* 12(1): 1–20.

———. 2006. *Scapegoats of September 11th: Hate Crimes and State Crimes in the War on Terror*. New Brunswick: Rutgers University Press.

———. 2008. "Foucault in a Post-9/11 World: Excursions into Security, Territory, Population." *Carceral Notebooks* 4: 225–40.

———. 2009a. *Crimes of Power and States of Impunity: The U.S. Response to Terror*. New Brunswick: Rutgers University Press.

———. 2009b. "American Pain-ology in the War on Terror: A Critique of 'Scientific' Torture." *Theoretical Criminology* 13(4): 451–74.

———. 2010a. "Pastoral Power as Penal Resistance: Foucault and the Groupe d'Information sur les Prisons." *Punishment and Society: The International Journal of Penology* 12(1): 47–63.

———. 2010b. "Detained in Occupied Iraq: Deciphering the Narratives for Neocolonial Internment." *Punishment and Society: International Journal of Penology* 12(2): 123–46.

———. 2011a. *Corrections: A Critical Approach, 3rd Edition*. New York: Routledge.

———. 2011b. "Counterveillance: How Foucault and the Groupe d'Information sur les Prisons Reversed the Optics." *Theoretical Criminology* 15(3): 301–13.

———. 2011c. "Illusions in Truth Seeking: The Perils of Interrogation and Torture in the War on Terror." *Social Justice: A Journal of Crime, Conflict, and World Order*, 37(2–3): 123–48.

———. 2012. "Penal Tourism and the 'Dream of Order': Exhibiting Early Penology in Argentina and Australia." *Punishment and Society: The International Journal of Penology* 14(5): 584–615.

———. 2013. "Penal Tourism and A Tale of Four Cities: Reflecting on the Museum Effect in London, Sydney, Melbourne, and Buenos Aires." *Criminology and Criminal Justice: An International Journal* 13(5): 479–505.

———. 2015. *Escape to Prison: Penal Tourism and the Pull of Punishment*. Oakland: University of California Press.

———. 2016a. "Political Imprisonment and the Sanctity of Death: Performing Heritage in 'Troubled' Ireland." *International Journal of Heritage Studies* 22: 664–78.

———. 2016b. Review of *An Archaeology of the Troubles: The Dark Heritage of Long Kesh/Maze Prison* by Laura McAtackney (Oxford: Oxford University Press, 2014). *Irish Political Studies* 31(2): 334–36.

———. 2016c. "Clinical Torture: Drifting in the Atrocity Triangle." *Oñati Socio-Legal Series* 6(4): 957–74.

———. 2017a. Review of *Corrections and Collections: Architecture for Art and Crime* by Joe Day (New York: Routledge, 2013). *International Criminal Justice Review* 27(3): 230–31.

———. 2017b. "Penal Tourism and the Paradox of (In)Humane Punishment." In *The Palgrave Handbook of Prison Tourism*, edited by J. Wilson, S. Hodgkinson, J. Piche, and K. Walby. London: Palgrave Macmillan.

———. 2017c. "'Doing Special Things to Special People in Special Places': Psychologists in the CIA Torture Program." *Prison Journal* 97(6), 729–49.

———. 2019. "Signs of Trouble: Semiotics, Streetscapes, and the Republican Struggle in the North of Ireland." *Crime, Media, Culture: An International Journal* 16(1): 7–32.

———. 2020. "In the Sites of Operation Condor: Memory and Afterlives of Clandestine Detention Centers." *Social Justice: A Journal of Crime, Conflict, and World Order* 47(1–2): 1–38.

Welch, M., and M. Macuare. 2011. "Penal Tourism in Argentina: Bridging Foucauldian and Neo-Durkheimian Perspectives." *Theoretical Criminology* 15(4): 401–25.

Whicker's World. 2018. "Whicker's World: Alfredo Stroessner." https://www.youtube.com/watch?v=8uEB-Vs8m-8.

Whitman, J. Q. 2003. *Harsh Justice*. New York: Oxford University Press.

Windrem, R. 2013. "US Government Considered Nelson Mandela a Terrorist until 2008." *NBC News*, December 7. https://www.nbcnews.com/news/world/us-government-considered-nelson-mandela-terrorist-until-2008-flna2D11708787.

Wilde, A. 1999. "Irruptions of Memory." *Journal of Latin American Studies* 31(2): 473–500.

Williams, P. 2007. *Memorial Museums*. Oxford: Berg.

Wilson, D. A. 1989. *The Irish in Canada*. Ottawa: Canadian Historical Association.

Wylie, D. 2004. *The Maze*. London: Granta.

Young, A. 1978. "Political Prisoners in U.S., Young Says." *Le Matin*, July 12. https://www
.nytimes.com/1978/07/13/archives/political-prisoners-in-us-young-says-un-envoy-in
-geneva-compares.html.
Zysman, D. 2017. "Punishment, Democracy, and Transitional Justice in Argentina
(1983–2015)." *International Journal for Crime, Justice, and Social Democracy* 6(1): 88–102.